PENGUIN AFRICAN LIBRARY

Africa in Prose

O. R. DATHORNE AND WILLFRIED FEUSER

Africa in Prose

EDITED BY O. R. DATHORNE
AND WILLFRIED FEUSER

Penguin Books

Penguin Books Ltd, Harmondsworth, Middlesex, England
Penguin Books Inc., 7110 Ambassador Road, Baltimore,
Maryland 21207, U.S.A.
Penguin Books Australia Ltd, Ringwood, Victoria, Australia

This collection published in Penguin Books 1969
Introduction copyright © O. R. Dathorne, 1969

Made and printed in Great Britain by
C. Nicholls & Company Ltd
Set in Monotype Plantin

Contents

Contents

Contents

Acknowledgements

For permission to publish or reproduce the material in this anthology, acknowledgement is made to the following sources and copyright holders:

1 SALIM BIN ABAKARI 'A Journey to Russia and Siberia in 1896'. Translated from Swahili and published in German in 1901. English translation taken from *Swahili Prose Texts*, ed. Lyndon Harries (Oxford University Press, 1956) pp. 263–7.

2 JOHN MENSAH SARBAH 'Coup' from *Fanti National Constitution* (William Clowes & Son, 1906) pp. 42–8.

3 A. B. C. SIBTHORPE 'The *Black Joke*' from *Oration on the Centenary of the Abolition of the Slave Trade* (1907) in Paul Edwards's *West African Narrative* (Nelson, 1963) pp. 138–50.

4 E. CASELY-HAYFORD 'An Early Train Journey' from *Ethiopia Unbound* (London, C. M. Phillips, 1911) pp. 121–6.

5 SOL T. PLAATJE 'Native Life in South Africa' from *Native Life in South Africa* (London, P. S. King & Son, 1916) pp. 17–28.

6 R. R. R. DHLOMO 'The Rake' from *An African Tragedy* (Lovedale, South Africa, Lovedale Mission Press, 1928) pp. 1–12.

7 ISAAC B. THOMAS 'Segilola: The Lady with the Delicate Eye-Balls' from *The Autobiography of Segilola* (Lagos, C.M.S. Bookshops, 1930) copyright © 1929 by Isaac B. Thomas. Translated from Yoruba by Razak Solaja.

8 SOL T. PLAATJE 'Mhudi and Umnandi' from *Mhudi* (Lovedale Mission Press, 1930) pp. 185–99.

9 OUSMANE SOCÉ 'Courting in Saint-Louis'. Translated

from Karim (Paris, Imprimerie Marcel Puyfourçat, 1935) pp. 26–9.

10 PAUL HAZOUMÉ 'A Message to the Ancestors'. Translated from *Doguicimi* (Paris, Larose, 1938) pp. 374–8.

11 AKIGA 'Justice' from *Akiga's Story* (Oxford University Press, 1939) pp. 277–82. Translated from Tiv by Rupert East.

12 E. E. OBENG 'Konaduwa's Trial' from *Eighteenpence* (London, Stockwell, 1943) pp. 37–44.

13 S. Y. NTARA 'The Visitor' from *Headman's Enterprise* (Lutterworth Press, 1949) pp. 109–114. Translated from Cewa by Cullen Young.

14 ADELAIDE CASELY-HAYFORD 'Reminiscences' from 'The Life and Times of Adelaide Casely-Hayford', *West African Review*, Vol. XXIV, No. 313 (October 1953) pp. 1058–60.

15 JEAN MALONGA 'Mambéké's Creed'. Translated from *Coeur d'Aryenne* in *Trois Ecrivains Noirs* (Paris, Présence Africaine 16, 1954) pp. 268–71.

16 ABDOULAYE SADJI 'Nini in Distress'. Translated from *Nini, mulâtresse du Sénégal* in *Trois Ecrivains Noirs* (Paris, Présence Africaine 16, 1954) pp. 409–12.

17 DAVID ANANOU '... and reel to the brink of the grave which awaits you'. Translated from *Le Fils du fétiche* (Paris, Nouvelles Editions Latines, 1955) pp. 160–66.

18 FERDINAND OYONO 'The Medal'. Translated from *Le Vieux Nègre et la médaille* (Paris, Julliard, 1956) pp. 110–19.

19 MONGO BETI 'Saving Souls in Tala Land'. Translated from *Le Pauvre Christ de Bomba* (Paris, Robert Laffont, 1956) pp. 50–7.

20 SÉKOU TOURÉ 'Speech Delivered on the Occasion of President de Gaulle's Arrival at Conakry, 1958'. Translated from *Expérience Guinéenne et unité africaine* (Paris, Présence Africaine, 1961) pp. 79–82.

21 KENULE TSARO-WIWA 'High Life'.

22 TIMOTHY WANGUSA 'How Fast We Are Moving'.

23 SPEEDY ERIC 'How Mabel Learnt' from *Mabel the Sweet Honey* (printed by Trinity Printing Press, 34 Moore St, P.O.

Box 538, Onitsha, Nigeria, and obtainable from A. Onwudiwe & Sons, P.O. Box 214, Onitsha, 1963) pp. 15–24.

24 MILLER O. ALBERT 'Rosemary and the Taxi Driver' from *Rosemary and the Taxi Driver* (printed by Chinyelu Printing Press, Iweka Road, Onitsha, 1963) pp. 6–14.

25 OKENWA OLISA 'Lumumba's Last Days' from *How Lumumba Suffered and Died in Katanga* (printed by Okwuno Printing Press, 38 Moore St, Onitsha, and obtainable from P. E. Unaigwe, 6 Bida Road, Onitsha, 1964) pp. 2–8.

26 SEMBÈNE OUSMANE 'Strike'. Translated from *Les Bouts de bois de Dieu* (Paris, Le Livre Contemporain, 1960) pp. 60–63.

27 CASTRO SOROMENHO 'Chief Xa-Mucuari's Grievance'. Translated from *Terra Morta* (Lisbon, Editôra Arcádia, 1961) pp. 42–9.

28 CASEY MOTSISI 'Riot' from *Classic* Vol. I, No. 2 (P.O. Box 6434, Johannesburg) pp. 69–74.

29 AKÉ LOBA 'Kocoumbo and the Stowaway'. Translated from *Kocoumbo, l'étudiant noir* (Paris, Flammarion, 1960), pp. 60–68.

30 ALEX LA GUMA 'Death in the City' from *A Walk in the Night* (Ibadan, Mbari, 1962) pp. 18–25.

31 D. N. MALINWA 'Everything Under the Sun'.

32 AMOS TUTUOLA 'Remember the Day After Tomorrow'.

33 EDWARD BABATUNDE HORATIO-JONES 'Mourner's Progress'.

34 EZEKIEL MPHAHLELE 'A Ballad of Oyo'.

35 LUIS BERNARDO HONWANA 'The Old Woman'. Translated from Portuguese by D. Guedes.

36 NAZI BONI 'The Meeting'. Translated from *Crépuscule des temps anciens* (Paris, Présence Africaine, 1962) pp.109–14.

37 JAMES NGUGI 'Limits' from *The River Between* (Heinemann, 1965) pp. 82–5.

38 JONATHAN KARIARA 'The Initiation' from David Cook, *Origin East Africa: A Makerere Anthology* (Heinemann, 1965) pp. 94–8.

39 SADRU KASSAM 'The House'.

40 LÉOPOLD SÉDAR SENGHOR '*Négritude* and Marxism'. Translated from *Pierre Teilhard de Chardin et la politique*

Acknowledgements

   africaine (Paris, Editions du Seuil, 1962) pp. 17–21.
41 RALPH OPARA 'Lagos Interlude' from *Reflections*, ed.
   Frances Ademola (A.U.P. Lagos, 1962) pp. 108–13.
42 WOLE SOYINKA 'Salutations to the Gut' from *Reflections*,
   ed. Frances Ademola (A.U.P. Lagos, 1962) pp. 117–23.
43 BAKARE GBADAMOSI 'A Wise Man Solves His Own Problems'. Translated from Yoruba by Ulli Beier.
44 CHEIKH HAMIDOU KANE 'The City of the Future'. Translated from *L'Aventure ambiguë* (Paris, Julliard, 1961) pp.
   93–101.

Every effort has been made to trace copyright holders, but
in a few cases this has proved impossible. The publishers
would be interested to hear from any copyright holders not
here acknowledged.

Introduction

At first sight there seems scant justification for yet another anthology of African prose, since there have, we ourselves believe, been too many African anthologies chasing too few writers. The same material has appeared time and time again with embarrassing regularity, and in large measure the pieces have been put together in a manner which did little more than indicate that Africans had written.

We have sought in this collection to show that there is a recognizable prose tradition that goes back to the beginning of this century. At the start there was the anthropological concern with tribe, and later with the coming of the white man. Early writers extolled the Christian way of life and the virtues that the missionaries preached. This can be explained, though only in part, by remarking that in Southern Africa the vernacular presses at Lovedale and Morija were missionary controlled and insisted on a suitably moral content for the literature they published.

When the novel does emerge in English and French, it contains a carry-over of the sociological concern and therefore much documentation. Ousmane Socé and Paul Hazoumé cast nostalgic looks at their societies; R. R. R. Dhlomo documents the evils of city life and upholds Christian virtues, whereas Sol T. Plaatje celebrates the courage of women in the historic wars of their menfolk. This is like the literature that the Southern African mission presses were turning out; but the more recent South African novel, perhaps wrongly dubbed a novel of protest, has turned away from these concerns. Instead its theme is cultural emancipation, which in the hands of some writers tends to distort the material of recall into the declarations of a propaganda leaflet.

Introduction

With the West African novel, there is a similar clearly defined break between the early and later novels. The first two imaginative prose works in English, E. Casely-Hayford's *Ethiopia Unbound* (which cannot properly be termed a novel) and E. E. Obeng's *Eighteenpence*, both show a certain obsession with tribal law and custom. There was no vernacular writing on which to draw, and these writers used a rigid moral vision to help them express something of the national sentiment that was taking shape.

In both South and West Africa, and more recently in East Africa, there emerges the theme of the individual struggling against the pressures of the tribe and breaking out of the enclave in which custom would seek to restrict him. Latterly there has been a concern in depth with the person, his private predicament in a world he seeks to salvage from the chaos of a divided inheritance.

Oral traditional literature in Africa does not make a hard and fast division between 'fact' and 'fiction', and the African writer has integrated large elements of biography (not always with enough concern for form) into his imaginative material. The prejudiced viewpoint all too readily emerges in some of the pieces ostensibly describing objective social issues. Perhaps this is an understandable reaction from the oral literature which masked the artist behind the anonymity of folk-belief.

Our anthology marks the development of this literature in English and French and to a lesser extent in Portuguese as well as in some vernacular languages. With a single exception (that of Castro Soromenho) we have used only the works of black African writers. We hope that in this way there may be demonstrated the unity and diversity of black African writing. As far as possible we have avoided using extracts from works of writers in English which are easily accessible to the interested reader. This has meant that some popular names have been omitted since our overall concern was not with the novel but with the development of prose on the continent during this century.

We hope that what emerges is varied. We have not set out to assemble neat little pieces of fine prose nor, indeed, to display the fruits of artistic endeavour. Our intention has been to give a coherent view of African prose from the beginning of this century. Our survey is not comprehensive; it is merely a pointer towards possibilities.

O. R. DATHORNE

1

Salim bin Abakari

A Journey to Russia and Siberia in 1896

The main interest of this piece is not only that it was published in 1901, as a result of a journey undertaken in 1896, but that it presents a viewpoint unique in African writing. African literature has frequently been marred by too close a proximity to the local, and few writers have ventured abroad, away from the village or the metropolitan centres to which the colonized communities belong. Salim bin Abakari did venture, and he showed himself in the process as an observer with a keen and careful eye.

Salim is in some ways an innocent abroad; he is easily amazed and quickly gratified. At the centre of what he says, however, there is always an extremely lonely figure, equally estranged from his German employers and from the alien people in whose society he found himself. That he set down his account in Swahili shows that he was alive to the historical circumstance of his journey in the literature of his continent.

A Journey to Russia and Siberia in 1896

When we reached Petersburg I was at once aware that now we were in another country. The clothes there are different from those worn in European countries, and the carriages were of a different kind. Inside, their droshkies were very small, and the drivers were dressed like old women. Truly when a person is on a journey he learns many things, and he increases his knowledge.

We left the Customs and went off to the Hotel Europa. When we went there we had a rest. Afterwards my employer left to go out, and he told me that when I had finished work and had something to eat I could go off and take a walk. So when my work was done I went to the dining-room to get something to eat. And I didn't know any Russian; when I wanted to ask for something they could not understand me. So I got up and went to call the German interpreter, and he came to tell them (the waiters) what things I wanted, and that is how they understood.

And the majority of waiters in the hotel were not Russian, most of them were Germans or Tartars, and the Tartars are Muslims. They were very surprised at the way I ordered my food and what I wanted to drink, and they asked, 'Why don't you eat pork and drink wine?' I told them, 'I don't drink wine nor eat pork because I am a Muslim.' And they replied that they too were Muslims. I thought they were having me on, and I said, 'How could it be that you are Muslims in this country?' And they said to me, 'We are Tartars by tribe, and the Tartars are Muslims.' I did not believe it, and thought they were telling a lie, so I rang the bell and a waiter came who knew German. I asked him, 'What sort of people are these who wait at table?' He told me, 'They are Tartars.' I said to him, 'What is their religion?'

He told me, 'Islam.' I was amazed to find that in a white man's country there were Muslims like this.

I went out to go round the town, and I knew nothing of the language, I knew nobody. I went to the commissionaire of our hotel and I asked him to tell me of a place where one could watch an entertainment or walk around. And he described for me every place of entertainment. And I said to him, 'Give me a letter, and write for me in Russian, and put the name of the hotel on the back, so that if I get lost I can take a cab and come home.' And he gave me the letter.

I took a tram to go to the Zoo and look at the wild animals. And I stayed there looking at the different things and the wild animals, and I remained until eight o'clock in the evening, and what a wonderful thing I saw. I left at nine o'clock and at ten o'clock at night the sun was still shining. I was much astonished, because in Europe during the summer the sun delays its setting, the sun goes beneath the water about nine o'clock in the evening, but in Russia the sun goes down at midnight, and at two o'clock in the morning it is rising again. And for two months the night is only half an hour long. And during the summer the people there sleep a lot in the daytime, they go about at night, because it is very hot in the day.

The people of Russia have a sterner temperament than other white people, for other whites work well and are well disposed to being taught, and have much more method than the Russians. In my opinion the Russians are well behind other white people, because in other white countries every white person is taught to read and write, but in Russia more people do not know how to read than those who do, because they do not like studying, and it seems to me it is their laziness.

There was a Tsar who gave a ruling that each of his subjects must go to school to be taught to read and write. The Russians in the rural areas refused to accept his ruling, and because of their refusal he ordered his soldiers, telling them 'I want you to go into the whole country and look for people who are refusing my command to be taught to read and write, and everyone who refuses my command, lock him up, send him to the cold country to a criminal gaol.' And the soldiers went and harassed the whole country, asking the people, (and saying), 'Whoever wants to read and write must send his children to school.' Some said they wanted it, and others said they did not. Those who did not were taken away and sent to the cold country, Siberia by name. They were imprisoned in chains to do (hard) labour for life.

In the whole of Europe kings may not pass judgement on a man, but their judgements are effected through judges. No one is more respected in Europe and more obeyed than the judge, because Europeans respect the law. According to European law it is possible to pass judgement on a ruler, but there is no ruler who can pass judgement on another man without the due processes of the law, everyone is judged by the (appointed) judges. But in Russia their custom is that anything the ruler wishes, that is what they do, even though the ruler follows no law, they must do what he wants. Even a person who is favoured by the Emperor of Russia can do anything he wants, the judges have no power whatsoever. Anything the Emperor disapproves of, they dare not do it. But in Germany and France and England, in the whole of Europe, a judge has more power to pass judgement than the ruler.

Let us go back to our mention of Siberia. Anyone sent to that country is lucky to return. Most people die there from (their) shackles and from rheumatism. There is nothing but ice, but they dig silver and gold and iron there. What is there is every kind of metal. And no country is more subject to sickness than one with minerals for the people who work (extracting the minerals) in the hills.

When I went from Petersburg to Moscow in a Russian train, I saw that things were very different from what they are in Germany or France. Their trains are not good like those in Europe, because they are very dirty in their trains, and the clerks are not trustworthy. In Europe what is ordered by the head of the rail-service must be carried out, but in Russia every man does what he likes, because the drivers and the clerks both steal. Because a person can journey and go to a place a long way off where the fare is a hundred rupees, but if you can give the clerk four or five rupees in private he will let you journey for five rupees without telling anybody else, and you say to him, 'I want to go to such-

and-such a place,' he will let you go for five rupees clandestinely given, without your paying the hundred rupees, because he steals the fare. But in Europe you cannot give a clerk a little something and get him to take you, you must show him your ticket.

And as for the dirt of their carriages, as many as twenty or thirty loads can be brought into the passenger compartment, but in Europe this is not allowed, for there is a luggage van as well as a passenger compartment. But in Russia they take on loads at every place and they spit in the compartment; it is very dirty, so much so that one cannot eat when travelling with them.

When we arrived in Moscow, we went to the hotel Safleski Bazar, and we stayed six days. I couldn't get anybody to go around with me, so I had to go along with my employer. And as I had heard the praises of Moscow, I wanted very much to visit the town and look around, but I didn't know Russian, so I had to take a cab to get about. I couldn't make myself understood with the drivers, I simply had to use my hands as though I were deaf and dumb. And there are no scoundrels to beat the cab-drivers in Russia. European cabbies are not allowed to accept more money than that for the time you are in the cab. Every European cab has a tariff, it is written in the cab, so that if the driver defrauds you of a single ha'penny you can look at the time, you will know what it is right to give him. But in Russia they do not have a fixed tariff, nor do they have a table of fares in their cabs. If you take a cab for a journey of two or three minutes, the driver will tell you that he wants four roubles, because he knows that you are a visitor, you don't know the language and you don't know the usual thing, he wants to defraud you. But a person of intelligence doesn't agree to give him the money he wants.

And if you don't know Russian and you take a cab, look well at your watch and the distance you have been when you have got down from the cab. It is no use asking the driver, just give him the usual fare that you heard of in the town, and go your way. The driver will make an awful row at you for you to give him a lot of money, but don't give in. He will tell you, 'I am calling the police.' Let him call them, the police are liars just the same, they do not speak the truth, for the drivers will tell the policeman,

'We will divide the money between us afterwards.' And these drivers do not know how to read nor how to count. If you say to one, 'Take me to such-and-such a house,' he will take you to some other house.

There are no people as religious as the Russians. Everywhere when he passes near a church, a Russian will inevitably bow down, he can't pass without an act of worship. On their screens they have pictures, they put pictures of the Prophet Jesus, and when he goes out in the morning first a Russian bows to the picture and worships it. Then he drinks coffee. When he has had his coffee, he goes off to bow before the picture of Jesus, and when they go to bed, they must bow down before the picture of Jesus; this is their confession of faith, whether it be adult or child, they all behave in the same way.

One day I went to the theatre-garden. Throughout Europe no one can get in to a theatre without paying money, but in Russia if you give the attendants who take the tickets a little money in private, you will be able to get inside all right. Because when I went I paid four roubles to go in. After about half an hour I saw some other people coming who had no ticket for the theatre, then they winked at the attendant (and said), 'We have no ticket to get in here, and we want to see the play, so take a quarter and put us somewhere.' At once the attendant took the quarter and put the three people in the seats priced four roubles. I was amazed, because in Europe you can't do a thing like this; if you do so you will be severely judged and the attendant will get the greater punishment, because it is like thieving.

And Moscow is the oldest Russian city. Long ago it was the ruling city, but now the capital city of Russia is Petersburg. But Moscow is healthier than Petersburg, because in the latter town there is a lot of fever, but the country districts of Petersburg are very fine. The important people of Petersburg mostly live in the country, because the air is better there than in the town.

And the old city of Moscow was burned down. The Russians set fire to it themselves on purpose, because of the French when they went to fight there. Now it has been built anew, it is much finer than the old city.

And Moscow is an important trade-centre, more so than

Petersburg, it is more famous throughout all the states in this respect than Petersburg. Most of the trade there comes from Asia and Persia and Bokhara. The people of those countries bring their wares to Moscow, mats and sheep-skins and the skins of wild animals are brought to be sold in Moscow. Each year there is a very big market, for much business is transacted in Moscow because traders from all over Europe come and buy things there and sell them at a high price in their own land.

And Moscow is the place of the leading Russian clergy, and their churches are magnificent, but their religion is of a different kind (from that of other people), though they worship the same Prophet as other white people. And there are many Muslims, and the food of Muslims there is horse-meat. I was astonished, because we at home regard horse-meat as unlawful, but there it is lawful. And their Muslims are Sunnis, they pray a lot and study.

And they are great people for bargaining. In their trade dealings they exchange things, old clothes for new clothes and skins, they exchange every kind of thing to get a profit. If you give a trader some old thing, he exchanges it for something new. And the trade of the Tartars is like that of the Indians, they also wear the same hats as the Indians, and they are better at trading than the Russians themselves, indeed they are smarter in appearance than the Russians.

2

John Mensah Sarbah

Coup

Five years after this extract appeared in 1906, the first West African novel in English was to be published. These two works show the obsession of Ghanaians with legal fiction, with the imaginative exposition of law and order. This section from *Fanti National Constitution* has contemporary as well as vintage interest. It suggests that 'totalitarianism' and 'democracy' are not necessarily conflicting ideologies, but can complement each other, given a specific context and the sanction of society.

Since this writing belongs to an early era of African literature in English, it seems appropriate to add a few words on the manner of execution. The factual nature of the matter necessitated a certain punctiliousness on the part of the writer, and this emerges in the scrupulous use he makes of words and ideas. There is little that seems *personal* here, and indeed this in itself makes one suspicious, until it is realized that here is a writer adroit enough to disengage himself completely from the irrelevancies of his experience. He has the cast of the expatriate, but he speaks with the knowledge and authority of the indigenous. This was no small effort for a man who had been educated away from his culture, but who could nevertheless re-enter it (before it had become something of a fetish to do so) and find much that was rewarding there.

Coup

Some misconception exists in connexion with the removal of a ruler or of the head of a family. The right of removing a ruler belongs to the people immediately connected with the stool; in the case of the head of a family the right is in the senior members, and the act of the majority is binding on the rest.

The grounds on which a ruler may be removed from his office or position are: (1) Adultery: this must be notorious and habitual; for the second and third offence he is generally made to give satisfaction in money equivalent to (where the amount is not fixed) what he would receive if he were the injured husband. (2) Habitual drunkenness and disorderly conduct which degrades him. (3) Habitually opposing the councillors and disregarding their advice without just cause. (4) Theft and general misconduct, such as constantly provoking strife by acts and words, and stirring up bad blood between his people and other rulers; inability to uphold the dignity and good reputation of the stool. (5) Perverting justice when hearing cases, and inflicting extortionable fines and penalties; failing to protect his subjects or to espouse their cause. (6) Cowardice in war. (7) Extravagance and persistently involving his people in debt and other liabilities improperly contracted or incurred. (8) Conduct derogatory and unworthy of his position; e.g. one Aban, ruler of Adjumaku, was removed from his office for holding a canopy umbrella over Edu, king of Mankesim, and for going to the public market to purchase provisions.

A subordinate ruler is removed from his office on complaint by the people of the town, the councillors, or the family. By the first he is charged before the councillors and the principal members of his family; by the second, before the elders of the town and principal members of the family; and by the third, before the elders of the town and councillors; but when the plaint is by the people of the town, including the councillors, the superior ruler and his council hear of it.

Complaint against a ruler, whether superior or subordinate, is the last remedy of those under him, for one must rest assured that before this step is taken the offending ruler had been warned and remonstrated with many a time. For some offences, such as cowardice, theft, and conduct deemed by his subjects derogatory, he can be removed at once if his defence or explanation be found unsatisfactory. In the other cases, if after two or three warnings he does not reform, he may be removed.

Where a ruler who is summoned to answer complaints against him fails to attend the hearing, and does not give good reasons for his absence, he may be removed. A subordinate ruler may be removed by his subjects, but he has the right to appeal to the superior ruler, who may investigate the matter afterwards. Should he find him in the wrong, the removal is confirmed; if the subordinate ruler be found in the right, but the subjects will not have him at any price, he is nevertheless removed, but his people are bound to pay all expenses he may have incurred in respect of the stool.

The practice in the case of a subordinate ruler is that if on complaint laid against him before the superior ruler he refuses or fails without good reason to obey the summons to appear and answer the same, he is liable without further warning to be removed as a punishment for his offence against the superior. Moreover, the original complaint can be investigated, and if the finding be against him, he can be degraded and set aside. He who refuses to obey his superior is guilty of an offence, which, unpardoned, is punishable by a fine; but in cases of public importance, where the complaint laid refers to misgovernment, the welfare of the public is the chief consideration, therefore the superior ruler, with the councillors, first investigates the grounds of such complaint and decides accordingly; afterwards he deals with the alleged contempt.

Before giving instances of certain typical trials in very recent times, the earliest extant report of a trial in the year 1600 is worth repetition. At that time

every man tells his tale (for they have no lawyers) by turns without interruption (which they specially forbid upon pain of corporal punishment) before the judge who, having heard both sides, gives his own judgment, which they must stand to without appeal. If there be any forfeiture to the king, it must be paid presently, or the party must be banished from his majesty's jurisdiction, with all his relations, until it is paid. If it be a controversy among the nobility, they come to combat, who engage side against side, the plaintiff and the defendant fighting in the middle of them. He that is beaten must suffer, and if he runneth away to another little king's dominion, he must be delivered up to the wife of the dead man to be disposed of, or it comes to a war.

In most matters the plaintiff certifieth the captain, who causes a drum to be beaten by one of his slaves, who carrieth it about his neck, and two boys with cow-bells (a sign that justice is to be done), whereupon the captain and his armed gentlemen sit round the market-place, whither the people flock, not knowing what is to be done, until the accused party is called, and bound to answer all the allegations against him, or pay the penalty with his purse or freedom (for they buy their lives there with money), divided among the MORNANS.*

I was present at this case. A man came from one town to another to gather up his debts, which man a year before had lain with another man's wife; and the same woman was by chance come to the market, and seeing him, went straight and complained to the Aene, i.e. the chief officer, who presently ordered his apprehension. The good woman complained he had forced her, and not paid according to his promise; he made answer, he did it with her good will. After a great contest, the Fetistero – or the priest that hath to do with their Fetistoes [gods] – came hither with a certain drink in a pot, and set it down before the captain, as they call their magistrates, where arms are the law. The woman took the pot and drank of it to justify he had not satisfied her for the loss of her honour; and if the man durst have drunk thereof before the woman, he had been acquitted, but knowing his guilt, he paid his three *bendas*, that is, six ounces of gold. But in case a man deserveth death and cannot pay a fine, he dieth without any more ado.

Basayin was a few years ago the ruler of Mansu district under Ohene Enimil of Wassaw Amenfi. His drunken habits and other

*This word seems to be meant for Oman, the council

conduct were so unsatisfactory that his subjects, some time in 1902, sent messengers to inform Ohene Enimil that they wished to remove him from the stool. Ohene Enimil said Basayin had done him no wrong, therefore he could not consent to his deposition. The people, however, exercising their inherent right, removed him and reported to the Ohene what they had done. Basayin also reported to the Ohene what had befallen him; thereupon the representatives of the people were ordered by the Ohene to appear before him at Bensu, his town. They did so. Before the Ohene and his council the reasons for removing Basayin were demanded. Thirty and three grounds were enumerated, and several warnings were also proved. Of these only two did Basayin deny, but admitted many more. The Gyasi and councillors retired to confer, and, on their return, found against Basayin. Enimil interceded for him to be given another chance, but not succeeding, he confirmed the deposition, and since then Kweku Pong has been placed on the Mansu stool.

In 1901, while Ohene Enimil of Wassaw Amenfi, and all his subordinate rulers, linguists, and councillors, were at Axim for the Chidda case, complaint was laid against one of the subordinate rulers, by name Kweku Inkruma of Pepisa Dompim, by his people, who sought for his degradation from his office on the following grounds, namely, misconduct with the wives of his subjects and others; insolence to his subjects for that he frequently called them his slaves and pawns; obtaining fetish and some charms with intent to kill or otherwise injure persons disliked by him; and lastly, stealing at Axim, for which he was convicted and imprisoned. The blood relatives of Inkruma were present at the trial. Yansu of Simpa, the second subordinate ruler of Mansa, and the councillors, laid the complaint and proved the charges. After Inkruma had been heard in his defence he was found guilty. Enimil suggested that he might be pardoned, but his people replied they did not want him any longer, and he was thereupon degraded and ordered to give up the stool. What he was sitting on was handed to his superior ruler for safe keeping, and in due course Ewusi was selected and placed on the stool, and is now the ruler of Dompim Pepisa.

In the early part of 1903, Etien, the successor of Bimfu, the ruler of Tumentu in Gwira, was degraded and removed from his office by the councillors and people of the stool on the ground that for several years he had neglected his district by residing permanently at Axim, squandered and spent for his own use the rents and monies paid for concessions, and otherwise wasted the stool revenue. To all messages from his councillors and people begging him to return home and look after them he had turned a deaf ear. The representatives of the council and people were sent to him at his residence, laid the charges against him, and his defence being unsatisfactory, he was degraded from and dismissed his office. In addition, all his goods and chattels were removed and taken away. The ruler of Axim, being the nominal superior, had the right to summon the people and councillors before him if he felt aggrieved. This, however, he did not do.

On the acquittal of a stoolholder from charges brought against him, the unsuccessful complainants are bound to sacrifice to and purify the stool. This is done either by killing a sheep and pouring libations, or paying money the equivalent thereof. In addition a fee [*mpatadzi*] to pacify him is paid, and the parties solemnly swear to each other to forgive and forget, and act harmoniously.

Whenever a stoolholder occupies a public position his private status is merged in the public office, and on his death the people of the stool have the right to take part in the ceremonies with the selection of a fit and proper person as his successor; for the good government of the general public has the priority and preference over all other considerations and claims. His self-acquired property, undisposed of by him, becomes stool property on his demise. Where through dispute or misunderstanding some members of the family have left the family abode and have informally severed their connexion with the stoolholder, their followers cannot lawfully take part in the selection of the successor, without the permission of those who remained in their allegiance to the stool. Generally before a successor is placed on a family stool the members of the family adjust any differences existing amongst them so as to be able to act harmoniously, and give full support to him.

3

A. B. C. Sibthorpe

The Black Joke

A. B. C. Sibthorpe was a Sierra Leonean. His interest and his laughter were different from those of the two previous writers. His was not straight history: it was biased, ironical, cruel. The sudden switch in approach might be a little bewildering at first, but his seriousness of purpose is always uppermost, and it is this which prevents the writing from straining too high towards a pitch of inaudible wordiness.

The remarks of his 'European gentleman' (which misled at least one previous anthologist into believing that the work was not entirely Sibthorpe's) is a way of cleverly disengaging himself from the account. It is through the so-called European's eyes that the unkindness of man to man is seen; and Sibthorpe subtly manages to introduce some of the speaker's own prejudices as well, as when he makes him refer to the 'apathy of the African'. The writer has twice distanced himself from the object of recall. He may be said to have created the very character out of which history manifests itself.

The *Black Joke*

Their distribution through the colony was determined according to the plans in progress for peopling the particular districts of the peninsula. The manager of a certain district was informed that a certain number would be consigned to his management, and selected spots within his province for their location. Each liberated slave received an outfit of a piece of cotton; and the government allowed an iron pot for boiling rice, a spoon, and a few additional implements of similar simplicity and usefulness. He reared a hut, with assistance from his neighbours; it was a square shed, supported by a framework resting on eight or a dozen poles, interlaid with dry grass or twigs, plastered with mud, and was thatched with dry boughs. Its construction occupied a few days to a month. Nails and hinges were supplied with him, and his wealth was further increased by a cutlass and a hoe. Round his rude dwelling the newly naturalized British subject obtained a grant of land, limited to about half a rood. Being now established, and having started into civilized British life under the same auspices and advantages as others enjoyed before him, he was from henceforth left to his own management. The habit of system, the sense of security, the advantages of barter in a regular market, by degrees wear off the rough edges of savage characters; and many a man so adopted into the English colony lived to appreciate his altered situation, to value improvement, to advance in intellectual and moral grade, to become a useful unit in the social aggregate.

In comparing the British with the American policy, in the location and treatment of the liberated in the two colonies of Sierra Leone and Liberia, the advantage in some respects would seem to lie with the latter. The emancipated in the English settlement received half a rood of ground, and no more could be obtained. This sufficed for personal subsistence, but precluded extensive agriculture. The face of the peninsula was speckled with innumerable half-roods of cassava, yams, cocoa, and plantain in endless repetition. Farms are discountenanced by this system; the more valuable produce of the soil cannot be reared; and, further than this, the few days required to cultivate so small a garden left the remainder of the year an indolent holiday. As yet the wild unclaimed bush, or forest, pressed upon the black colonists; and when industry and taste for agriculture develop themselves, free use will be made of the unappropriated land. By this means the rich soil of the valleys will often be cleared of its wood, and industrious hands will plant useful roots and raise fruit-trees. This was, however, permitted, not encouraged. Ground so appropriated and cultivated might be taken from the useful trespasser, and allotted in grants upon the first fresh importation of captives sent to be located in the district.

The patrons of Liberia acted otherwise; they were, perhaps, enabled to do so from the much greater extent of territory at their command. With the intention of providing, not only for the immediate wants of the black colonist, but also for the permanent and progressive prosperity of the settlement, each settler had assigned to him a grant of fifty acres of land, with the privilege of claiming an addition of the same extent on payment of twenty-five cents per acre, after five years of residence and steady labour. This stimulus to exertion and enterprise operated favourably. But the free blacks of Liberia had a greater inducement to the pursuit of agriculture, such, indeed, as must ultimately render the colony valuable to the mother country and rich in itself. A donation of 500 acres was given to any black, or association of blacks, upon the simple condition that it should be devoted to the cultivation of coffee, sugar and cotton.

To return, however, to the process of liberation in Sierra Leone. 'I had an opportunity,' says a European gentleman, 'of observing its details as an eyewitness.

'One fine day in May 1834, the signal-gun told of the approach of a vessel, which the looker-out on the signal hill announced, by the usual mode of hoisting a coloured ball to the top of a staff, to be a schooner or brig from the south. A sharp-built schooner with crowded canvas glanced up the estuary like lightning. Her nature was obvious. She was a prize. A painful interest prompted me to visit as speedily as possible this prison-ship. A friend offered the advantage of his company to a scene which has some-times so completely overwhelmed a novice as to render the sup-port of a friend advantageous. The Timani crew of the official boat swiftly shot us alongside. The craft showed Spanish colours, and was named *La Pantica*. We easily leaped on board, as she lay low in the water. The first hasty glance around caused a sudden sickness and faintness, followed by an indignation more intense than discreet. Before us, lying in a heap, huddled together at the foremast, on the bare and filthy deck, lay several human beings in the last stage of emaciation – dying. The ship fore and aft was thronged with men, women, and children, all entirely naked, and disgusting with disease. The stench was nearly insupportable, cleanliness being impossible. I stepped to the hatchway; it was secured by iron bars and cross bars, and pressed against them were the heads of slaves below. It appeared that the crowd on deck formed one third only of the cargo, two thirds being stowed in a sitting posture below between-decks, the men forward, the women aft. Two hundred and seventy-four were at this moment in the little schooner. When captured, three hundred and fifteen had been found on board; forty had died during the voyage from the Old Calabar, where she had been captured by H.M S. *Fair Rosamond*, and one had drowned himself on arrival, probably in fear of being eaten (yammed) by the English. It was not, how-ever, until the second visit, on the following day, that the misery which reigns in a slave ship was fully understood.

'The rainy season had commenced, and during the night rain had poured heavily down. Nearly a hundred slaves had been exposed to the weather on deck, and amongst them the heap of dying skeletons at the foremast. After making my way through the clustered mass of women on the quarter-deck, I discovered the slave captain, who had also been part owner, comfortably asleep in his cot, undisturbed by the horrors around him. The captives were now counted; their numbers, sex, and age written down for the information of the Court of Mixed Commission. The task was repulsive. As the hold had been divided for the separation of the men and the women, those on deck were first counted; they were then driven forward, crowded as much as possible, and the women were drawn up through the small hatchway from their hot, dark confinement. A black boatswain seized them one by one, dragging them before us for a moment, when the proper officer at a glance decided the age, whether above or under fourteen; and they were instantly swung again by the arm into their loathsome hell, where another black boatswain sat with a whip or stick and forced them to resume the bent and painful attitude necessary for the storage of so large a number.

'The unfortunate women and girls, in general, submitted with quiet resignation when absence of disease and the use of their limbs permitted. A month had made their condition familiar to them. One or two were less philosophical, or suffered more acutely than the rest. Their shrieks rose faintly from their hidden prison as violent compulsion alone squeezed them into their nook against the curve of the ship's side. I attempted to descend, in order to see the accommodation. The height between the floor and ceiling was about twenty-two inches. The agony of the position of the crouching slaves may be imagined, especially that of the men, whose heads and necks are bent down by the boarding above them. Once so fixed, relief by motion or change of posture is unattainable. The body frequently stiffens into a permanent curve; and in the streets of Freetown I have seen liberated slaves in every conceivable state of distortion. One I remember who trailed along his body with his back to the ground by means of his hands and ankles. Many can never resume the upright posture.

'*La Pantica* was condemned. The "slaves", so designated in the official order of the acting registrar, after their emancipation, were brought ashore. Their comfort was yet little consulted; fifty were conveyed in each canoe, one expired during the transit, and another, a few minutes after landing, died before my eyes. The apathy of the African here displayed itself. Shuddering at the sight of the gasping man, whose fixed and glazing eye, emaciated body, and rattle in the throat indicated coming dissolution, I requested a constable of the King's Yard, who stood by, to raise the dying slave from the mud and pool of water into which he had been carelessly laid down, and desired him to spread a mat for him on the dry ground under the shed. The request was not granted. The constable walked away, simply remarking, "He no good. He go for die!"

'The men and children were first brought into the Liberated Yard, and, being ranged in a line, a piece of cotton was given each. Several had no idea of the purpose for which it was intended. Few of the children seemed to approve of the new uncomfortable fashion. Decency had suggested the distribution of the scanty checked chemises to the women previous to their landing. When clothed and again counted, the whole were marched across the street from the Liberated Yard to the King's Yard, to await their final distribution as soldiers, wives, apprentices, and country gentlemen.

'To the King's Yard I paid frequent visits, and found an interest awakened in behalf of the people. The young children soon recovered from their sufferings, and their elastic spirits seemed little injured. The men next rallied, but several died in the shed devoted to the most sickly, chiefly from dysentery; they were wrapped in a coarse grass mat, carried away, and buried without ceremony. Of the women, many were dispatched to the hospital at Kissey, victims to raging fever; others had become insane. I was informed that insanity is the frequent fate of the women captives, and that it chiefly comes upon such as at first exhibit most intellectual development and greatest liveliness of disposition. Instances were pointed out to me. The women sustain their bodily sufferings with more silent fortitude than the men, and seldom destroy themselves; but they brood more over their misfortunes, until the sense is lost in madness . . .

'The slaves had been principally brought from the Old Calabar River, but consisted of contributions from many nations. None understood English; and the interpreter, Ogoon, an Ebo by birth, now a useful officer in the Liberated Yard, who spoke several languages, found those of the majority unintelligible to himself; I had therefore small means of ascertaining the general impressions of the liberated. No joy at the fact of liberation was perceptible. In more cases than one a strong desire to return to the ship was expressed; they certainly did not attribute their woes to the Spanish captain. Indifference both with regard to the past and the future seems general; the Foulahs are fatalists, and probably their pagan countrymen submit to circumstances on the same principle. They are not, however, destitute of feeling. On one occasion it was displayed in an interesting manner. A visit of some of the English prize officers to the Yard had evidently given pleasure to several of their late charge. It happened, however, that when the ship stock of yams and pepper was brought to the King's Yard, one of the black boatswains, a most ugly Kroo named Bottle of Beer, who had superintended the slaves in their voyage, accompanied the sailors who brought the food. No sooner was the good-humoured, merry face of the hideous Bottle of Beer perceived than a general rush took place from all quarters of the yard. All gathered round, laughing and shouting his name. The women and children pressed upon him; at least a dozen seized him at once by the hands, arms, and knees. A little girl climbed up his back to kiss him; the women tenderly wiped the perspiration from his face, and the throng threatened to suffocate him with fondness. Even the invalids, hearing the name of their friend, rose from the mats and tottered from their sheds to greet him. He had been kind to them when kindness had little power to lessen their misery. Such gratitude, in such a place, was touching.

'Their hours were spent idly; preparation of food was their sole occupation. The young children alone showed active ingenuity. This they did in two ways; they had at first submitted to the innovation of the cotton wrapper, but before a day had elapsed I found many freed from the encumbrance, carrying instead of it little wallets suspended round their necks and formed of the calico. The young creatures had torn it into small squares; by twisting the unravelled fibres they had made thread, and, by means of a sharp stone or pointed stick picked from the ground, had sewn the edges together firmly and neatly. One bag so made by a child of six or seven years had two compartments, cleverly divided by the insertion of another square of calico. In the place of ribbon they had drawn out the long grass from their matting and plaited it.

'Their other employment was laughable, even to themselves.

The propensity of the African to gash and tattoo the face has been observed. Here a substitute for the knife and burnt stick presented itself in the mortar of the walls and shed. With a lump of this material moistened in water an elder girl continued through a morning chalking into grotesque patterns the jetty face of a grinning little maid, who sat on the ground enduring the operation with much glee. Circles and vandykes, perpendicular and horizontal lines half an inch in breadth, white upon black ground, precisely like the markings of a zebra, put nearly all the children into masquerade. The sight of these variegated creatures in their evening dance would have forced smiles from an anchorite.

'At my last visit the children wore circular tin plates, stamped and numbered, tied around their necks. They had been allotted as apprentices to different applicants. Their mirth was to end; the bond of fellowship, bound in days of misery, was to be loosened; the "ship friends" were to be separated. The badge of appropriation looked ill; it savoured of slavery. The settler who first explained to me the purport, said the tin plates were to show to what master each "slave" belonged.

'The last place in which romance and poetry would be sought is the King's Yard at Sierra Leone; yet there they certainly did throw their soft inspiration over a boy and girl, each in the poetic period of African life. Calabar appeared to be sixteen years of age; he had an intelligent countenance, a fine expression. He alone had learnt some English on board the slaver, owing, perhaps, to more frequent intercourse with the officers, which resulted from his superior bearing and excellent conduct. He had been slave to the notorious Duke Ephraim, but detested restraint, and sighing for independence, he had used an Irish mode of obtaining it by escaping from the black Duke and delivering himself up to the Spanish captain, at that time taking in his complement of slaves for the Brazilian market. He had made himself useful on board, and was useful in the Yard also, maintaining an ascendancy over all the boys, and marshalling them to order.

'Amongst the young girls, one had early attracted my interest by a singular maidenly grace and dignity; her person was exquisitely moulded; her countenance beaming but gentle. I had recommended an English lady to apply for the beautiful Faye-nawon in order that she might educate her as a substitute for the terrific object who officiated as lady's-maid, and, as a mark of this possible approbation, I had tied a bright red handkerchief round the child's head. Ignorant of my intention, Fayenawon had innocently considered it as a mere ornament and proof of kindness; and ever afterwards, on my entering the yard, would leave the throng of her companions, and even her plantain and rice, to meet me. It needed little observation to discover that an attachment had grown between Calabar and Fayenawon. They were constantly walking together with her arm resting on his shoulder, and he proved a very knight of the old school of chivalry, daring dangers to gratify his little lady. Africans are much terrified at a horse; none of these slaves had before seen one. Horror-stricken when I first rode into the Yard, one and all had rushed for safety into the shed on my advance, and Calabar as nimbly as the rest. Fayenawon alone lingered at the entrance of her shed, without courage to meet the monster, yet desirous of presenting herself before me. I called her; she came forward a step, then hastily retreated; Calabar ran to the child, and taking her hand, cautiously led her towards me. On dismounting, I told the boy to hold the horse; after a pause he did so, to the high gratification of little Fayenawon. Being desirous to discover how far the young savage could conquer his terror, I ordered him to mount. He looked long at Fayenawon, but at last placing his foot in the stirrup, leaped into the saddle, to the astonishment of the slaves; he turned his eyes proudly towards his favourite, and soon rejoined her. On the distribution of apprentices, Calabar and his Fayenawon were, of course, separated. The timid girl is now probably in the severe labour of some hard black task-mistress, and liable to the frequent castigations of the thorn-stick [*largbar*]. The lot of Calabar depended on his age; if classed amongst the boys he, too, is an apprentice in some part of the colony; if amongst the men, he is either employed in the barracks, or on public works, or farming his half-rood of ground. It is within the scope of possibility that both of them have been carried off, again battened down between the decks of the slave ship, and are again on their way to the slave markets of Rio de Janeiro or Havana.'

Thirteen British men-of-war watched the coast, cruising for slaves. The headquarters and residence of the Admiral were at the Cape of Good Hope, scarcely the most favourable spot, if the exclusive use of the squadron were for the suppression of the slave trade. The rivers of Guinea, frequented by the slave ships, were too remote from the Cape to permit rapid and constant exchange of intelligence, and the slave trade was by treaty *legal* to the south of the line. The vessels employed for its suppression were small frigates and gun-brigs commissioned for three years' service. The ship which captured a prize received the price it brought by auction; and prize money was, moreover, awarded according to the number of slaves released.

The chances of capture and of consequent prize money, the excitements of search, of chase, of occasional exchange of shots, combined to soften down the afflictions of the climate. The excellent band of meritorious and energetic officers and men who were then employed on the station did as much as could possibly be done to check the traffic. Experience, however, proved the system to be totally inadequate. But a small proportion of slave ships were captured; by far the greater number eluded detection, and arrived safely at their destination. Captures were, with few exceptions, the result of mere accident. The low, sharp, rakish schooner of the pirates could sometimes walk round the dignified square ships of the service, and in light winds invariably distance them; if they were taken after a long chase, it was in consequence of the better skill of the British sailing master. Thus the *Pantica* was captured by a happy chance. The *Fair Rosamond* had entered the Calabar River, and dropped anchor on a dark, foggy night. When morning broke, the slave ship was discovered close by; they had unconsciously lain as neighbours side by side. The *Pantica* had been loaded with slaves, and was ready to weigh anchor at sunrise for America. A rocket was fired over her, and she had no alternative but to strike her colours.

Some years since, we find a plan adopted of arming these captured schooners, and employing them as cruisers. The result was one of singular success. The far-famed *Black Joke* was of this description. She had been a slave ship of the finest model, captured by Sir F. Collier in the Sinylle, and, armed with a long swivel, she became the terror of the slave merchants throughout the coast. Her speed was unequalled by anything that ever made trial against her. In a year she alone captured nearly as many slave ships as the whole squadron. Her fame does not rest upon her speed; as long as gallantry of the highest order is esteemed, her deeds and encounters will be remembered. The ultimate benefit to be derived from such employment of armed slavers cannot be known, the Admiralty having decided against their further use.

The *Black Joke* was finally condemned and burnt, and a melancholy sight have I considered it when passing by her long-eighteen, that still stood above water in the Kroo bay at half-tide. It recalled the stories of her heroic doings, which had often excited men in distant England, long before they dreamed that it would ever be their lot to glide by the remains of that gallant barque.

So efficient were her services, that many a black who had been liberated by her was said to have wept on beholding the conflagration; and it is notorious that, from the Rio Pongas to the Callenas, feasts and rejoicing amongst the slave merchants bore witness to the feelings with which they regarded the destruction of their scourge.

4

E. Casely-Hayford

An Early Train Journey

Ethiopia Unbound (1911), from which this extract is taken, was written by a Ghanaian, E. Casely-Hayford. The 'novel' is at logger-heads with itself, since Kwamankra, the chief character, is unknowingly the first 'divided man' – a theme of so many subsequent African writers in English. Kwamankra is honestly concerned with racial rediscovery, with African unity, with human rights, but his way back to his origins is difficult to justify. He journeys to England to have books printed in the indigenous language he hopes will be the medium of instruction in his national university. In true 'classical' manner he visits the under-world to see his dead wife. He addresses his son in the language of an educated Victorian gentleman. This extract is not indicative of the book's general pattern, but it is worthwhile reproducing, as a rare early example of African laughter in literature – laughter, incidentally, which was to become a phenomenon.

An Early Train Journey

'I say, boys, what class are you travelling?' shouted Aban to Tandor-Kuma and Kwamankra.

'I go neither first nor second,' returned Tandor-Kuma; and as the Gold Coast Government Railway boasts of only two classes, Kwamankra said, 'Look here, you fellows, I am a man of peace. If you are going to have any larks, I would rather take the down train twenty-four hours hence.'

By this time the bell announcing the hour for the departure of the train had sounded. So Kwamankra rushed to secure a first-class ticket, leaving the 'Professor' and Tandor-Kuma to their own devices. When he returned, the two had occupied seats in the first-class compartment and started to make themselves merry with the good things which Kwamankra had provided for the journey.

'Here's to you and another five hundred a year, as the chaps over the water say' – this as the 'Professor' raised his glass in the direction of Kwamankra. Seeing there was no alternative, the latter resigned himself to the situation, and good-humouredly toasted the company round.

'Teekeets! teekeets!' shouted the collector from the second-class end of the 'composite carriage'. Of course, you know what a 'composite carriage' is? If you don't, I will enlighten you. It is the kind of thing on this particular railway in which the whites travel at one end, their servants and the black élite at the other end, while the ordinary blacks are packed like sardines in a detached carriage, labelled 'second-class'. Not that there is any rule prohibiting black gentlemen from using a first-class carriage, but the fact is the class referred to know better, and have too much self-respect to travel first, except on rare occasions when they can have a carriage all to themselves.

To resume, 'teekeets! teekeets!' sounded nearer. By this time the 'Professor' was in the middle of a Mississippi story, and his brush with buffaloes and other hair-breadth escapes. After taking a cheap degree, with his usual erratic disposition, Aban had been travelling, often supporting himself by odd jobs, and had included in his experiences an acquaintance with the Japs of whom he was never tired of speaking. The ticket collector eyed the three gentlemen furtively once or twice, and seemed to have come to a mental resolve not to disturb them for the nonce, nor did the trio disturb him by so much as a momentary notice of his presence.

Just as he was about retreating to the second-class compartment, Kwamankra shouted after him, 'I say, collector, won't you have a drink?' holding out to him some whisky and soda – 'the others do it, you know,' and this with a knowing wink.

The collector was human. He hesitated, then made up his mind, took the drink, and went away. Presently he returned and became communicative.

'I don't know, Sar, if any of you, Sar, be lawyer man, Sar?'

Tandor-Kuma chuckled. 'What next,' demanded the 'Professor' sternly. Kwamankra held his peace, appearing not to listen.

'I don't know, Sar, but I bin tink say I da go show you di rules which say di collector mus examin ebery gentman him teekeet.'

Kwamankra began to fumble in his pockets. 'My good man,' said the 'Professor' to the collector, 'I have made it a rule never to give up my ticket on this line till I have landed safely at my destination, do you understand?'

The emphasis seemed to upset the equilibrium of the collector. He sneaked away, may be, to reflect upon the advantage of an emphasis, and sure enough, he was soon heard letting off steam in the second-class compartment at the expense of an inoffensive Fanti.

By this time the train had passed Mansu. Shortly after leaving that station there was some trouble with one of the vans getting off the rails; and it was a matter of half an hour before it was set right. Half-way between Mansu and Ashieme, some timber was taken, and as they steamed away in the twilight, the train with its composite appendages was a full furlong long! Soon they were in thick darkness.

'Light, collector, light!' – this from Kwamankra, for in the detached carriage could be heard yells and shrieks of women and children.

'I say, collector, light! Do you hear? Light!' and this with an expletive or two from the 'Professor'. The expletive did its work. The collector made his way to the composite carriage amid a scene of much confusion.

'You had better go and fetch the Inspector to see about this mess, or I will report the whole lot of you fellows, white and black alike. It is perfectly disgraceful, this kind of thing,' said Tandor-Kuma.

The Inspector, who had, in the meantime, been hurried to the detached compartment by the shrieks of the women and children, had by this time got into the composite carriage.

'What the deuce are you doing not having yet lighted the carriage,' he said to the collector with an offended air.

'I no get mach, Sar! Railway no buy me mach, Sar!'

The Inspector made as if he would knock the collector down, but thought better of the matter, and, snatching a borrowed match box, quickly tried to light the lamp. Puff! went out the light.

'Try again, Sir,' suggested Kwamankra dryly. 'There may be a drop of water in the oil.' Puff! went out the light the second time.

'Try again! try again!' came from all sides. 'Shall I get out and buy you some paraffin, Mr Inspector? You know this is perfectly disgraceful. Thirteen shillings for thirty-nine miles and no oil,' said Tandor-Kuma.

'Try again! try again! knock him down, teach him a lesson,' shouted some roughs. It was getting a bit exciting. The Inspector beat a hasty retreat.

'They call dis di Govmont railway. It is di dirtiest hole I have been in. South Africa, East Africa, North Africa, they be countries. Dis country is disgraceful to the British Govmont,' put in a Frenchman at the corner.

Pu! pu! pu! piyu!! Pu! pu! piyu!! came the heartbreaking

49

snort from the nostrils of the iron horse. It reminded one of an overworked omnibus horse at midnight in Oxford Street. First backwards, then downwards, up the incline, and down the gradient, toyed the iron horse, and as Tandor-Kuma thought of his wife, and children waiting dinner in the cosy little room across the bridge, he could not help inwardly bestowing a blessing upon the devil and all his works. It was not until 9.30 p.m. that the terminus was made, the party having left on their thirty-nine miles run at 2.30 p.m. As the trio walked the lonely streets, where black men are scarcely seen after sunset, the 'Professor', as a parting reminder, said to Kwamankra, 'On principle I never pay for a ticket on this line until I have made the terminus, and if you are a wise man, you will take my tip.'

5

Sol T. Plaatje

Native Life in South Africa

It is ironical, but scarcely surprising, when the African equips himself with the cudgels of the conqueror in order to defend himself. Sol T. Plaatje, a South African, did just this. For a great deal of South African writing towards the end of the last century had been marred by attempts at posturing as 'good' Africans. The mission presses encouraged this type of literature, by which the African hero saw in his culture only what was to be shunned, and his role became that of a messiah, leading his people away from 'ignorance'.

All this seems rather old-fashioned now; but if today black South African writing seems unduly weighted on the other side, with its creators over-anxious to demonstrate strength and tolerance (virtues that are denied them in their societies), then the reasons for these preoccupations are literary as well as political. Plaatje was one of the earliest writers to revolt against the clover world of mission literature and begin forcefully expressing what 'civilization' had come to mean for his own people and their literature.

The immediate reason for this book was the Land Act of 1913, by which land that could be owned by Africans was formally restricted to 13 per cent of the country, and the promotion of a migrant labour force, to serve white mining, industry and agriculture, correspondingly advanced. Plaatje visited farms during this period and so his account is a first-hand one.

Native Life in South Africa

Awaking on Friday morning, 20 June 1913, the South African Native found himself, not actually a slave, but a pariah in the land of his birth.

The 4,500,000 black South Africans are domiciled as follows: one and three-quarter millions in Locations and Reserves, over half a million within municipalities or in urban areas, and nearly a million as squatters on farms owned by Europeans. The remainder are employed either on the public roads or railway lines, or as servants by European farmers, qualifying, that is, by hard work and saving to start farming on their own account.

A squatter in South Africa is a native who owns some livestock and, having no land of his own, hires a farm or grazing and ploughing rights from a landowner, to raise grain for his own use and feed his stock. Hence, these squatters are hit very hard by an Act which passed both Houses of Parliament during the session of 1913, received the signature of the Governor-General on 16 June, was gazetted on 19 June, and forthwith came into operation. It may here be mentioned that on that day Lord Gladstone signed no fewer than sixteen new Acts of Parliament – some of them being rather voluminous – while three days earlier, His Excellency signed another batch of eight, of which the bulk was beyond the capability of any mortal to read and digest in four days.

But the great revolutionary change thus wrought by a single stroke of the pen, in the condition of the Native, was not realized by him until about the end of June. As a rule many farm tenancies expire at the end of the half-year, so that in June 1913, not knowing that it was impracticable to make fresh contracts, some Natives unwittingly went to search for new places of abode, which some farmers, ignorant of the law, quite as unwittingly accorded them. It was only when they went to register the new tenancies that the law officers of the Crown laid bare the cruel fact that to provide a landless Native with accommodation was forbidden under a penalty of £100, or six months' imprisonment. Then only was the situation realized.

Other Natives who had taken up fresh places on European farms under verbal contracts, which needed no registration actually founded new homes in spite of the law, neither the white farmer nor the native tenant being aware of the serious penalties they were exposed to by their verbal contracts.

In justice to the Government, it must be stated that no police officers scoured the country in search of lawbreakers, to prosecute them under this law. Had this been done, many £100 cheques would have passed into the Government coffers during that black July, the first month after Lord Gladstone affixed his signature to the Natives' Land Act, No. 27 of 1913.

The complication of this cruel law is made manifest by the fact that it was found necessary for a high officer of the Government to tour the Provinces soon after the Act came into force, with the object of 'teaching' Magistrates how to administer it. A Congress of Magistrates – a most unusual thing – was also called in Pretoria to find a way for carrying out the King's writ in the face of the difficulties arising from this tangle of the Act. We may add that nearly all white lawyers in South Africa, to whom we spoke about this measure, had either not seen the Act at all, or had not read it carefully, so that in both cases they could not tell exactly for whose benefit it had been passed. The study of this law required a much longer time than the lawyers, unless specially briefed, could devote to it, so that they hardly knew what all the trouble was about. It was the Native in the four Provinces who knew all about it, for he had not read it in books but had himself been through its mill, which like an automatic machine ground him relentlessly since the end of the month of June. Not the least, but one of the cruellest and most ironical phases – and nearly every clause of this Act teems with irony – is the Schedule or appendix giving the so-called Scheduled Native Areas; and what are these 'Scheduled Native Areas'?

They are the Native Locations which were reserved for the

exclusive use of certain native clans. They are inalienable and cannot be bought or sold, yet the Act says that in these 'Scheduled Native Areas' Natives only may buy land. The areas being inalienable, not even members of the clans, for whose benefit the locations are held in trust, can buy land therein. The areas could only be sold if the whole clan rebelled; in that case the location would be confiscated. But as long as the clans of the location remain loyal to the Government, nobody can buy any land within these areas. Under the respective charters of these areas, not even a member of the clan can get a separate title as owner in an area – let alone a native outsider who had grown up among white people and done all his farming on white man's land.

If we exclude the arid tracts of Bechuanaland, these Locations appear to have been granted on such a small scale that each of them got so overcrowded that much of the population had to go out and settle on the farms of white farmers through lack of space in the Locations. Yet a majority of the legislators, although well aware of all these limitations, and without remedying any of them, legislates, shall we say, 'with its tongue in its cheek' that only Natives may buy land in Native Locations.

Again, the Locations form but one eighteenth of the total area of the Union. Theoretically, then, the 4,500,000 Natives may 'buy' land in only one eighteenth part of the Union, leaving the remaining seventeen parts for the one million whites. It is moreover true that, numerically, the Act was passed by the consent of a majority of both Houses of Parliament, but it is equally true that it was steam-rolled into the statute book against the bitterest opposition of the best brains of both Houses. A most curious aspect of this singular law is that even the Minister, since deceased, who introduced it, subsequently declared himself against it, adding that he only forced it through in order to stave off something worse. Indeed, it is correct to say that Mr Sauer, who introduced the Bill, spoke against it repeatedly in the House; he deleted the milder provisions, inserted more drastic amendments, spoke repeatedly against his own amendments, then in conclusion he would combat his own arguments by calling the ministerial steam-roller to support the Government and vote for the drastic amendments. The only explanation of the puzzle constituted as such by these 'hot-and-cold' methods is that Mr Sauer was legislating for an electorate, at the expense of another section of the population which was without direct representation in Parliament. None of the non-European races in the Provinces of Natal, Transvaal and the 'Free' State can exercise the franchise. They have no say in the selection of members for the Union Parliament. That right is only limited to white men, so that a large number of the members of Parliament who voted for this measure have no responsibility towards the black races.

Before reproducing this tyrannical enactment it would perhaps be well to recapitulate briefly the influences that led up to it. When the Union of the South African Colonies became an accomplished fact, a dread was expressed by ex-Republicans that the liberal native policy of the Cape would supersede the repressive policy of the old Republics, and they lost no time in taking definite steps to force down the throats of the Union Legislature, as it were, laws which the Dutch Presidents of pre-war days, with the British suzerainty over their heads, did not dare enforce against the Native people then under them. With the formation of the Union, the Imperial Government, for reasons which have never been satisfactorily explained, unreservedly handed over the Natives to the colonists, and these colonists, as a rule, are dominated by the Dutch Republican spirit. Thus the suzerainty of Great Britain, which under the reign of Her late Majesty Victoria, of blessed memory, was the Natives' only bulwark, has now apparently been withdrawn or relaxed, and the Republicans, like a lot of bloodhounds long held in the leash, use the free hand given by the Imperial Government not only to guard against a possible supersession of Cape ideals of toleration, but to effectively extend throughout the Union the drastic native policy pursued by the Province which is misnamed 'Free' State, and enforce it with the utmost rigour.

During the first year of the Union, it would seem that General Botha made an honest attempt to live up to his London promises, that are mentioned by Mr Merriman in his speech (reproduced elsewhere) on the second reading of the Bill in Parliament. It would seem that General Botha endeavoured to allay British apprehensions and concern for the welfare of the Native popula-

tion. In pursuance of this policy General Botha won the approbation of all Natives by appointing Hon. H. Burton, a Cape
Minister, to the portfolio of Native Affairs. That the appointment was a happy one, from the native point of view, became
manifest when Mr Burton signalized the ushering in of Union, by
releasing Chief Dinizulu-ka-Cetywayo, who at that time was
undergoing a sentence of imprisonment imposed by the Natal
Supreme Court, and by the restoration to Dinizulu of his pension
of £500 a year. Also, in deference to the wishes of the Native
Congress, Mr Burton abrogated two particularly obnoxious
Natal measures, one legalizing the 'Sibalo' system of forced
labour, the other prohibiting public meetings by Natives without the consent of the Government. These abrogations placed
the Natives of Natal in almost the same position as the Cape
Natives, though without giving them the franchise. So, too,
when a drastic Squatters' Bill was gazetted early in 1912, and
the recently formed Native National Congress sent a deputation
to interview Mr Burton in Capetown; after hearing the deputation, he graciously consented to withdraw the proposed measure,
pending the allotment of new Locations in which Natives evicted
by such a measure could find an asylum. In further deference to
the representations of the Native Congress, in which they were
supported by Senators the Hon. W. P. Schreiner, Colonel Stan-
ford, and Mr Krogh, the Union Government gazetted another
Bill in January 1911, to amend an anomaly which, at that time,
was peculiar to the 'Free' State: an anomaly under which a
Native can neither purchase nor lease land, and native landowners in the 'Free' State could only sell their land to the white
people.

The gazetted Bill proposed to legalize only in one district of
the Orange 'Free' State the sale of landed property by a Native
to another Native as well as to a white man, but it did not propose
to enable Natives to buy land from white men. The object of the
Bill was to remove a hardship, mentioned elsewhere in this
sketch, by which a 'Free' State Native was by law debarred
from inheriting landed property left to him under his uncle's
will. But against such small attempts at reform, proposed or
carried out by the Union Government in the interest of the

Natives, granted in small instalments of a teaspoonful at a time – reforms dictated solely by feelings of justice and equity – ex-Republicans were furious.

From platform, Press, and pulpit it was suggested that General Botha's administration was too pro-English and needed over-hauling. The Dutch peasants along the countryside were inflamed by hearing that their gallant leader desired to anglicize the country. Nothing was more repellent to the ideas of the backveld Dutch, and so at small meetings in the country districts resolutions were passed stating that the Botha administration had outlived its usefulness. These resolutions reaching the Press from day to day had the effect of stirring up the Dutch voters against the Ministry, and particularly against the head. At this time General Botha's sound policy began to weaken. He transferred Hon. H. Burton, first Minister of Natives, to the portfolio of Railways and Harbours, and appointed General Hertzog, of all people in the world, to the portfolio of Native Affairs.

The good-humoured indulgence of some Dutch and English farmers towards their native squatters, and the affectionate loyalty of some of these native squatters in return, will cause a keen observer, arriving at a South African farm, to be lost in admiration for this mutual good feeling. He will wonder as to the meaning of the fabled bugbear anent the alleged struggle between white and black, which in reality appears to exist only in the fertile brain of the politician. Thus let the new arrival go to one of the farms in the Bethlehem or Harrismith Districts for example, and see how willingly the Native toils in the fields; see him gathering in his crops and handing over the white farmer's share of the crop to the owner of the land; watch the farmer receiving his tribute from the native tenants, and see him deliver the first prize to the native tenant who raised the largest crop during that season; let him also see both the Natives and the landowning white farmers following to perfection the give-and-take policy of 'live and let live', and he will conclude that it would be gross sacrilege to attempt to disturb such harmonious relations between these people of different races and colours. But with a ruthless hand the Natives' Land Act has succeeded in remorselessly destroying those happy relations.

First of all, General Hertzog, the new Minister of Native Affairs, travelled up and down the country lecturing farmers on their folly in letting ground to the Natives; the racial extremists of his party hailed him as the right man for the post, for, as his conduct showed them, he would soon 'fix up' the Natives. At one or two places he was actually welcomed as the future Prime Minister of the Union. On the other hand, General Botha, who at that time seemed to have become visibly timid, endeavoured to ingratiate himself with his discontented supporters by joining his lieutenant in travelling to and fro, denouncing the Dutch farmers for not expelling the Natives from their farms and replacing them with poor whites. This became a regular Ministerial campaign against the Natives, so that it seemed clear that if any Native could still find a place in the land, it was not due to the action of the Government. In his campaign the Premier said other unhappy things which were diametrically opposed to his London speeches of two years before; and while the Dutch colonists railed at him for trying to anglicize the country, English speakers and writers justly accused him of speaking with two voices; cartoonists, too, caricatured him as having two heads – one, they said, for London, and the second one for South Africa.

The uncertain tenure by which Englishmen in the public service held their posts became the subject of debates in the Union Parliament, and the employment of Government servants of colour was decidedly precarious. They were swept out of the Railway and Postal Service with a strong racial broom, in order to make room for poor whites, mainly of Dutch descent. Concession after concession was wrung from the Government by fanatical Dutch postulants for office, for Government doles and other favours, who, like the daughters of the horse-leech in the Proverbs of Solomon, continually cried, 'Give, give.' By these events we had clearly turned the corner and were pacing backwards to pre-Union days, going back, back, and still further backward, to the conditions which prevailed in the old Republics, and (if a check is not applied) we shall steadily drift back to the days of the old Dutch East Indian administration.

The Bill which proposed to ameliorate the 'Free' State cruelty, to which reference has been made above, was dropped like a hot potato. Ministers made some wild and undignified speeches, of which the following spicy extract, from a speech by the Rt Hon. Abraham Fischer to his constituents at Bethlehem, is a typical sample:

'What is it you want?' he asked. 'We have passed all the coolie* laws and we have passed all the Kafir laws. The "Free" State has been safeguarded and all her colour laws have been adopted by Parliament. What more can the Government do for you?' And so the Union ship in this reactionary sea sailed on and on and on, until she struck an iceberg – the sudden dismissal of General Hertzog.

To the bitter sorrow of his admirers, General Hertzog, who is the fearless exponent of Dutch ideals, was relieved of his portfolios of Justice and Native Affairs – it was whispered as a result of a suggestion from London; and then the Dutch extremists, in consequence of their favourite's dismissal, gave vent to their anger in the most disagreeable manner. One could infer from their platform speeches that, from their point of view, scarcely any one else had any rights in South Africa, and least of all the man with a black skin.

In the face of this, the Government's timidity was almost unendurable. They played up to the desires of the racial extremists, with the result that a deadlock overtook the administration. Violent laws like the Immigration Law (against British Indians and alien Asiatics) and the Natives' Land were indecently hurried through Parliament to allay the susceptibilities of 'Free' State Republicans. No Minister found time to undertake such useful legislation as the Coloured People's Occupation Bill, the Native Disputes Bill, the Marriage Bill, the University Bill, etc., etc. An apology was demanded from the High Commissioner in London for delivering himself of sentiments which were felt to be too British for the palates of Dutch employers in South Africa, and the Prime Minister had almost to apologize for having at times so far forgotten himself as to act more like a Crown Minister than a simple Africander. 'Free' State demands became so persistent that Ministers seemed to have forgotten the assurances they gave His Majesty's Government in London re-

*A contemptuous South African term for Indians.

garding the safety of His Majesty's coloured subjects within the Union. They trampled under foot their own election pledges, made during the first Union General Election, guaranteeing justice and fair treatment to the law-abiding Natives.

The campaign, to compass the elimination of the blacks from the farms, was not at all popular with landowners, who made huge profits out of the renting of their farms to Natives. Platform speakers and newspaper writers coined an opprobrious phrase which designated this letting of farms to Natives as 'Kafir-farming', and attempted to prove that it was almost as immoral as 'baby-farming'. But landowners pocketed the annual rents, and showed no inclination to substitute the less industrious 'poor whites' for the more industrious Natives. Old Baas M—, a typical Dutch landowner of the 'Free' State, having collected his share of the crop of 1912, addressing a few words of encouragement to his native tenants, on the subject of expelling the blacks from the farms, said in the Taal: 'How dare any number of men, wearing tall hats and frock coats, living in Capetown hotels at the expense of other men, order me to evict my Natives? This is my ground; it cost my money, not Parliament's, and I will see them banged [barst] before I do it.'

It then became evident that the authority of Parliament would have to be sought to compel the obstinate landowners to get rid of their Natives. And the compliance of Parliament with this demand was the greatest Ministerial surrender to the Republican malcontents, resulting in the introduction and passage of the Natives' Land Act of 1913, inasmuch as the Act decreed, in the name of His Majesty the King, that pending the adoption of a report to be made by a commission, somewhere in the dim and unknown future, it shall be unlawful for Natives to buy or lease land, except in scheduled native areas. And under severe pains and penalties they were to be deprived of the bare human rights of living on the land, except as servants in the employ of the whites – rights which were never seriously challenged under the Republican régime, no matter how politicians raved against the Natives.

6

R. R. R. Dhlomo

The Rake

R. R. R. Dhlomo published the short novelette *An African Tragedy* in 1928, and it is from there that this extract has been taken. It was written in English and was the story of how Robert Zulu mistakenly left his village for the seedy life of Johannesburg. Robert Zulu's introduction to gambling and drinking is the beginning of his estrangement from the virtues of his tribal society. But neither Robert Zulu nor his creator are believers in the traditional world; Robert Zulu's marriage is a failure because he does not have the Christian virtues of his wife. Finally he is murdered and, in a melodramatic scene at the end, confesses his 'sins'.

Dhlomo contrasts strongly with Plaatje. Robert Zulu is as wrong when he is found without a pass as when he drinks and gambles. Dhlomo intentionally creates the 'bad' African so that by inference it can be seen how the 'good' African ought to behave. There is no irony, no interrogation. Dhlomo had absorbed the lessons of his masters, and it was not his purpose to question their values. What he found he accepted, and what he accepted he deemed good.

The Rake

Two reasons made Robert Zulu leave teaching at Siam Village School. The first was that he wanted to get married to Miss Jane Nhlauzeko as soon as possible. But as Jane's father had asked for a silly huge sum of money and other gifts for *Ilobolo*, Robert felt that he could not raise this sum quickly enough while teaching – teachers' salaries being anything but lucrative at that time.

So he made up his mind to leave teaching, and go to Johannesburg to look for work. He felt sure that there he could make more money in more ways than one, and that quickly too.

The second reason was that he thought, as most foolish young people think nowadays, that town life is better in every way than country life; and that for a young, educated man to die having not seen and enjoyed town life was a deplorable tragedy. These excuses made Robert deaf to all the efforts of his parents and friends to dissuade him from going to that most unreliable city of Johannesburg. His final decision therefore, to go to Johannesburg at all hazards, was a blow to his people, who had thought high of him, as a young Christian teacher in the Mission.

This blow was felt even more strongly by his future parents-in-law. But as Robert pointed out to his father-in-law that, unless he reduced his *Ilobolo*, there was no alternative open to him but that of going to Johannesburg to try and raise money quickly, his father-in-law did not argue any further.

He wanted money for his daughter. He had said: 'What business has Robert to ask my daughter's hand in marriage if he has no money to pay for her?' This is unfortunately the parrot-cry of many Christian fathers, the costly mistake which, in many cases, results in poor, and financially stranded homes, or driving the young lovers to the terrible alternative of a 'Special Licence', or running away from their homes with disastrous results all too well known.

Robert Zulu had been in Johannesburg for about two years – as our story begins. During this time, he had been engaged in all sorts of nefarious activities in pursuit of get-me-rich-quick methods. But all these activities, instead of getting him rich, only plunged him deeper and deeper in vice and evils.

The first disastrous step he took on his arrival in Johannesburg was that of his bad choice of companions. When he received his first monthly wages he usually bought himself a few necessaries, and then saved the rest for his future plans. But after his choice of companions his earnings and savings steadily but surely diminished.

He was now a reckless, dissolute young man. When he received his wages he no longer thought of sending part of it home or banking it. No, Goodness, what for? What fashionable young men, except they be fools, thought of banking their money in such a gay, rollicking city as that of Johannesburg? His first thoughts now were always on pleasure. That sort of pleasure for which Johannesburg is so notorious. Pleasure that has caused the sudden, terrible death of many a promising young man or woman. That was Robert's second mistake, which was subsequently to plunge him in terrible and heart-rending tragedies. Yet this error is so seemingly innocent that many young people still fall into it daily in spite of their education and faith. In his heart, Robert heard a soft, warning voice say:

'Do not! You will be ruined! Think of your duty to God. Think of those you left behind you. Be a man!' Yet another voice loud and insistent this time rang in his heart: 'Pleasure is the essence of young people's lives here in Johannesburg. Enjoy it, man! You will be loved and admired by lovely, dancing ladies of fashion, if you mix up with the gay throng and let your money and clothes advertise you!'

Robert Zulu soon made friends with a boy working next door. In the course of time they deceived themselves that they were fast and loyal friends. At least that is what Robert thought.

The young man, whose name was John Bolotwa, boasted

that what he didn't know in Johannesburg was not worth mentioning.

'Suggest a place, then, where we can enjoy ourselves tonight,' said Robert, in reply to this boast.

'Right you are,' agreed John eagerly. 'I shall call round for you this evening, and take you to a lively place just a few yards from Jeppestown. There, old man,' he continued, warming to his subject, 'we shall enjoy ourselves like lords for a mere shilling.'

When once a young person thinks of pleasure first, it never occurs to him or her that, where pleasure and vice abound, true and loyal friendship never exists. That evening Robert and John went out to enjoy themselves. They went to Prospect Township – a revolting immoral place; where the black sons and daughters of Africa are kicked about by their unbridled passions as a football is on the playfields. Here one may come across any kind of debased humanity. Ministers – in names and collars only – live in filthy closeness with loose women.

Murders and assaults are committed here with animalish ferocity, through the influence of drinks and faithless women.

Loose, morally depraved women, who parade the Township with uncovered bosoms; clothed in dirty robes. Women, whose sole aim in life is to get money at whatever costs or hazards, their chief traps or snares for obtaining this filthy lucre from the gullible mine boys and unwise educated people being their strong drinks and prostituted bodies.

No wonder Black Africa is cursed! At Prospect Township – which is, by the way, a matter of half a mile from the heart of the city of Johannesburg, and a matter of yards from the City Deep and Meyer and Charlton Gold Mines – in spite of the ceaseless activities of the Liquor Staff of the Prospect Township Police Station, to stamp out the Illicit Liquor Traffic – strong and violent drinks are brewed and sold in broad daylight.

To this place then Robert Zulu, the once promising young teacher and the future husband of a true, pure, faithful girl, came of his own free will, through his love of pleasure and his bad choice of companions. The room in which they found themselves was already half full with people of both sexes. The air was reeking with the evil smell of drinks and perspirations. As they entered, Robert shivered involuntarily. He had not bargained for such a scene of pleasure.

At one end of the room an organ was being hammered by a drunken youth. Couples – literally fastened to each other – were swaying giddily, wildly, to this barbaric time. In this mood young girls are deflowered in their youth. Yet we hear people wondering why there is so much licence among the young people.

Do these people who have the welfare of our nation at heart, ever visit these dark places and try to win back the straying young?

Carrying war only in clean and favourable surroundings; and preaching to the well-to-do and educated, is no remarkable and self-sacrificing warfare. War, if war it is, should be waged right into the enemies' lines where the source of all evils is.

For after all is said and done, what is the use of trying to unite our peoples when their offsprings wallow in the mud – so to speak? Do Christians who profess to love God, and seek to do His will ever visit such places – not as they do on Sunday afternoons when the people in the yards are already half mad with drinks and evil passions – but in the quiet during the week when these people are more amenable to reason?

Does it occur to their minds that these slaves of vice may be the sheep of whose welfare Christ spoke so eloquently and so feelingly in the 10th chapter of St John's Gospel: verse 16?

Pardon my digression, my poor effort being to write the story of Robert Zulu as he handed it to me for publication – not to presume to teach or preach.

Robert felt his heart sinking within him at this scene before him.

No! He did not think of going back – he went inside and sat down beside John on a long bench near the bed.

'Ma-Radebe!' called John, who was quite at home in such places, 'Give us two.'

The lady addressed as 'Ma-Radebe' was a stout, pretty looking woman of seven-and-twenty, with large, languishing eyes. A glance at her perfect, round, trim figure and at her pretty face gave one the impression that she was a married lady, and had her own, dear children somewhere in the background.

But when one again remarked her short, daring skirts; and marked her outrageous flirtations, one's opinion as to her being a mother was dashed against the rocks of impossibilities.

The truth was that she had left her lawful husband at Queenstown – and was now living with a 'kept' husband without moral or religious scruples.

When John ordered the drinks, he patted her on the shoulder affectionately, and she favoured him with a languishing glance, before she darted outside to execute her orders.

She approached an innocent looking ash-heap; and, after casting hurried glances round, dug quickly, and brought to the surface a small can full of Skokiaan. She poured a quantity of its contents into a jug, and, having replaced the can into the hole, she rearranged the ash-heap and went into the room. John took the jug. As he did so, all eyes were turned thirstily towards him. Eyes of confirmed slaves of Drink! Lost children of Light!

John handed the jug to Robert.

'Take a sip, man,' he said pleasantly. 'It will help to drive away all your doubts and fears.'

Robert took a step backward.

'I don't drink,' he said, in alarm.

'Who said you drink? I only said "Just a sip" – a sip is not a drink, surely.'

'Please, I'd rather not, old man,' protested Robert nervously.

John uttered an impatient oath under his breath.

'Do not be a fool, Bob' – he said persuasively. 'Take a sip, and act like a man.'

At this juncture the organ suddenly stopped – and Robert felt rather than saw, that he was the cynosure of all eyes. He grew hot all over. Beads of perspiration stood on his brow. Then he made a serious mistake, he hesitated perceptibly.

Hesitation!

When you are in a crisis, Robert, never, oh! never hesitate. Act on the first dictum of your heart! When John saw him hesitate, he knew he had won him.

He smiled grimly, as the serpent must have smiled in the

Garden of Eden, when Eve, instead of fleeing from its fascination, stood to parley with it.

'Sis!' exclaimed a young girl fashionably dressed. 'Isn't he a coward!'

'Perhaps he is thinking of his mother at home,' said another, calmly flicking the ash from her cigarette. 'John,' she added with a sneer, 'why did you bring a Christian here?'

'But to drink is no sin,' interjected a depraved young man. 'The Bible does not say it is a sin.'

There was a laugh at this irreverent talk. This laugh proved to be Robert's undoing. He took a step forward and thrust his face close to the depraved young man's.

'Say that again ... you ... you damn fool!'

The depraved one retreated in alarm at this unexpected terrible outburst.

'Don't run away, Jim,' cried the cigarette girl, 'stab him with your knife!'

John hastily stepped between them.

'No harm meant, Bob,' he said in a conciliating tone. 'Prove to these silly girls that you are no coward and drink this glass with me.'

There was a brief silence, during which the angels above held their breath in fear and dismay.

Then Robert – without a word – took the glass from John's hand, and drained it. This cool and manly act brought forth cries of delight from those in the room. The girls eagerly surrounded Robert, asking him to dance with them, which he did.

Robert Zulu was now lost. From that night, he had drunk and drunk until he became a hopeless drunkard. His physical health was now impaired. He mixed with loose women; enjoyed their company when their husbands were at work. Today young people marry to give chances to their rapacious brothers and sisters, who never hesitate to pay attentions to married young husbands or wives. The — Hall was now his favourite place of amusement. Here he was always sure to find a lonely girl, who would enjoy his company, although on the morrow she would be receiving the attentions of another young man.

These girls pride themselves that they can steal the husbands of any silly Christian girl once he puts his foot in the Dancing Hall – and his lips on the flowing bowl. They generally put their boasts into practice too – with tragical results to the newly married and quiet young girl.

It was only after the following ghastly tragedy that Robert began to think of his home and the faithful girl, whose letters still continued to arrive monthly. These he always answered profusely, and thus deceived the simple-minded country people. They thought he was still doing well, and consequently swallowed whatever he told them with child-like gullibility.

Then the terrible diversion came with the suddenness of a storm, and brought Robert Zulu to his distorted senses with a jerk, and incidentally, sent him dashing homewards as fast as the 8.45 p.m. express to Durban could carry him.

7

Isaac B. Thomas

Segilola: The Lady with the Delicate Eye-Balls

These letters were originally published in a Lagos newspaper between July 1929 and March 1930, and were probably written by Isaac Thomas, the editor of the paper. In all there were thirty of them, and, as the newspaper editor frankly admitted, he hoped that 'most of our readers will learn much'. The supposed Segilola is a Lagos prostitute who at the time of writing is forty-seven, and her letters describe her home life with her mother, her love affairs, her marriage. The narrative ends with her decision to become a prostitute.

Although the intention was didactic, Segilola's letters make better reading than Dhlomo's novel, partly because she exults in life and takes an obvious relish in recording her own failings. The story is delightfully ribald in parts, and manages to blend two traditions in African writing – the gloomy morality of mission press literature and the ethical emancipation of folk-tales. The literature of tutelage was beginning to free itself in another important way.

Segilola: The Lady with the Delicate Eye-Balls

Dear Editor,
Greetings!

I shall remain grateful to you throughout the remaining days of my life if you will grant that I, Segilola, the lady with the delicate eye-balls, the celebrated prostitute (married to a thousand husbands) may serialize my autobiography in your newspaper. Maybe by so doing I shall perform one good deed in the last days of my life – a life that has been all misery and waste – for there may be a few ones among the young men and, particularly, ladies, who may learn from my misdeeds and avoid regretting in their last days with bitter tears as I, Segilola, weep today for mistakes that cannot be repaired.

Alas! Alas! But things are never so bad that a miserable person lacks a comforter! Dear Editor, I beseech you to grant me this protection: never reveal my real names to anyone lest you make it impossible for me to move freely in Lagos, the land of my birth. I believe that you will stand by your promise that no one on earth will know my real names from you, while I am alive.

I, Segilola, the lady with the delicate eye-balls, come from a distinguished family in Lagos. I was born at Imaro Street on 9 September 1882, the sixth child of my parents. All other children died in their infancy, as I was told, and my parents were already old before I was born.

My mother told me that she lost my father when I was only one year and one and a half weeks old and since then she has been labouring alone with much hardship to bring me up as a good child who might support her in her last days. But I regret to confess that rather than become a source of comfort for the kind mother, I became an object of affliction. Maybe it is for this that God now punishes me, and my conscience troubles me all day long.

Oh! what a life! what tears for my fate! what lamentation! what sighs at this stage of my life!

Anyone who is taught, let her learn; anyone who has the benefit of parental training, let her know that she is being given an enduring legacy. See me now, the pitiful wretch! My mother taught me, but I was incorrigible; she warned me openly and privately but I chose to be deaf to her advice. Here I am now, an orphan, crying tears for my stubbornness, but my lamentations are belated for the good mother is no more.

But let me stop this wailing now, I have been overwhelmed with regret for my misdeed; oh my eyes are already full of tears as I write now. Therefore let me set aside my remorse and continue the story of my life.

My complexion was extremely fair; frankly I was one of those few women on whom God lavished beauty. It was the misuse of that beauty that has brought me into this misery.

My eye-balls are fairly big; that was why the wives of the family, in choosing the usual cognomen, called me 'Eleyinju-ege' meaning 'having delicate eye-balls'. Segilola ('Segi' means wealth) was the pet name which my grandmother gave me when I was a child. My mother told me that this was because my neck usually became more alluring whenever I wore a necklace made of *segi* beads. It is these two names that I have combined to form 'Segilola Eleyinju-ege'. As I proceed further with my story, all of you who do me the honour of reading this account will come to know how I married one thousand husbands in my single life.

I shall stop writing now until next week.

Yours sincerely,
Segilola.

LETTER XVI

Dear Editor,

Last week I promised to relate more about my marriage and how my first husband who married me in the church, was disappointed with our nuptial bed. All his relations, particularly his mother, expressed grave concern at the shameful discovery. But worst of all when my mother was informed, she fell ill immediately and was confined to bed for a long time.

What a day that was! A day of paradox. There I was as happy all day as any bride should be who had such a colourful society wedding; then came the night and gloom set in. How good it would have been if I had not given myself away so cheaply to the herbalist, Olojo of Okepopo.

All through the preparations for the marriage, whenever I recalled that frivolity, I wept secretly and at times prayed that 'something' might save me from the wedding-day disgrace. On the spinster's eve, as my friends and well-wishers surged round me and I swayed right and left, changing my clothes every half-hour and appearing rather elated, my conscience again and again seemed to remind me of a song:

> The face is a virgin
> Beneath is a woman

Then I would feel a bit nervous but as I had to face the ordeal, I quickly cheered myself up with another song:

> 'Tis an age-old custom
> 'Tis an age-old custom
> Having a husband
> And lovers besides.
> It did not start with us

With this song repeatedly in my mind I went on gay for the marriage day.

I had decided not to disclose the date of my marriage to avoid causing embarrassment to myself, but I have now changed the decision. I shall tell you the date and month of the marriage, but as for the year, I shall not describe it for such people as can make something out of it.

I was married on a Thursday, the sixth of November. It was exactly ten years later that a terrible incident occurred at Epetedo Area, Lagos, when an old man called Yesufa climbed into the ceiling of his house and shot a number of people dead. It gave rise to that song:

> O Yesufa the aged hunter
> O Yesufa the aged hunter
> The man-hunter lives in Epetedo
> 'Tis here he lived, the aged murderer.

In those days there were no motor-cars. I was driven to church in a horse-drawn carriage, accompanied by hundreds of my companions. Such a day could not be too long. After all I had taken an active part in other people's marriages. Our family-dress for the occasion was a very colourful print pattern, sewn into the design of a blouse called *buba-bonfo*, the craze of the day among the élites.

At last came the night, and the time for me to be taken to my new home. I was satisfied that I had at long last succeeded in getting a man to perform the legal church marriage with me and give me that precious wedding-ring. The rest should be well – somehow!

When the time came for her to hand me over to the envoys from my husband's home late in the night, my mother gave me her final words of advice. She called me by all my pet-names and cognomen and those of my ancestors. She was moved to tears as she advised me on many aspects of marriage life. Then she invoked the blessing of God on me in profuse terms.

This was repeated by my uncle Abiola and other elders who had been invited for the private ceremony. I could not help sobbing as I heard all these things from where I knelt on both knees and I felt the tragic importance of eternal separation from my family. As I rose up to go out my mother called my name again, rather softly, and expressed the hope that the news of my virtue on the marriage-bed would be the first thing to delight her on the following day. I was horrified but I quickly covered up with pretended coyness.

After all the blessing, I left with a large envoy of housewives for my new home. My main hostess was my brother-in-law's wife, Titilola, who was also married in church. I had my little niece with me as the 'bride's daughter'.

I was ushered into the bedroom which was beautifully furnished and soon it was time for the test. All the household, particularly my husband's mother, listened to hear the groan that should answer my success – but it never came.

When my husband asked me what had happened, I tried to plead with him that it was all due to my carelessness, that he should not be disturbed because what was most important was my bearing him children. But he would not be appeased, so I became aggressive and told him that no man should expect a woman of my beauty and fame to remain untouched. After all, as he loved me, so did many others. Seeing that he was still recalcitrant, I asked him: 'Do you really want to eat my virginity – to mix it with *gari*?'

It was like igniting gunpowder! He exploded at once and soon everybody was on me with unprintable invectives. But I was unmoved: I had already got the ring!

Have no fear, O lucky wife –
The ring is already yours.

So ran the song. I shall continue next week, kind Editor.

Yours sincerely,
Segilola.

8

Sol T. Plaatje

Mhudi and Umnandi

Sol Plaatje, the author of *Native Life in South Africa*, wrote *Mhudi*, the novel from which this extract is taken, before 1920, though it was not published until 1930. Written in English, *Mhudi* was a story of love and war, of heroism and sacrifices made by the women. Plaatje does not try to hide the strong streak of propaganda in his book. His own tribal loyalties emerge, but at times his characters subjugate these to their confrontation with the advancing Boers.

Mhudi is, however, not about hate but about love. The enmity between the Matabele and the Barolong takes second place to the love that Umnandi, wife of Mzilikazi, the Matabele king, has for Mhudi, wife of Ra-Thaga who is fighting against the Matabele. Courtship and marriage are treated in detail; between Ra-Thaga and Mhudi, and the two Boers Phil Jay (a close friend of Ra-Thaga's) and Annetje. The women in the story not only direct the course of action but symbolize the sentiments of courage, beauty and truth which are the novel's principal theme.

Mhudi and Umnandi

The friendship between Phil Jay and Ra-Thaga had not suffered in the least from the events of the past few days; so leaving the wagons among the trees near the dell, they went to
sit under a shady wild syringa, a little distance apart from the
camp.

Phil Jay examined and permanganated his wound once again;
and having readjusted the sling round his arm, he proceeded to
use his ramrod on his own rifle and that of his wounded black
friend. By the side of the kloof, not far from where they sat, was a
trickling fountain. The tiny perennial streamlets that oozed
from it had furrowed the escarpment, leading first through a
patch of bulrushes, then, widening and deepening its course, the
water wound its way underneath two rows of *modubu* trees down
to the dell below. Near the foot of the scarp the stream spouted
and widened into a creek whose banks were rich with the ver-
dant grass and other luxurious undergrowth. These provided
food and shelter for the numerous herds of game that quickened
the surrounding woods. Lilies and daisies along the glen had
long since succumbed to the cold breath of autumn and left
their tender stubbles to mark the spots where once they bloomed.
Fallen petals of withering wild poppies littered the earth beneath
the *mopane* trees, but the hardy marigolds survived the blast and
garnished both sides of the rivulet which, unmindful of the
seasons, wended its way beneath the water-lilies and rendered a
perennial tribute to the great Marico River some miles to the
west.

Leafy trees with creepers round their stout stems stood on the
fertile banks of the rustling creek, where their branches furnished
many an aerial tryst for birds of every plume. Nature had spread
a peaceful calm around the oasis, and it were gross sacrilege for

83

man to rupture this the sublimity of the wilderness with his everlasting squabbles.

'I do wish the Matebele would come,' said Phil, still pushing and tugging at the ramrod, cleaning the guns.

'And what would you do with them?' asked his sable companion.

Phil: 'I will catch Mzilikazi alive, and tie him to the wagon wheel; then Potgieter will make me his captain, and you will be my right-hand man.'

Ra-Thaga: 'That will not do, for your people will not tolerate me. If they get enraged by nothing more than a drink of water out of their water-pail, they are not likely to allow me a place near their Captain.'

Phil: 'But to tell the truth, I get on much better with you than with many of my own people. I owe you more than I could ever repay. But for you, Mogale's people would have killed me, or handed me to the Matebele as they did with Sarel Van Zyl. And since his disappearance, I realize all the more forcibly how much I am in your debt. If ever I become a Commander, you must come and stay near me.'

Ra-Thaga: 'Oh, no! I am not going to abide with a boy. You should get a wife first and take your place among men before thinking of that. What would my children think of me if I were to be the right-hand man of a wifeless youth?'

Phil: 'Are those your terms?'

Ra-Thaga: 'Without joking, it is time you did. Look at the advantages. Besides, marriage will give you two mothers – your own and the wife's; the latter the greatest of the two.'

Phil: 'Is that the reason why your people call them the plain mother and the fine mother respectively?'

Ra-Thaga: 'Yes, and let me tell you why I am so glad Mzilikazi is getting a beating. When he is killed, I shall return to Kunana, walk around the old place and venerate the ground where lived and worked my mother-in-law whom I never saw. I shall go down to the field of carnage, bestride the old battle-field, and say: Here fell the noble Rolong woman who gave life to my faithful Mhudi. Somewhere here lie the remains of the woman who mothered my wife, and nourished every fibre of her beautiful form. Then I will call to her spirit and say: Come down from the heights and approve of the feeble cares I am trying to bestow on the noble treasure thou hast bequeathed to me. My mother, O, cradle of my wife! That after all thy pains and nursing, thou shouldst have been hounded out of this life without receiving a pin from the worthless fellow who wived thy noble offspring!' (After a long pause.) 'Now, seriously, why don't you marry, Phil Jay?'

Phil: 'Well, you see, the girls are – er – er . . .'

Ra-Thaga: 'Are what? I have been to Moroka's Hoek and seen the Boer girls. They are all crazy about you. I heard several of them say so.'

Phil: 'Which one?'

Ra-Thaga: 'Everyone.'

Phil: 'But you know that I cannot marry them all.'

Again there was no answer, and Ra-Thaga continued:

'A man was not made to live alone. Had it not been for Mhudi, I don't think you would have known me at all. She made me what I am. I feel certain that your manhood will never be recognized as long as you remain wifeless. Marry a wife, Phil, and you will soon understand the Barolong, and – listen! After taking to yourself a wife, you will realize that you knew nothing at all about your own people, the Boers, for you will begin to understand them properly when your young wife has unbosomed herself to you. Now, Phil, why don't you marry Van Zyl's daughter?'

'Which one? Annetje? And why?' Phil's impatience was noticeable as he put the questions in rapid succession.

'I will tell you why,' said Ra-Thaga. 'I don't go about Moroka's Hoek with my eyes and ears shut. She has got a pair of bewitching eyes, and the moment you appear I have noticed that she always slips away like a mouse at the sight of a cat. She will either go to play at the far end of the camp or disappear into the interior of her mother's hut. Most of the time she spends working with elderly women, mending clothes, cooking food or boiling soap, and her ways are so admirable I have often said to myself that this daughter of Van Zyl is fit to marry the future King of the Boers.

'Do you remember when we returned from the spying trip?

85

<caption>Sol T. Plaatje</caption>

I noticed that many of the girls were openly shaking your hand and hugging you, glad to see you back. I was wondering where she was until I saw her in the interior of the hut, shyly devouring you with her dreamy eyes, but not daring to give vent to her raptures in public. Phil, that's the Nonnie for you! I tasted her roast meat only once since I have known you, and I think her cooking beats your mother's by far. And, oh! how beautiful she talks!'

Phil Jay, who had been listening to these rhapsodies, remained quiet for some little time. The silence of the moment and the girl's absence, hundreds of miles away, was to him symbolical of her retiring disposition. He felt a strange sensation all over him as thoughts of Annetje flitted across his mind. He could not account for these unaccustomed thrills. He mopped his brow, but that did not stop the flow of his perspiration. Modest and retiring as Annetje Van Zyl had always been, he could not forget the occasions on which he discovered her peeping coyly at him through the folds of her cappie; and how quickly she would get out of his way and feel embarrassed if he surprised her anywhere by herself. He saw again in imagination the pure white face, the tender blue eyes and gentle smile. He thought he heard her mellifluous voice, and there was a kind glow all about him, for Ra-Thaga's praises of her stimulated all these feelings. Finally he exclaimed: 'Man, Ra-Thaga, I always told you that you had a brown skin over a white heart, but you wouldn't believe me. Do you know I have been thinking of her too; I was too shy to ask anyone's opinion and now you have given me yours without asking. There are times I seem to lose my head over her. The night before last I was dreaming of her in the Camp. Now you have made me crazy and I will never get the frenzy out of my head.'

Suddenly the confabulation between Phil Jay and his solicitous match-maker was disturbed by a rush of men from the Camp. They ran forward to meet a party just arriving. Everybody wanted to be the first to meet the newcomers, and hear from them the very latest news from the front.

'Is Mzilikazi shot yet?' several voices asked.

Phil and Ra-Thaga jumped up and looked in the same direction. The piercing eyes of Ra-Thaga having at that distance established the identity of some of the new arrivals, he too raised his voice and shouted, 'Praise, Phil Jay, praise the God of the Boers.'

'What is the matter?' asked Phil Jay in surprise, still looking intently.

'The girl's brother!' replied Ra-Thaga.

'What girl?' queried Phil Jay, impatiently.

'Van Zyl, the spy we thought was killed; and there is Taolo who was with him.'

For a moment Phil did not know how to act; he seemed dazed with joy. He was not sure if in such circumstances his best course was to move forward or sit down again. He thought of Annetje far away at Moroka's Hoek. He remembered how she had wept over the supposed death of her lost brother, and he wondered if she would survive the reaction that must be caused by his reappearance. How he wished he could be the first bearer of the glad news and break it to her very gently. He knew not how to meet the returned friend, and so Ra-Thaga again rose to the occasion.

'You don't seem to believe that this is the brother of the Nonnie we have been speaking about,' said he.

'Now, what would you have me do?' inquired Phil, rather sheepishly.

'Go and offer him your good wishes,' replied Ra-Thaga. 'Tell him how sorry we are that we missed him when he came in search of us. Offer him some food, and, while he eats, relate to him the experiences of our mission of espionage. I will be there to supplement your remarks wherever necessary.'

Phil at once darted forward, and was soon struggling in the crowd that hurried to reach Van Zyl, whom he succeeded in monopolizing. They strolled about together a little among the wagons, being the while immersed in discussing their adventures. After refreshments which Phil procured for his friend, they listened to his story of the sudden condemnation to death and dramatic reprieve of the spies after their captors had heard a rifle shot; how they were retained in order to teach the Matebele the use of the gun; and how they wasted their ammunition and asked to be allowed to go for a fresh supply. How after repeated refusals

Moremi was sent, Van Zyl and Taolo being detained at the Matebele capital.

'He was a long time in coming back but we postponed the fatal day,' said Van Zyl, 'by constantly reminding our captors that Colesberg, where the powder comes from, takes months and months to reach. If the Allies' attack had been delayed much longer, we must certainly have been put to death, for the Matebele patience was well nigh exhausted. However, when the alarm was raised, and panicky reports arrived about the defeat of the Matebele armies, pandemonium reigned in the city and with the aid of some Bahurutshe cattlemen we took advantage of the confusion and effected our escape.'

The conversation was interrupted by a sensational movement in the camp. '*Basadi, basadi!*' [women! women!] shouted the crowd.

Everybody looked round and saw a small party arriving near one of the wagons with three women among them. Ra-Thaga and Phil Jay were dumbfounded to recognize Mhudi among the new arrivals.

Glad as Ra-Thaga was to see his wife, he found himself repressing a feeling of anger. He inwardly resented her appearance, because he feared that he would in future be chaffed by other men and called the poltroon who took his wife to war.

Ra-Thaga, still carrying his arm in a sling, came up to the wagon and hiding these feelings, affectionately greeted his wife. 'Have you come to show us how to kill the Matebele, Mhudi? Could you not have trusted us men to do the work? Now, sit down and let us hear how you are going to do it.' They carried on a dialogue.

She laughed and replied. 'I am not after Matebele, I am after you. What's the matter with your arm?'

'Where are the children?' he asked, without answering her question.

'At home with their aunts.'

'How did you manage to get here?' he asked again.

'Have I not the use of my legs and both arms? What's the matter with your arm?'

'Come over here, sit down and have some meat, then tell us all the news.'

Mhudi and her friends having had refreshments, she said in answer to Ra-Thaga's questions that she had been very restless since he left. She became indisposed and as the doctors failed to cure her she thought she would go and find her husband. So leaving the children with her relatives she departed, and the sickness left her the day she set out on her journey.

'Alone?' exclaimed Ra-Thaga in amazement.

'Yes, alone,' she replied.

'Silly woman! And did they allow you to do it? Where did they expect you would land?'

'Exactly where I am now,' replied Mhudi triumphantly. 'I did not ask anybody's permission. Besides, the wake of the army is unmistakable unless one deliberately intended to get lost. After a weary tramp of four days through a dreary country I overtook some Dutch wagons and travelled with them till after we crossed the Great River. Parties returning from the front with cattle were often met with and their good reports about the fight excited everybody. But some of them told us you had been killed. Thereafter the wagons travelled too slow for me and I left the Boers behind. I am thankful to them, however, for I could hardly have crossed the Great River alone. Besides, they provisioned me for several days.'

'I thought you always found the Boers such awful people?' said her husband with a smile.

'Wait until I tell you what happened at the river,' she retorted.

'And what was that?' asked Ra-Thaga.

'As we were crossing the Lekwa, I sat in the rear of one of the wagons. Behind us, the Hottentot leader of the next wagon's team swam so near that he often touched the brake of our wagon. I could easily speak to him from where I sat. Suddenly something went wrong with his team. Two of the middle oxen got entangled with their yoke and chain and the wagon stopped amid stream. His name was angrily shouted and abuses were hurled at him by nearly every Boer, each trying to outdo the others in their expletives. It was Dancer this, Dancer that and Dancer again and again, in a chorus of profanity that conveyed to me

89

much meaning but very little intelligence. The Boers in our wagon also shouted their imprecations at Dancer – they frightened me terribly, for I feared they were going to fling me into the water. Perhaps they might have done so if the trouble had been among our oxen. Fortunately we got through and they unhooked our team and extricated the next wagon with the two teams of oxen.

'As soon as the convoy got through, Dancer was tied to the wagon wheel and flogged till he was half dead. For the life of me I cannot understand why a leader, any more than the other people in the wagon, should be flogged for a tangle among the bullocks. But that was not all. After Dancer was beaten, there were loud calls for another little Hottentot. I never found out what was his crime, but the Boers called out, "Jan, Jan!" Poor little Jan who was minding some sheep hard by, was dragged along, tied up and mercilessly punished.

'A pretty Boer girl in the wagon in which I came remonstrated with her mother for keeping quiet while Jan was being beaten for no cause whatever. The Boers are cruel but they sometimes breed angels,' concluded Mhudi, 'and Annetje is one of them.'

'What is her name?' asked Ra-Thaga quickly.

'Annetje,' replied Mhudi, 'the girl whose brother was killed by the Matebele while out spying with Taolo and Moremi.'

'And where did you leave their wagon?' he asked impatiently.

'I believe the name of the river is Matloasane, two days' drive this side of the great Lekwa.'

'And who are your friends?' inquired her husband, looking at the two women with whom Mhudi shared her food.

'This beautiful lady,' she said, 'is Queen of the Matebele –'

Ra-Thaga started. 'What! Mzilikazi's wife? Where did you find her, and what does she want among us?'

'Sh-sh, not so loud or you might frighten her. This good lady was turned out of their city through the evil influences of her rivals three summers ago, and she has been hiding among Mogale's people; but hearing of her people's plight she felt she must at all hazards return to them. She is on her way to find her husband, take her place by his side and share in all his troubles.'

'What a noble woman!' exclaimed Ra-Thaga in admiration. 'She is as well-bred as she is fair of countenance. But how will she get through? Mzilikazi is probably killed by now. Still death has become so tame that I am yet alive after having been twice accounted dead. Mzilikazi too might be just as fortunate, notwithstanding that report has killed him about six times during this campaign. Where did you meet her?'

'I met her two days ago, and being on the same quest we quickly fell in love with each other. The other one is a Rolong girl who has been captive among the Matebele since her childhood when Kunana was sacked. She wept for very joy on seeing me and talking once again to one of her own folk in her mother tongue after so many moons; but so attached has she become to this noble Queen, that she realized the inhumanity of deserting her now in this war-devastated wilderness. After my own alarming experiences I cannot but encourage the girl in her sympathy for the lonely Queen, for indeed it is a shame that one so dear and so good-hearted should be a Matebele.'

Ra-Thaga abruptly broke the interview with his wife and ran after a young Boer.

Umnandi, the Matebele Queen, shuddered on seeing him start off. She thought he was going to betray her to the Boers. Mhudi however assured her that her husband, unlike many men, did not have a heart of stone.

'What is your wife after?' inquired Phil Jay, who stopped in answer to Ra-Thaga's call.

'She has come to tell us that Annetje is not hundreds of miles away as you said a while ago, but only a day or two's ride from here.'

This was greater news to Phil Jay than the expected information from the front. He was at once overwhelmed with ideas. His head was reeling with excitement and he wished to fly and meet Annetje. He could not desert the commando without disgracing himself, and possibly losing Annetje in the bargain – the natural punishment for such unmanly behaviour. He could not hope to disappear for two days and return to camp before he was wanted. What then was to be done? Oh! If he could only persuade the Field Cornet to send him back with the next field-post, he might be the first to break to Annetje the news of the dramatic return of her brother who was supposed to be dead. How could he manage this?

In due course the scouts reported that the woods were clear of the Matebele *impis*. The news of their rout being established, Potgieter gathered his burgers to his laager outside the ruins of Inzwinyani, where they held a service of thanksgiving to the God of the Boers.

'You know,' Ra-Thaga used to say, 'the Boers can do many things in this world but singing is not one of them. On that day, however, the Boers sang as they never did before or since. I have been to Grahamstown and heard English congregations sing with a huge pipe organ that shook the building with its sound, like the pipes and brass horns of English soldiers on the march; I have been to Morija and heard Pastor Mabille, the best singer that ever held a church service, and the Basuto congregations render their beautiful hymns in answer to the signal he gave; I have been to Bethany and heard the most perfect singing by Native choristers under German leadership; but touched as I was by the rhythm of their drum-like voices, they always left something to be desired, when I thought of the manner in which those Boers sang that morning in the level valley bottom near Inzwinyani ruins, their old hymn "*Juich aarde, juich alom den Heer*".'

Even those who knew not their language felt that they were listening to a stirring song of deliverance expressed by the souls of a people who, for the time being at any rate, felt profoundly grateful to their God.

By daybreak next day a detachment of Barolong were ordered to return with some cattle, and Phil Jay was placed in charge of the company and ordered to relate to the Boers all the news about the war. Ra-Thaga, who was one of the company, returned home with his wife – she had been deftly attending to his wound, which had now healed. Before their departure, Mhudi took an affecting farewell from Umnandi and wished her a safe journey and reunion with her consort.

'Good-bye, my sister,' she said. 'I am returning to Thaba Ncho for I have found my husband: mayest thou be as fortunate in the search for thine own.'

'Umnandi salutes thee also and thanks thee for the brief but happy time we have spent together. Thou hast a welcome destination in Thaba Ncho while I (supposing I meet my husband) know not what the future may have in store for me.'

'Nay, not so, my Matebele sister, for the gods who protected thee from the wrath of Mzilikazi will surely accompany thee in the search; seek him and when thou hast recovered the lost favour of thy royal lord, urge him to give up wars and adopt a more happy form of manly sport. In that he could surely do much more than my husband who is no king.'

'Nay,' retorted Umnandi ruefully. 'Thine is a royal husband, the king of the morrow, with a home and a country to go to. What is my lord without his throne, for what is a defeated king with his city burnt? It is no bright destiny I look forward to, but a blank gloom. I shared the glory of Mzilikazi when his subjects came and prostrated themselves before him for then they always called at my dwelling to do me homage. The jealous machinations of my rivals drove me from out the city and forced me abroad to seek for shelter; but now that I hear Mzilikazi's glory is overthrown, I regard it my duty to seek him and share his doom if he will but permit me.'

'How wretched,' cried Mhudi, sorrowfully, 'that with so many wild animals in the woods, men in whose counsels we have no share, should constantly wage war, drain women's eyes of tears and saturate the earth with God's best creation – the blood of the sons of women. What will convince them of the worthlessness of this game, I wonder?'

'Nothing, my sister,' moaned Umnandi with a sigh, 'so long as there are two men left on earth I am afraid there will be war.'

'Already the dust-clouds of the wagons are receding in the distance; the darkness will overtake us ere I reach them and make it difficult for me to trail my people; so we must part. Good-bye, my sister,' continued Mhudi as the two women clasped each other. 'Farewell, thou first Matebele with a human heart that ever crossed my way. Mayest thou be as successful in thy quest as I have been in mine. May the gods be forgiving to thy lord and make him deserve thy nobility, and may the god of rain shower blessings upon thy reunion. Good-bye, my Matebele sister; may there be no more war but plenty of rain instead.'

'Oh, that I could share thy hopes,' rejoined Umnandi plaintively. 'Good-bye, my beloved friend. Peace be to thee and thy husband. I am going into the wilderness and will not rest till I have found Mzilikazi. *Sala kahle*, my Mlolweni Sister.'

'That thou wouldest find him, is the ardent wish of Mhudi. Urge him, even as I would urge all men of my race, to gather more sense and cease warring against their kind. Depart in peace, my sister. *Tsamaea Sentle.*'

9

Ousmane Socé

Courting in Saint-Louis

Ousmane Socé Diop – Ousmane Socé for short – is commonly considered the author of the first French African novel, though he himself gives the credit to his more obscure predecessor and compatriot, Bakary Diallo, whose autobiographical novel, *Force-Bonté*, appeared in French in 1926.

Socé's *Karim* is the prototype of the African urban novel. With *Mirages de Paris* (1937) its author also took the lead in the novel of culture conflict and exile which is still vigorously alive in the 1960s (Cheikh Hamidou Kane, Aké Loba, Camara Laye's *Dramouss*, 1966). At the same time *Mirages de Paris* represents a unique document of the *Négritude* movement.

Karim is a young, generous Wolof white-collar worker in Guet N'dar (or Saint-Louis), a city depicted here as a haven for time-honoured Islamic-African customs and contrasted with a strongly Europeanized Dakar, where Karim runs wild on occasion. But finally he settles down in the place of his first wooing, to share in the ancient wisdom of his community.

Courting in Saint-Louis

Karim woke up, his heart brimming over with joy as he remembered his first visit to Marième. All had worked out according to his wishes; the girl had been polite and a good hostess, too, and he himself had created a good impression by his lavish spending.

He stretched his limbs twice, then put on his caftan. He washed his face without using soap, took a shirt from his coat-peg to dry himself, and went off to work.

At the office he gave his colleagues an account of the most exciting features of his 'campaign'. His mind was not on his work all day. The long columns of figures he had to add up bored him. Only the picture of the girl absorbed his thoughts and made him dreamy . . .

Fatum, Marième's friend, came to see him. 'Marième has sent me to tell you that her female *griots* will come to salute you in her house tonight.'

'Agreed,' he consented.

Karim was flattered by what he had just learned. But there would be some money needed for the reception, and he had only fifty francs left. He drew a letter from his pocket, tore off the blank page it happened to contain and scribbled on it:

Good for three hundred francs to be deducted from this month's salary.

Saint-Louis, 12 January 193 . .
KARIM

At nightfall he went to Marième, accompanied by his *diali*.★

The air in the room was saturated with the fumes of frankincense, which in a delightful way made breathing difficult. The beds had been carefully made and provided with beautiful white sheets.

★ Guitar-player.

Karim was touched by these tokens of high esteem. He took off his slippers and stretched out full length on the brass bed. His stiffly starched costume was puffed up and at his slightest movement gave off a rustle which he found not in the least unpleasant.

The *griots* had only waited for Karim's arrival to start singing Marième's praise.

'Marième, if you were a man, you would be a *damel*.'*

'If you were a horse, you would have the nobility of the thoroughbred.'

'But we don't deplore your being a woman. You are the star among those of your sex by virtue of your beauty, generosity and conduct. We fix our hopes on you, and you will not disappoint us.'

'Marième, our *guère*!† He who wants to be your friend must also be ours. Nobody can part us.'

Karim understood the allusion and in deference to Senegalese custom gave one hundred francs to prove himself a worthy lover of the girl whose eulogy was being sung.

The singers, surprised and overjoyed, now turned to reciting their thanks without paying any attention to one another, and the resultant confusion of their speech was quite exhilarating.

Their leader nevertheless managed to impose her role.

'What is your name, my Lord?'

'Karim Guèye.'

'Your generosity no longer surprises me,' she went on. 'It is a heritage come down to you from your gallant ancestors, who in battle, when the enemy was superior in strength, would fill their baggy trousers with sand and stand rooted to the ground so as to be unable to flee should their agony cause them to lose control over their actions. When a great disgrace befell them in their private lives, they would lie down, take the barrel of their *dibi* between their teeth, and working the trigger with their toes, blow their brains out in order not to survive their honour!... *Niàye ala Gayenago!* The elephant has no keeper!'

'*Samba-Linguère!*' the *griots* chimed in to show their admiration.

---

* Emperor of the Senegalese province of Cayor.
† Lord; title of nobility.

They left the party still singing their thanks, and their eulogy could be heard even after they had reached the street . . .

Marième turned to the only table, placed against the wall, on which soup-tureens, toilet articles, scissors, and a deck of cards were arranged in an orderly manner.

She took a calabash from the table, removed the piece of cloth with which it was covered, poured milk into small enamel cups and distributed them. While they were enjoying their refreshments, they carried on a rambling conversation.

Afterwards, [Karim and his supporters], in true *Samba-Linguère* style, each dropped a twenty-five franc note in a saucer.

At midnight the guests departed.

On the way home, they confided their secrets to each other, just to kill time.

'You know, Karim, I haven't got a farthing left. I've spent everything on your "campaign". I can't even buy tobacco.'

'Tomorrow I'll give you an I.O.U. and you can buy our brand from my Syrian trader.'

'I still haven't given my parents anything,' a second friend complained.

'You'll pick up a sack of rice from the "Cayor Company". That'll keep them happy for the moment.'

'I have to collect two pairs of trousers from my tailor,' a third fellow chimed in.

'Oh, just wait till next month . . .'

Thus they all sacrificed their own needs and those of their parents to the *griots* and to their friends. People should not be able to say about them that they were miserly or even thrifty. As far as they were concerned, charity did not begin at home.

This mentality of theirs originated from the zest for ostentation which is inborn in the Senegalese. Outside your father's home you had to attract attention by your costume, spending habits and behaviour . . . you had to pass for a *samba-linguère*.

They arrived at the intersection where they usually parted. Karim returned home followed by his *diali*, whose tunes accompanied him as he walked along. He lay down, and the guitarist stayed by his bedside, lulling him to sleep with his music.

10

Paul Hazoumé

A Message to the Ancestors

When Paul Hazoumé was born in the French coastal protectorate of Porto-Novo in 1890, the colonial power was preparing to dismantle the throne and realm of Béhanzin, the redoubtable king of the hinterland. After it had been for a long time denounced by missionaries and self-righteous colonial apologists for its human sacrifices, the kingdom of Dahomey, precariously poised between French, British, and German ambitions, was brought down in 1893 by the faithful mulatto servant of the Third Republic, General Dodds. Hazoumé was to revive it in the sober light of an anthropologist's mind.

For twenty-five years he associated with the old people of his country; by extracting every scrap of information that he could from them and by consulting all written records that he could lay hands on, he recreated the Dahomey of the first half of the nineteenth century, centred around King Ghezo and the heroic Princess Doguicimi. Slow-moving and over-documented, his novel gives nonetheless an authentic view of an old African kingdom.

The passage which follows shows the ambiguity of human sacrifice in a particular historical situation: as a religious custom and as a gesture of political defiance.

A Message to the Ancestors

The envoys sat down again around the table. Mêwou went out followed by the girls who had been lining up along the wall.

They returned carrying copper, bronze, and silver trays on which were various liqueurs the whites drink, glasses, and silver and gold pitchers filled with cold water.

While some arranged the glasses in front of the envoys, others uncorked the liqueur bottles, and some of them served the whites by asking them their preference with an engaging smile, presenting several bottles at a time.

Though they were in a great flurry, the girls, who were innocence itself, performed their duties, which after all they were doing for the first time in their lives, with comparative adroitness. Some laughed secretly at the clumsiness of two or three of their companions who had almost knocked over some glasses. Far from becoming indignant, the latter promised in a low voice to do better the next day . . .

A maidservant made the round of the table, glancing at all the glasses and making sure that they were all filled. She left and the long train of serving girls followed gracefully behind her, leaving in the room the perfume of the cream with which they had anointed their bodies and of the film of white paint which they had rubbed on their necks and busts, and some members of the delegation kept casting glances at them until they had reached the far end of the courtyard. Their neighbours had to nudge them discreetly with their elbows to break the spell and to remind them of their duty to offer a toast to the king.

The pride in seeing those eyes full of desire riveted on them and also the hope that at the end of their days they would be able to recall that in their youth they had been distinguished by their beauty and selected for the honour of serving at table an important mission which had come from the land of the whites, had lit up the faces of all these girls; some young princesses not excepted. The thought that it was customary to give a young girl to every one of the whites coming to the court of Abomey made some happy but saddened those who considered the whites behind whom they had been posted not particularly handsome . . .

The delegates were so thirsty that almost all the glasses had come back empty from their lips. Some felt sorry that the maidens were no longer there to fill up the glasses again. 'They have most certainly gone to get some food,' an interpreter whispered into an envoy's ear.

The secretaries of the delegation were ready to take down the king's declaration and to submit it immediately for the signature of the court.

Outside, the drumming and singing had suddenly come to a stop. The vague buzzing of voices which followed it was not strong enough to trouble the impressive silence which ruled inside.

The envoys had turned towards the throne and were waiting anxiously for the moment when the king of Dahomey would renounce on behalf of himself and his successors, wars, slavery, and human sacrifice, which were banned by the law of the people from whom they had come to convince, so they thought, the king and his court.

Upon a signal from Guézo, the Lady Keeper of the Spittoon approached. Her assistant then wiped the royal lips. The queens kissed the ground at the foot of the throne as a thanksgiving for the honour which the King of the Spirit had just bestowed on them by allowing them to touch his venerable lips.

The king uttered two muffled 'hum-hums', which were answered by deafening coughs from the ranks of courtiers while the queens kept saying, 'Easy, go easy.'

Was the king getting ready to speak? All glances were hanging so to speak on his lips. Hardly had the coughing died down when menservants entered like a whirlwind and lined up on the table the trays which had served to bring the envoys their refreshments but which now held the heads of the pure young girls who just a little while ago had so gracefully poured them drinks and who by the smiles some of the men had given them had been complimented on their youth, beauty, and innocence. On all these cut-off heads, the faces still retained a semblance of life and showed eloquently what had been the entreating attitude of these innocent victims at the moment of execution. The looks of the first few were full of anguish; tears were flowing freely to implore pity. The eyes of the next group were reddened and wild-looking. On other faces the eyelids tried in vain to open so that their eyes might see for the last time the things that were about to cease existing for them. Still others, three, four, five, so many of them, had their blood-tinged tongues hanging out, half cut by the jaws which must have clamped down violently on them. Some lips twitched convulsively, foreheads wrinkled up, faces grimaced. A mouth opened, the tongue darted out, moved, withdrew, and came out again; the maiden continued crying. One could not hear her any more, but one understood her: she cried out her innocence, she cried out her right to live, she implored pity for her youth. Not having succeeded in moving the executioner, who was listening only to the grim voice of his heart, she started to call at the top of her voice – as the expression on her face clearly showed – for the vengeance of her ancestors and her gods on Dahomey. On one tray the abrupt opening of a lower jaw turned over a head, a thin jet of blood squirted out into the air and fell on to the tablecloth.

One of the envoys fainted with a piercing cry; others turned away, threw their arms in the direction of those heads, and with their hands performed jerky gestures as if they wanted to repel the spectacle.

Nigan, whose exit they had not noticed, returned noisily, clutching his huge, bloody scimitar. His face with its glittering eyes, its dilated nostrils, its dimples and protruding jaw, smeared with blood all over like his garments, had assumed the furious appearance of a gorilla provoked into anger, coming with his mouth foaming and his fangs threatening.

Some envoys trembled, others threw themselves against their neighbours, overturning them. One, maddened with fear, ran to the far end of the hall. Two or three hid under the table.

Turning to their leader, the executioner said with a sardonic smile, 'You dressed people, you are asking that Dahomey should tie her own hands in order to become easy prey for her enemies. You want this kingdom to elevate its slaves to the station of their masters who are born free. You want the King of the Universe not to honour any longer the memory of his ancestors by human sacrifices, that is to say that he should bring down misfortunes on himself by giving up a custom which has lasted for six reigns and which until now has received the approval of all our ancestors. You want Dahomey to be ruined by abandoning the slave trade, and you want her to allow strangers to roam this country, free to sow disease and disorder among our people?

'The Predestined King had first decided to send you personally on the errand of taking your proposals before his ancestors. At the last moment he chose to delegate in your stead the young girls who had listened to your words with the greatest of attention. If the ancestors of the Lord of the World approve of your demands, they will unfailingly send back these messengers to let you know. So you had better await their return.'

The leader of the delegation could not articulate a word because fear was tightening his throat. Then the triumphant executioner put down his scimitar with a flourish on the heads lying on the two trays in the middle and prostrated himself at the foot of the throne. The king withdrew. The princes and princesses crowding in the courtyard poured sarcastic remarks on these sea-animals rendered pitiable by fear. 'Is it really the fate of our victims that brought these white elephant trunks to Dahomey? Isn't it rather because they don't have the stamina to see blood being spilt that they have come to advise us to give up war, human sacrifice, and slavery?' somebody in the crowd scoffed.

'Then why do they want to send all those sabres, rifles, carronades, and gunpowder to Dahomey?' pursued a prince.

'The sabres are supposed to be used for fighting the mosquitoes, the rifles to knock down the fruits from the trees, the carronades to sit down on during our palaver meetings or to rest our heads on during the siesta, and the powder is probably for us to lick,' a princess sneered.

The crowd outside, which had learned what had happened, praised the king's wit loudly and jeered at the fright the sea-animals were showing. Drums and cannon joined the courtiers in praising the king and underlined the caustic remarks aimed at the envoys.

It would not be three days before all Dahomeans, including the babes at their mothers' breasts, knew the ingenious answer which the Lord of the World had given the Glincis* who had come to request Houegbaja's Dahomey to commit suicide.† Tradition would preserve it to keep awake in the generations to come the distrust of the Glincis, the sworn enemies of Dahomey.

Guézo refused the presents from the king of the Glincis. The delegation obtained the permission to set off again for Gléhoué‡ the next morning. 'We have to get away as fast as we can from this kingdom so pregnant with crimes that it proves rebellious to any idea of humanity,' the head of the delegation explained to his colleagues, who would have liked to have a day of rest at Abomey.

* English.
† Houegbaja, the second king of the Dahomean dynasty, defeated Dan and founded Abomey, capital of Dahomey, 'in the belly of Dan'.
‡ Ouidah.

11

Akiga

Justice

African prose is surfeited with documentation, partly because so much of it has been addressed to a curious and alien audience. Yet it seems odd that *Akiga's Story*, from which this extract is taken, and which was published in 1939, should have been as concerned with advertising Tiv custom as it is. For this book was taken down originally in Tiv. There is no pretence in the book that this is anything but a painstaking chronicling of events, at times mundane, at times indicative of awareness in a larger involvement.

Justice

At that time the whole land of Tiv was shaken. When the Tiv saw that the Shitire elders were severely dealt with by the District Officer they were glad, for they were given a great chance to avenge themselves on their enemies, by falsely accusing them before him. One would come and say, 'So-and-so killed my brother to set right an *imborivungu*.' When the District Officer heard this he would send to the chief to have the man brought in. The policemen went to fetch him, and before they even started from his home they would give him a thorough beating. When they brought him in, the white man asked him where was the *imborivungu* for which he had killed the man. When he began to deny it, the District Officer violently upbraided him and accused him of hiding the truth, until finally he admitted his guilt and asked to be allowed to go and fetch it. Policemen were sent with him. In some cases, when the man arrived at his home he would ask to be allowed to go into his house, and when he found nothing which he could give up, took an arrow and stabbed himself, saying that death was better than so much undeserved misery. Another would enter his house and set it alight, thinking to be burnt to death inside, and had to be dragged out by force. Some had a real *imborivungu*, or medicine, and brought it in; others, being unable to find anything, took a bone or some other thing, covered it with wax, stuck hair on it and red beans, and said that it was an *imborivungu*. By giving this up they obtained relief from their troubles. Some who said they had nothing were lying, but after they had been well punished they cunningly went and found something quite different to bring in. This they said was the medicine which they had for killing men, and the District Officer and the chiefs accepted their story. (At that time many of the chiefs were assembled at Katsina

Ala.) The chiefs, of course, were perfectly aware of all this, but they wanted to find favour with the District Officer; so even when people brought in what was quite spurious they said it was the real thing.

Sometimes a man was said to own a Poor, and to be *tsav*, but when the white man told him to bring the human skulls which he was keeping he was unable to produce any. When he failed to find any skulls the police gave him such a beating that even if he returned home his strength was exhausted, and he died. But if a man was wise, when the white man told him to bring the skull of the man he had killed he did not deny it, but set off at once to go and dig up the grave of someone who had died many years ago. Taking out the head, he brought it back in an old sack, gave it to the white man and the chiefs, and all would go well with him. But the man who had no sense, and truthfully protested his innocence, brought enough trouble on himself to last him his lifetime, and often did not survive it. The people who suffered most were the two sections of Shitire and Ikurav, Ugondo, Kunav, and Turan.

The white man knew little of the suffering which occurred in the clans affected by the Haakaa. The trouble was made much worse by the mutual incriminations that took place when he first called in all the chiefs to Katsina Ala. Everyone who was indicted for having instruments of the *mbatsav* turned round and accused his enemies, so that in any one case five men suffered. The thing which the white man was most anxious to get was a complete human skin. He said that a human skin must be brought, but no one could produce one. When the District Officer went on leave, and another took his place, Tseva, of Ikado in Ukum, said that if the white man would give him the chieftainship of Ukum on condition that he brought him a human skin, he would find one. The white man agreed, and Tseva sought with all his power, and all his knowledge, but he never found one. People in the end began to laugh at him, saying that he was looking for a thing which did not exist.

At the time when the white man and Tseva were making every effort to find a human skin, there was a certain man and his wife who perhaps suffered worse than any one. The man's name was

Justice

Atserve, his wife was called Tungwa, and their son Agundu, who was a very beautiful child. Agundu died, and about the time of his death it was said that Tsofo, the son of Zaki Biam, had in his possession a human skin. So the white man ordered Gana, his foreign messenger, and a policeman called Igbudu to go and arrest Tsofo, and make him give up the human skin. Tsofo denied having one, but asserted that Atserve had killed his son and skinned him. Gana stayed at Zaki Biam, and sent policemen to seize Atserve. Atserve was then beaten till he could no longer cry out, and his whole body was covered with sores. They told him to bring the skin of his son Agundu. When he saw no escape he lied to them, and said that he had indeed killed Agundu, and would bring his skin. So they untied him and told him to go and fetch it. Everyone was glad, thinking that at last they were going to see a human skin. The police went with him, but nothing was found. So they brought him back again, beating him as they went. When they came back, and Gana questioned him, he put the blame on his wife, Tungwa, saying that he was actually fetching it, but she had prevented him. So Gana sent them to arrest Tungwa and bring her in. They beat Tungwa till she screamed and could scream no more, while her husband lay on the ground and watched his wife's sufferings. Then they caught hold of him and started beating him again. When they had beaten him for a long time, he said that if they would let him go he would fetch the skin, and fool no longer. So they untied him and took him back again. He told the police to wait outside while he went into the house to get it. So they waited. He entered his house, took an arrow, and stabbed himself in the thigh. Then he sat down to await the death which seemed to him a better thing than the trouble that had come upon him without cause. The policemen, having waited in vain for him to come out, went into the house, and there found him on the point of death, with the arrow stuck in his thigh. They took him, and quickly applied remedies, and sent word to Gana. Gana was afraid, and released his wife, who was still lying bound in the middle of the village. The man did not die, but he and his wife still bear the marks of their beating. A few months after this Gana gave up his post, but I do not know the reason. I afterwards, however, met him in

Abinsi, and he told me that he would rather be left to live in poverty than undertake *mbatsav* work again.

At that time all the officials working under the European claimed to have a good knowledge of the Tiv, and the white man acted on their advice without question. In this way they had great opportunities to hoodwink him, and many obtained promotion in consequence. One day the white man sent his policeman, Abaivo, to Chief Yaakur in Ugondo, telling him to go with him and seize the *mbatsav*, and to take their bad things from them. Abaivo went, and they came and stopped at Ugba's old village. (Ugba was then living at Kaduna.) Ugba's brother, Igase, was away at the time, but the labourers who were working on the road from Zaki Biam to Tombo were staying in his village and going to their work from there. The name of their headman was Korinya of Akaa in Kusuv. That day, as they went to work, two eagles were fighting in a tree, and they saw them fall off into the grass at the side of the road, on the site of the present Ugba market. The road workers ran to the spot. One of the eagles got up, but the other was caught by one of the young labourers (his name was Uwogba of Ugondo), who took it to Korinya, his headman. Korinya handed it over to Yaakur, who was drinking beer together with his chief men and Abaivo. Abaivo took the eagle and said, 'I will go and tell the white man that I took Igase's box with the instruments of the *mbatsav* in it, and that I caught this eagle as it came to take it away from me.' Chief Yaakur agreed to tell the same story if he were asked by the white man. So they tied a string to the eagle, and three days later, when Igase returned, they told him that they were waiting for him to give them the box in which he kept the bad things. Igase denied having any *mbatsav* instruments, but they beat him, went in and took one of his boxes by force, and put into it some *mbatsav* instruments out of another box which they had previously confiscated. Then they set out for Katsina Ala to give their evidence. When they arrived, Abaivo told the white man his story, and Yaakur, on being questioned, supported him. Everyone praised Abaivo for the power of his *tsav*, by means of which he had been able to catch the eagle. The white man plucked the eagle's feathers and put them in the place at Katsina Ala where the bad things were kept. Abaivo's fame spread to all parts of Tivland. Men came from a distance to see the eagle, and, having seen it, paid homage to the greatness of Abaivo. This pleased Abaivo beyond measure.

Then there was the case of the human slaughter-slab. The Tiv originally knew nothing of a slab for cutting up human flesh; they always said that the *mbatsav* found a big tree, bent it down to the ground and cut up the meat on its leaves. But when the Haakaa came, Ukum started the idea of the slaughter-slab. This was sewn like the cloth which is put over a horse's back. It was made of black material, at the corners of which were attached human hair and phylacteries, and it had blood on it which, they said, was human blood. Every slaughter-slab, moreover, had a small butcher's knife attached to it. This thing also at first caused the Tiv the greatest suffering, until they discovered a way out of the trouble. Afterwards, when a man was seized and told to bring a slaughter-slab, he did not argue, but asked to be allowed to go and fetch it. Then he went and sewed together an old black blanket and strip of cloth, and attached to it all the things which he had seen on another one. For blood, he squeezed out some juice from the bark of the *ikpine* tree and let it dry. Then he took it to the white man, and said it was a human slaughter-slab.

12

E. E. Obeng

Konaduwa's Trial

Eighteenpence (1943) was the first true West African novel written in English. It is really extended allegory, with the author, E. E. Obeng, a Ghanaian, extolling the virtues of a large family, honesty and the rural life.

His hero Akrofi, in order to repay the eighteenpence he had borrowed to buy a cutlass with which to begin farming, agrees to work free for his creditor. A series of incidents follow one upon the other, with almost every one leading up to a law suit. The farmer's wife, Konaduwa, falsely accuses Akrofi of raping her. Before he is tried, she is accused of failing to report a case of rape. On her way from the 'native' court to see the District Commissioner, she insults a policeman and is brought to court once more.

Then her husband is tried for employing slave-labour, and Akrofi for attempted rape. Later on, after general acquittal, Akrofi begins a successful farm by using 'European' methods, but makes still another appearance in court for failing to report that he had found treasure.

Akrofi is not a person but a repository of virtues. He successfully brings up his son Sam to take a job with the government and instils worthiness into his three daughters, Violet, Lily and Rose, around whose names he delivers an engaging homily. The section reproduced here describes the true rebel of the book. Konaduwa has none of the boring piety of Akrofi. She is Obeng's single success in character-creation.

Konaduwa's Trial

When the assembly broke up, Konaduwa hastened away, meaning to go to Asiakwa to report the case to the District Commissioners. But at Anyinam the Birem had overflowed its banks, and the ferryman exacted a toll of sixpence from every passenger. When Konaduwa was asked by one of the ferrymen to pay the amount, she parted her lips in a brilliant smile, displaying her teeth, which had a gap at the centre of the upper row.

'What exceptionally fine teeth this woman has!' the ferryman exclaimed. 'Keep your sixpence,' he added, 'and I will pay it for you.'

Konaduwa thanked him with a bow, and tied the coin up in a corner of her handkerchief.

He then asked some of his friends to help him with her luggage aboard the pontoon. There was a crowd of passengers, and some of them were eager to push past her. Suddenly it began to rain. The other ferrymen remained in the hut on the other bank of the river, thatched with palm leaves. They had a small fire, and round this they squatted, their hands spread over the flames, to keep themselves warm. As it was still raining, the passengers remained on the far bank, and they shouted entreaties to the ferrymen to bring the pontoon to take them over.

The toll-collector said that because of the attractive woman he would go with the pontoon. He did so, assisted by one of his friends. When they reached the other side of the river, they found that everyone was soaked to the skin. Konaduwa's teeth were chattering and she was trembling with fever. She was taken by the hand and led on the pontoon. Her belongings were removed safely and, because of her illness, care was taken that the vessel should not be overloaded. But the other passengers, frozen with the cold, rushed aboard, and one man knocked her portmanteau into the river. A boy saw the occurrence and drew the man's attention to it. When they landed and it was found that Konaduwa's portmanteau was missing, the boy pointed out the culprit, who admitted the charge but said he had not done it intentionally.

The ferryman said that if it did not contain much wealth, the man should buy her another one, for they could not dive into the water after it. But Konaduwa told them that she was involved in a case which might cost her over a hundred pounds, so she was on her way to Asiakwa to request the District Commissioner either to dismiss the case or to minimize the fine. In view of the situation, she had obtained a loan of a hundred and fifty pounds, partly in cash and partly in jewels which she could dispose of for cash if needful. She could not, therefore, go to Asiakwa without the portmanteau and its valuable contents.

On hearing this, divers jumped into the river in search of it, but all returned empty-handed. It was sunset, and it was still raining, so the men dispersed one by one, like people who had come to buy or sell at a market. Konaduwa became infuriated, and, though she was ill and cold, she flung herself on the ground and rolled about, shouting and screaming, and refusing to be soothed.

The offender, who had not thought the loss was so great, stood looking at her, and, seeing her anguish, nearly drowned himself. When he became calmer, he stated that a man had hired him for three shillings to go to Dodowa to buy two young hogs and a young pig for him. He had received a shilling in advance, and his employer gave him fifteen shillings to pay for the pigs. All he had on him, therefore, was sixteen shillings, less his ferry fare.

The case was taken to the Odekuro of Anyinam, who ordered that both Konaduwa and the man should be sent to Kyebi. She demanded to see the District Commissioner before going to Kyebi to see the Omanhene of Abuakwa; but the messengers of the Odekuro did not permit this, and the couple went direct to Kyebi.

According to custom, they had to see an Okyeame before going to the Omanhene; so they went to the house of Okyeame Aninkora, who took them to the Palace. The messengers explained their errand, and after the parties had been questioned regarding the amount of money involved, the Omanhene told them he had no jurisdiction over a case involving a hundred and fifty pounds, so he asked his Chief Sword Bearer to send them to the District Commissioner at Asiakwa. Before they departed, he gave them some palm-wine to sustain them. The Anyinam messengers returned to their village, and the Omanhene's man and the two litigants, together with their witnesses, went to Asiakwa.

The Sergeant in charge of the Police Barracks was sought out, and the Omanhene's messenger told him his errand. Next, Konaduwa was asked to make her statement. She did so. The man who had knocked the portmanteau overboard did the same. On the following day the charge-book was put before the District Commissioner.

The Commissioner inquired whether it was a mere complaint or a summons. Konaduwa said she had no more money on her to cover the costs of the summons, and entreated him to collect her hundred and fifty pounds for her. He then asked why she should travel with so much money, when she did not mean to transact business.

This gave her the chance to relate her whole story. She sent for another bag which formed part of her luggage, and emptied the contents, which were the leg-bones of the many sheep slaughtered in Kwahu in connexion with her case. At this, he told her to go home and wait until she heard from the Omanhene of Kwahu regarding the matter. The District Commissioner drafted a letter to the Omanhene in order to obtain information about one Konaduwa, who had come to him with the bones of many sheep which she alleged were slaughtered against her. The letter was written and sent to the Asiakwahene for immediate despatch.

The next morning the District Commissioner came to Court to examine the affair of the lost portmanteau. When he had heard Konaduwa's statement, he asked the man how he could replace the amount. The man replied that he did not think she had had all that money with her, and believed she only said so after the portmanteau was lost. He added that he could not replace it, and the Court would have to punish him in some other way; he

would submit to whatever decision was made. At this, Konaduwa became intensely angry, and began to shower abuse on
him and on the Court in general. A constable ordered her to be
silent. She turned on him and said that if he had lost a hundred
and fifty pounds through another's folly, would he like to be
shouted at with 'Silence'? The constable was so annoyed that
he referred the matter to the Commissioner and threatened to
beat the woman when the Court had risen, for, as a woman, she
had no right to charge him with being a fool, according to the
established customs of the Akans.

'Are you deaf, or what is wrong with you?' she retorted.
'When did I charge you with being a fool, you stupid one?'

The constable again told the Commissioner what she said, and
he, in turn, ordered that she should be charged at once.

Mr Richard Jones, the Registrar, then conferred with the
Commissioner for a few minutes, after which he sat down to
frame the charge. This ran as follows:

'Rex versus Konaduwa.

'That you, on the fourteenth day of July 1913, at Asiakwa, did
insult and abuse Constable Musa Buzanga during the execution
of his duty, thus committing contempt of the King's Court. Are
you guilty or not guilty?'

'Is this what the English Court is like?' she demanded with
astonishment. 'When a case has not been tried, how can one say
whether one is guilty or not. Even if the case has been tried, how
can you expect one to pronounce judgment against oneself?
Tell the Commissioner that I cannot possibly answer that question.'

When he heard this the Commissioner said:

'Konaduwa, you are making matters worse. At first you committed contempt of the King's Court and now you are committing the same misdemeanour towards the King's Judge. Mr
Jones, frame the second charge and commit her for trial.'

The Registrar hastened to obey, writing out and reading aloud
the following charge:

'Rex versus Konaduwa.

'That you on the fourteenth day of July 1913, at Asiakwa, did
speak against the established procedure of the British Court, and

also against the District Commissioner, who is the King's Judge. Are you guilty or not guilty?'

'If you ask me this question a hundred times, I will still make no reply. Even if I knew I were guilty, I should never admit it and ask you to pronounce judgment upon me. If I say I am not guilty, you would not let me go scot free; but if I say I am guilty, you will pronounce judgment at once. The Governor sent you here to decide cases before you get your pay, and if you have not fully learnt how to try cases, and want to ask me how you should pronounce judgment, you should go back to your own country to learn your law properly and find out how to conduct your business, without perplexing a woman by asking her if she is guilty or not guilty.'

'I believe that the accused is of unsound mind,' said the Commissioner to Mr Jones.

'I think so too, sir,' replied Mr Jones.

'In that case, she should be sent to Accra for mental examination, and if the Medical Officer thinks it is right, she should be sent to the asylum.'

Konaduwa was then handcuffed and handed over to the police, who would escort her to Accra.

The man she had accused, who was captivated by her beauty, her teeth, and above all by her stammering, approached the Commissioner and begged that she might be punished in some other way, offering to bear the punishment himself, for he believed that her stubbornness was due to the loss of her property. The Commissioner was inclined to agree, but he could not revoke his own orders, so off the police went with their prisoner.

When they were a few miles outside the town, they met a man carrying a pot of palm-wine. One of the constables offered to buy it, but when they had emptied the pot they went off without paying for it. The owner, on demanding payment, was given a blow that sent him reeling.

'What?' cried Konaduwa. 'Do you policemen act in this way? Did not your master give you some money to pay your way? When the Asantehene's servants did the same thing, your master came and took him away. If that was bad, why are you doing what they did?'

'Be quiet, or I will beat you,' said one of the constables.

'You are afraid to,' she retorted. 'If you dare, you will see that you are playing with fire.'

The Corporal hushed the man, and said: 'This woman is as dangerous as a loaded gun; so be careful, as she can charge you and have you sent to prison.'

They did not speak to her again.

Amoako, the ferryman, who was bewitched by her, followed them to Accra and to the Principal Medical Officer's office, where he boldly explained the situation. When the doctor examined her he found she was not mad but that she suffered from some mental depression which, in his opinion, had caused her impudence. She was taken back to Asiakwa. There the District Commissioner told her he would not try her again on the old charges, and asked the police to withdraw these and give her the benefit of the doubt. He added that she must go back to her own country to be tried by the Elders of her State. When she asked what had become of the money she lost, he told her that the accused did not believe she had had that amount in her portmanteau, but as she insisted on claiming it, the Omanhene of Kwahu would be instructed to examine the case.

13

S. Y. Ntara

The Visitor

S. Y. Ntara is the main author in the Nyanja language, of which Cewa, in which he writes, is a dialect. Writing in the vernacular languages, for a home audience, tends to be less expository. Writers take more for granted, straining neither to allure nor antagonize the alien audience.

The Visitor

Msyamboza and his people travelled easily, without any need to inquire from anyone about the path or about anything else of that sort, since now they were well acquainted with the route. It was a happy journey; plenty of food and meat with no lack of water, since they had a large earthenware water pot which one of Leza's wives had given to one of Msyamboza's. Just as we have noted the experiences of the earlier travel, so now we hear that, on the return, they were well received at the villages right up to the edge of their own country where they, of course, knew everyone.

On the day when they reached the home territory they had rested in the hot hours by a running stream to await the sun's decline. The women busied themselves getting ready some food and Masakhumbira got wood for a fire, taking some of the dried meat and grilling it to eat with the porridge. Then, food finished, they lay in the shade of a tree to straighten their backs and, after a little time of rest, they espied other travellers belonging to a village not far from Cibanzi who drew near and, coming over to them, made themselves known. One of them, after greeting, said:

'And where has this travelling company of yours come from, Chief Msyamboza?'

'Ha!' replied Msyamboza, 'we have been far away at Band-awe; to Chief Leza's in Kanyenda's territory.'

'Kanyenda?' queried the man, 'which Kanyenda? That one near by here?'

'We went to the land of Kanyenda at Nkhunga. And what about yourselves? How was our village when you left? Was there any word of sickness?'

'Well,' replied the man, 'just at this present time things are fairly pleasant but, of course, one hears of sickness ever and again. During the days of the late moon people have felt a lot of sore-throat. Not a hut silent without someone, adult or child, coughing!'

'Yes,' agreed Msyamboza, 'that was an unfortunate moon: even there where we were a lot of the people were really ill. Some of our travelling company felt unwell, too, but not to cause them to lie down sick. They just kept on, however unwell they felt.'

'Well now,' said the man, 'you must not be angry with me, but there is something to puzzle and worry you at your village. A European is there, whose name is Bwana Swann. The name that the people give him is "Kamkamba" owing to the smallness of his body. He came from Kota Kota the day before yesterday and he is after taxes!'

'A European at my village!' exclaimed Msyamboza.

'Yes, indeed: there he most certainly is.'

'And what then,' asked Msyamboza, 'is this "taxes"?'

'Even I also do not know the answer to that,' said the man, 'because very many of the men are off into the bush, fleeing from this European. I have not gone there, believe me! Indeed I just came away without knowing anything about the man except that he has been asking for you. "Where is the chief?" he says. And the people say, "He has gone on a journey."'

'Well,' said Msyamboza, 'we have, as a matter of fact, our-selves met some of these Europeans and have seen that they are a good kind of person.' And then they commenced to talk of this and that in their journey until, when they had finished the talk and made farewells, Msyamboza said to Masakhumbira:

'Come on now! Let us get going on our way that we do not arrive after people have gone to lie down, but while it is still light and we can avoid going to sleep hungry.'

So they started off and still had not arrived when the sun went in; but on they plodded, strengthened by the sharp air and a fine little wind. Thus, darkness being not yet fully fallen, Msyamboza and his people reached Cibanzi with joy. Crowds greeted their arrival and immediately the chief began to make inquiry about his cattle, 'How are they keeping?' and about his workers in the dry-season food plots, 'How have they been doing?' and about the seeds and plants – the beans, sweet potatoes, onions, bananas – 'How are they all thriving?' Then, when he had finished all his questions, he went to lie down.

Yet, ere going to sleep, he said to a wife: 'On the way yonder where we halted, a certain one put news before us of a Bwana Swann, a European from Kota Kota. Has this European gone, or is he here?'

'He has not gone,' replied the wife, 'he is here, since he awaits you. He is not at all far off, but has fixed his house of cloth in which he sleeps. Each day he summons people, and when his *capitao* has written and written on a paper he tears it off [i.e. from its counterfoil in the tax-receipt book] and gives to each male. Then he says things to the man; I do not know whither they tend, the things he says. You yourself will hear tomorrow if you go there.'

'Who did the European come with?' asked Msyamboza.

'With his *capitao* and other men who carried his house and many loads; also cooking things and food of one kind and another. So far as our foods go, he eats meat, and the milk from these cows of yours, and eggs.'

'I will greet him, then, in the morning, because my feet ache with the stones and sand of the journey, and furthermore I am nodding with sleep even as I talk.' And having so spoken with that wife of his, he lay and slept so that people who came to give a greeting did not have any chance to do so.

But when it was light in the morning, Msyamboza called a youth and said: 'Get a goat that we may go and see the European who is here at our village. We just heard yesterday as we were arriving, that a European is here.' And when the lad came with the goat they went together to the European and greeted him, saying:

'We see you, Bwana!'

'And who,' said Mr Swann, 'are you?'

'I am Msyamboza, chief of this place. I had gone off to a distance and got back home last evening. As soon as I arrived I heard that you were here. Thus I come this morning to see you and I bring this small goat that you may put it on your fire and eat it, along with your men.'

'I am grateful. I am glad indeed to see you. I have stayed at your village for several days. And what a village! Are all here your people, or are there some who belong elsewhere?'

'There are those,' replied Msyamboza, 'who are of my tribe, but there are those, too, whom I bought in the past with ivory. This I have given up and all the people here are in freedom. They may hoe where they wish and live after their own desire.'

'You have done well,' said the European. 'Now the reason for my coming is tax. We are going to look after this land and we want to find men who will go and take employment at Blantyre. They will work for a period and will then get a chit to certify that they are free of debt to the Government.'

'Have you then,' asked Msyamboza, 'found any men?'

'I have indeed: men have come to me to be enrolled to go for work at Blantyre.'

Then, when all the talk was over, the European uprooted his hut, presented some salt to Msyamboza, and started off on his further journey to Dzoole. Later came the news, as the fame of the European spread, that he had arrived at Doozle's, who had given him a number of tusks, and had then gone back to Kota Kota.

14

Adelaide Casely-Hayford

Reminiscences

Adelaide Casely-Hayford was the wife of E. Casely-Hayford, the Ghanaian author of *Ethiopia Unbound*. She had a distinctly 'European' sensibility, with her interests, her feelings and her prejudices those of the people amongst whom she had grown up. She was probably the Mansa of her husband's work, an African woman who 'discovers' herself in Germany. Her daughter Gladys, who is mentioned, has emerged as a poet of some talent; but her best poems have been written in Krio and not in the toffy-tainted style her mother admired.

'The Life and Times of Adelaide Casely-Hayford' appeared in the magazine *West Africa* in 1953 when the author was old. The extracts give a charming period glimpse of a world seen through eyes very much the author's own.

Reminiscences

I do not know his name, but that is immaterial. It happened in 1885, when I was seventeen, and little was known of Africans in Germany. So, I occupied the priority place of Curio No. 1. Of course, the old Colonel heard about me in Oehringen, the little town where we lived, and insisted on my visiting him. So I went, but at ninety one's sight can be pretty dim: as a matter of fact, he was almost blind, and made me sit on a footstool, while he passed his gentle hand over my face. He was definitely eccentric, especially about bathing, when he would jump into the bath fully dressed, accompanied by his attendant, fully dressed also.

But on one topic – his beloved Emperor William the Great – he was absolutely sane. 'My child,' he said, 'I have only one wish in life – to see my Emperor before I die. He and I are the only two survivors from the famous battle of — .' (I must confess that I cannot now remember what battle it was.) I wondered at the time whether his wish would materialize. And it did. It was announced that the Emperor would hold a review at Stuttgart, some two hours' journey by train, in a couple of weeks. So arrangements went ahead. The old Colonel, in full regimental regalia, drove to the parade ground in a landau, whilst the ninety-year-old Emperor dismounted from his magnificent white charger, and there they stood, bare-headed, with the breeze playing about their sparse locks, and clasped each other's hands. It was a poignant moment, this meeting between two old campaigners, their battles behind them, and eternity before them. They died within a few days of each other, not long afterwards.

*

I must narrate this, because at eighteen everything seems so tremendously important. At least, it seemed so in those days, when life was so simple and unsophisticated. The modern miss is not like that, indeed she is often quite blasé.

I was busily studying, and happily ensconced in my *pension* at Stuttgart, when I received a letter from the bride, Fraulein Matilda Bazlen, my beloved teacher, who had shepherded me and brought me to Germany. 'I am getting married in a week's time, and you must come to the wedding. I simply won't get married without you.'

Now, she was in Oehringen, and I at Stuttgart. So, I had to consider travelling expenses. Then, I had no suitable clothes. At that time, weddings in Germany were very complicated. There were generally about twelve bridesmaids, each accompanied by her groom, all in evening dress, and they made a lovely picture as they followed the couple up the aisle, forming a semi-circle round the altar. Now, evening dress in those days was a kind of mystic rite, when the beauty of neck, shoulders and arms, otherwise discreetly covered, was exposed to the public eye – so different from today, when all mystery about the female form is no more. I had to decline the invitation, for lack of suitable clothing. A telegram arrived: 'Come as you are', to which I replied, 'I am not coming.' Imagine my consternation, when my foster-father, Herr Bazlen, marched in a day or two after, with instructions from his daughter to bring me by force. And how nice they all were! Nobody seemed to notice either my colour or my morning dress. As I had no groom attendant, Matilda's brother-in-law shepherded two of us, one on each arm, and I was by no means left out in the cold.

At the *Polter Abend* – the night before the wedding, which is devoted to feasting, orations, and many expressions of felicity – somebody read out a poem, about 'the little stranger within their gates', whose presence had added so much to their enjoyment. I was overwhelmed with embarrassment and simply had to hide my head. What a Germany it was in those days!

*

As a teenager, I was terribly shy – probably because I was too race conscious – and in a white country I felt so conspicuous that

I always wanted to hide my head. Consequently, it was a terrible trial to go out alone.

At fifteen, a batch of us from the Jersey Ladies College, where I was one of the foundation pupils, were invited to a lecture given by George Macdonald, who, though one of the minor poets, was very renowned in his day. 'Alice,' I said to my companion, 'when the lecture is over, I am going to shake hands with him.' Alice gasped in astonishment. 'You, Adelaide, a little mouse like you, I don't believe you! I am prepared to bet you won't do it!'

A bar of chocolate was the wager decided upon. Then, slyly, like the little mouse I had been called, I approached the great man from behind, and coughed discreetly. He turned round, and was taken aback to see a little black girl standing there. I seized my opportunity. 'Please, may I shake hands with you?' I asked. 'Why, certainly!' he said, and he gave me a grip, which was quite all right then, but which would have been all wrong now with my acute rheumatism. I won my bet.

*

America is not only a country of adventure, of enormous financial opportunities, and of costly experiments of a lien on human nature, but it is also a country of freaks, especially in the line of religious sects. What other country could have given birth to 'The Holy Rollers', or 'Burning Bush'. Their titles speak for themselves. But the 'Bahais', of whom I had never heard till I crossed the Atlantic, are wonderful people. Their founder, Abdul Bahai, was a Persian – a 'miracle worker' who attracted a large following, who hailed him as the promised Redeemer. Never have I been so lavishly entertained. The Bahai repasts could rightly be designated 'Love-feasts', because of the atmosphere which prevailed. On one occasion, in spite of, or possibly because of my black skin, I was given the seat of honour next to the late founder's nephew. Certainly racial discrimination was absolutely taboo. One devoted adherent gave me a beautiful sketch she had drawn of Abdul Bahai, which was of so much greater value to her than to me, that I subsequently returned it. But to my everlasting regret it never reached her, because of change of address.

*

Yes, I knew about the Salvation Army. In those initial days it achieved its aim as it does today, by catering for the outcasts of society, so we unmitigated little snobs strongly disapproved of my father, a very highly respected member of the community, sneaking out to enjoy a little 'knee-drill'. If he managed to emerge unnoticed, he was invariably caught on his return, and treated to large doses of cold shoulder. That did not detract from subscribing to the *War Cry*, and if our welcome to the vendors was somewhat stand-offish and patronizing, they came all the same. One day they invited us to attend a meeting to be conducted by the great General himself, who was combining business with pleasure by taking a holiday in lovely little Jersey. He was a magnetic personality, with his hawk-like features and uncompromising jaw. When he turned his penetrating black eyes on you, it was like an X-ray searching the hidden precincts of your soul.

I was very young at the time, and possibly passed quite unnoticed, but in later years I realized that the colossal success of this amazing movement was largely due to the amazing faith and indomitable grit of its founder. He was one of the ships that greeted me in passing.

*

After my first adieu to the Gold Coast, I arrived in Freetown in May 1914, with my little daughter Gladys May, and went to live with my young nephew, Dr Charles Farrell Easmon, who had just joined the Government Service. When war broke out four months later, he was drafted to the Cameroons as a surgeon.

I felt I must put my surplus energy to use, so I obtained a teaching job as Music mistress at the Annie Walsh Memorial School. In those days there were no buses, and no cars, so my mode of transport was a little Japanese rickshaw. I always felt that my last moment had come when I ventured on that rickshaw, but I arrived at my destination unharmed. I had to contend with something like one hundred and twenty teenagers, divided into two classes, with an immense capacity for staring and taking in details, and very little for music. I quite enjoyed it and my income was enriched by the sum of 2s. 6d. an afternoon, twice a week, for singing lessons, with a few private pupils thrown in.

In those days, much more stress was laid upon what we could give, rather than what we could get, with the result that although our pockets were light, we were much happier than the present-day teacher. Teaching is very strenuous, because it makes heavy demands on every part of the personality, having no mercy on brain, heart, physique or talents. But it has its own reward, 'It blesseth him that gives and him that takes.'

*

Some time in 1923, Sierra Leone was honoured by a visit from a squadron of battleships including the *Hood*, the *Repulse*, the *Renown*, etc., under the command of Admiral Sir Frederick Field. He invited us to inspect the *Hood*, later giving a magnificent reception which remains in the memory of Sierra Leoneans. This visit was the forerunner of a visit from H.R.H. the Prince of Wales, which took place the following year. That was a red-letter day for Freetown, and the Prince was very approachable and nice to all.

The inability of many of the guests to obtain gloves for the reception at Government House came to his ears, and he immediately issued a statement that he himself would go without. Such considerate, unselfish little acts are unforgettable, especially in a hot climate, where shaking perspiring hands becomes a mixed blessing.

The Prince seemed to be bored to extinction by the ceremonial: indeed, the only time I saw him laugh was when a group of little Brownies performed before him.

Prior to his arrival I had approached all the principal African ladies, whom I knew would be asked to meet him, begging them to put on native costume. I pointed out that it would be so much more picturesque, and would not only enhance our appearance but would show that we were proud of being Africans. They all turned me down. Nothing daunted, I wore for the occasion a plain black satin *lappah*, and a most beautifully embroidered *boobah*, worked by black men right up at Pujehun. The effect was, I think, altogether charming. The Prince then sent an A.D.C. to

inform five or six of us that he would like a few minutes' conver
sation. H.R.H. asked me where I had been educated and what
was doing in Freetown. To which I replied, 'I am teaching.'

'Teaching?' said the Prince. 'I would never have taken you
for a teacher.' To this day, I wonder whether that was a compli
ment or not.

The Prince also asked where my husband was. I was non-
plussed for the moment, but the A.D.C. came to my rescue –
'Oh,' he said, 'you will meet Mr Casely-Hayford when you go
down to the Gold Coast. He is a member of the Legislative
Council there.'

How times have changed. The outlook has altered completely
Instead of blindly copying European fashions, which are made to
suit a white woman's personality, our women now have come to
realize that every race has its own distinctive dress, with its
own appeal – and its own suitability for particular climatic
conditions.

15

Jean Malonga

Mambéké's Creed

The River Congo, murky and crocodile-infested, meanders throug the underbrush of love, intrigue, lust and death which is Malonga *Cœur d'Aryenne*. When the story opens, young Mambéké, with courageous plunge from his father's canoe, saves Solange, the litt daughter of the white exploiter, from drowning. Solange – or Arya Heart as she is fondly called – becomes Mambéké's mistress and th mother of his child, kills her brute of a father, and takes a last despera plunge into the Congo.

Apparently inspired by a *Paul et Virginie* style exoticism, this fir interracial love-story in modern African literature (apart from th somewhat special case of *Nini*) is a literary concomitant of the 'Unid *Française*' of the 1940s and 50s, in which Jean Malonga took a leadin part. Like Mambéké, and the high-ranking French educationist i Brazzaville who sees him through school, the novel itself epitomize the desirable attitudes of sympathy and tolerance, which are expecte to make the experiment in racial co-existence a reality.

While in full agreement with the French-type lay school, the autho using Mambéké as his mouthpiece, launches a full-scale attack o missionary education and missionary practices in general.

Mambéké's Creed

On the occasion of this courtesy visit, Father Hux, who was curious to know the intimate thoughts of the boy whose soul he had violated not so long ago, realized that he was coming to grips with a trenchant, logical mind when the young teacher started refuting Catholicism, and especially the conduct of the missionaries in charge of spreading this faith among the 'Gentiles' of Central Africa and all other tradition-bound continents. The old priest was utterly scandalized by the severe judgement of Mambéké, whom he accused without foundation of sectarian atheism. He refused to have any discussion with his visitor.

'You are certainly mistaken, Father,' the young man defended himself, happy to see the priest who had so often criticized him blush under the barrage of his sharp retorts. 'You are doubtless mistaken about me, Father, for I assure you and can prove to you that I'm by no means an atheist. I wonder – and I think I have a perfect right to do so – I only wonder, as I said, in which God I should believe: yours or mine. For we should at last come to understand each other once and for all. Personally I think there are a lot of points we can never agree on. Let's start with the Decalogue, if that's all right with you. In the first commandment, from which, if I remember rightly, all the other commandments spring, God enjoins His creatures to worship only Him, and not to offer sacrifices to false idols or images painted by the hand of man. But in all the churches I go I see statues and portraits, images and symbols, in front of which the faithful prostrate themselves in ecstasy. I find places of pilgrimage where the churchgoers and the exalted kneel by the thousands to burn candles and incense, where hundreds or even thousands of infirm and sick are publicly displayed while expecting to be cured by a hypothetical miracle. But what happens among recent converts elsewhere? Their amulets are burnt, their liturgical incantations condemned, and they are given scapulars, rosaries, and consecrated medals instead. God says: 'Love one another.' But at Pointe Noire, at Libreville, and at Léopoldville, where I happened to pass through, I found that coloured priests were systematically relegated to living in huts with their grandfathers, the fetish priests, so that they stayed in squalid hovels and did not eat together with their white fellow-priests. In the schools run by the Church, white children are separated from black. People have even gone to the extent of creating an intermediate race, the mulattoes, leading a marginal existence between the two others and inflated with pride. Even if this attitude does not render relations between the members of the young generation altogether impossible, at least it makes association between them difficult, though what young people really want is to get to know each other and to fraternize. The religion of love and charity is taught through the persuasion of assault and whipping and through abductions which create trouble in tribal families and spread the venom of hate in a society established for thousands of years. I witnessed this myself in missions where I saw girls and women who had been dragged away from their parents' or husbands' homes to be locked up in a convent; I saw children of all ages and both sexes recruited to places thousands of miles away from home on the pretext that they were to be given an education and upbringing necessary to their spiritual uplift, but who were in actual fact employed in clearing fields for the planting of fruit-trees, vegetables, groundnuts, coconut palms, and banana trees, yams and potatoes, all of which they were strictly forbidden to touch themselves. In like manner they were supplying unpaid labour to profit-making brickyards and joiners' shops. Within the same Christianity, dispensations are granted to the privileged and the priests themselves. On this point, I remember that in our totems and in all our intransigent sects, what is forbidden for the neophyte and what is a sin for the disciple, whether rich or poor, is equally forbidden for the priest or even the patriarch, although this may only be intended as an example to be emulated by the others.

'When I consider all these disillusioning discoveries, is it not my right, or rather my definite duty, to ask myself whether those responsible are not harming the future growth and purity of Catholicism? One really wonders who is right, God or His envoy. Is a critical mind not allowed to have a moment's hesitation before taking the apostle's sincerity for granted? We are not rebelling against religion itself, which is perhaps necessary and maybe – or maybe not – indispensable to society, but we are only wondering whether those responsible are not taking pleasure in sabotaging it, in transforming it so as to suit their own cause and make it fit for the exclusive consumption of the less enlightened peoples, that is, of the so-called primitives.'

'Stop! I would be an accessory to your blasphemies if I were to let you continue. In all you've said, my son, I can see only pride and vanity. It's a pride with which the evil spirit has inspired you. I myself am distressed to discover (since we are concerned with discoveries) that the entire religious instruction you received from me has not done you much good. The undenominational school has made another person out of you, and you are no longer your old self. In short, if I understand what you've been saying, you don't believe in God any more, do you?'

'Oh, how you've misunderstood me, Father. Is it because I don't know how to express myself clearly in your language? If that's why, would you please let me make some more comments in Likuba? I'm sure we would then understand each other better.'

'Don't bother! I can see quite clearly that you have become a little demon. Whether you speak French or Likuba makes no difference.'

'Well, then let me go on. I'll try my best to tell you quietly what I think. You cannot condemn the person I have become merely because I now know how to reason and to ask why things are the way they are. Please, if you tried to, Father, could you tell me what in your opinion has been the purpose of all the education and training you gave me, that you mentioned a while ago? Why in fact are you an enemy of reasoning and of an inquiring mind? But that's not the point here. Let me tell you once more, it is not the existence of God we should discuss now but the ways of teaching how to get to know Him as proposed by you. For you have to admit, I never told you I didn't believe in God any more. Above all, don't forget that I'm first and foremost an African. That means a lot. Yes, I do believe in a supernatural power which rules the universe. I also believe in the brotherhood of man. I believe in the existence of visible and invisible beings. I believe in the beauty of the world, in everything that is great, noble, and good. I believe in the spirits of water, wind, fire, and of the planets. I believe in a better world for my race so forgotten down here. The things I believe in constitute a coherent whole which can be explained. This is my Credo.

'I believe in this God because He is possible, because I feel Him, because He is accessible to all His creatures, to the whole human species. *My* God does not refuse His forgiveness to the sinner because of his green colour while granting it more readily to somebody who is violet, because this God of mine does not reject anyone from His bosom, does not make any distinction between any of His creatures, and does not shut His door to the poor wretch who has no golden key as have the torch-bearers of a Christianity which was sublime at the beginning, universal and uniform in its whole doctrine, but nowadays tends towards a spirit of segregation that I can only deplore. Yes, Father. Yes ... I do believe in God, but in the One I defend with all the strength of my soul, that is, in the infinitely good One, the infinitely equitable One who is fair towards the whole world and who, like a father who is impartial to his violet and green children, is not concerned with their colour which is, after all, only a cosmic accident. Is *your* God all this, Father Hux?'

'That's enough! Get out of here at once, Satan! I'm not going to speak to you any more. I don't want to hear any more of this and I don't want to see you here for another second. My God! ... Is that the way to pay back the debt of gratitude you owe to the missionary that brought you up, by becoming a militant atheist, a raving, stubborn communist who feels free to insult God and His ministers?'

'Father, listen to me carefully. You're about to make a dreadful mistake. You're about to drive me out of your house when all I'm asking is that you enlighten me. I swear that a priest from my own country who happened to be in your place, and who finds nothing to hide in his religion, which he derives from the same God as you, would have told me everything in an attempt to convince me. Be careful, Father, be careful. I'm afraid you are acting contrary to all you want to defend. No, Father Hux, I'm insulting neither the missionaries nor God. On the contrary, I want to save the prestige and good name of the one, and to defend in your stead the greatness and purity of the other.'

'Enough, I'm telling you. Get out, child of the Devil!'

Our good Rev. Father Hux could not be helped. For him, to reason, to refuse, to contest the pertinence of a claim or the unjustified boldness of a concept, was tantamount to declaring oneself an atheist and a communist, to insulting God Almighty. Amen.

16

Abdoulaye Sadji

Nini in Distress

As in Ousmane Socé's *Karim*, Saint-Louis is the scene for this novel of manners. Here, however, the author does not deal with the healthy traditional way of life such as attracted even an enterprising beau like Karim; he singles out a segment of the city's society which, at least in the colonial situation, keeps aloof from the rest of the indigenous population – the mulattoes.

Despite her flat little nose and bee-stung lips, Nini considers herself a Nordic. She is fair-haired and blue-eyed; 'her eyes and the name of her family place her somewhere closer to the North Pole than to the Equator'. Nini is not just a beautiful, conceited, and reasonably efficient office-girl in Saint-Louis who also happens to be a mulatto. The author wants her to be 'the eternal moral portrait of the mulatto woman'. And that is where Sadji, notwithstanding a wealth of sharply observed detail, goes astray. Partly because of his constant pedantic intrusions, his Nini never moves us as a character, but turns out a literary type whom the author either 'debunks' or blandly pities as a victim of time, place and environment.

Nihi is wooed by N'diaye Matar, a member of the rising black élite; but she considers his advances an outrage and prefers the favours of a young Frenchman who finally deserts her.

Nini in Distress

The next morning Nini got up, washed and put on her make-up as usual, and left for work without touching again upon the questions discussed the night before. Her aunt, seeing her in a more cheerful mood, thought she had regained control of herself and had calmed down.

At the office she got started with her work and busied herself with her typewriter without showing the least sign of irritation. Then suddenly she stopped typing and addressed the private secretary, who had his back turned to her.

'Excuse me, sir,' she said, 'for interrupting you just now when you're probably very busy. But I should like to ask you for some information. Will you let me ask you a question?'

'But of course, Miss Maerle. If I can be of any help to you, just go ahead.'

'Sir, I'd like to know under what conditions I've been given a government contract.'

The private secretary reflected for a moment and then shrugged his shoulders in a gesture of helplessness. 'I'm sorry, Miss Maerle, believe me if I tell you that I haven't any more information than you on this point. I only know that when you were taken on, you were posted to my office to take the place of a certain Mrs Rémy, who was getting too old and whose contract was about to expire. Listen, you could maybe ask the personnel manager. Wasn't it he who got you to sign your contract?'

'Yes, sir, but he didn't want to tell me to whom I owed this job.'

'I'm sorry, Miss Maerle, but he's the only one who's in a position to give you this information.'

'Sir, could you give me permission to be absent for a while so that I could make an appointment with him?'

'Most certainly. I know that you're not behind with your work and that you'd bring it up to date anyway.'

So Nini left her typewriter and went to ask for an appointment with the little old man who had received her so politely the first day and signed her up on contract.

As soon as she was in his presence, the old man, used to the bile of civil servants feeling wronged and to the changing expressions on their more or less tense faces, guessed that all was not right with the mulatto girl. 'What can I do for you?' he asked, almost capitulating before her.

'Sir, I should like to ask you once more to whom I owe the contract job I have.'

The little old man looked up, knitted his brows, and striking his little fist on the minister-size desk asked, 'Oh yes, I remember. What's your name again?'

'Virginie Maerle.'

'That's right.' He rang a bell. A man appeared, a white man who undoubtedly fulfilled the functions of a secretary. 'Would you please give me the file of Miss . . .'

'Virginie Maerle,' Nini said.

'Yes, the file of Miss Virginie Maerle,' the personnel manager concluded.

'I'll get it right away, sir,' the man consented. Less than a minute later the file was on the personnel manager's desk.

'So what is it you want, Miss Maerle?'

'I want to know who the individual – beg your pardon, the man – is to whom I owe my post.'

'But I've already told you several times, if I remember rightly, that he doesn't want his identity disclosed.'

'In that case, sir, I'm obliged to hand in my resignation. People are making too much fun of me in town. They're saying a lot of unpleasant things about me.'

'Come, come, that's unbelievable. A lot of unpleasant things just because you have a nice contract? But your references entitle you to it. We have got our information from reliable quarters. There has been no illegal manipulation, neither by you nor by ourselves. Some people are so wicked! Miss Maerle, why don't you just laugh at everything these people say and keep your post in spite of and in defiance of them all. Come now, you want to resign because there are jealous and envious people around you who talk a lot of nonsense?'

'Well, yes, sir,' Nini admitted, 'but if I could at least know who the man is who recommended me to you.'

'All I can tell you about this – but what importance can it have – is that this man is a celebrity among your people, I mean an African in a very high position, whose help is completely disinterested, believe me.'

'An African?' Nini cried, full of indignation.

'But Miss Maerle, calm yourself. Why should you be so astonished? Are you afraid something unpleasant might happen to you because of his intercession?'

'Sir,' Nini hurled at the frightened little man, 'I can't accept the fact that I owe my position to a black man, even if he should be the most illustrious of his whole race. I'm sorry, but I'm going to hand in my resignation to you right away.'

After leaving the office of the personnel manager, Nini went back to the private secretary's office where she usually worked. She drew up her resignation in a few lines, typing it in duplicate, signed it, and handed it to her boss.

'Why, Miss Maerle, you're resigning?' the private secretary asked in amazement.

'Yes, sir, I can't avoid it. Everywhere in town people are saying that I owe my job to a black man, and I've just learned that it's true. Besides, they add a lot of unpleasant things...I can no longer put up with such an affront. Moreover, I'm engaged to be married and my fiancé, who's in France at present, will soon come back to Sénégal. Then we'll get married and I'll be all right. I won't have to work any more.'

'Can I give you a piece of advice? Think it over for a little while before sending in your resignation.'

'I've thought it over carefully, sir ...'

17

David Ananou

'...and reel to the brink of the grave
which awaits you'

Old Sodji is a man of the Toobgan tribe in Southern Ghana who has settled in Togoland. The mainstay of his old age is his son Dansou, 'the son of Dan'. Dan is the serpent, 'the god of miracles', to whom Sodji and his childless wife Avlessi vowed to dedicate the child he was to grant them. The heir was born almost three years after their visit to the god's shrine and barely eleven months after Avlessi had been treated by a white doctor. But, as old uncle Aholou said, the doctor could not have achieved anything without the god's intercession.

Dansou becomes in turn a farmer, fisherman, basket-maker, money-lender, and on the artistic side, improviser and composer of music, poet and sage. He retains powerful charms given to him by his father. When Sodji dies, Dansou seems to be cut out for the rôle of leader of his community. But inventive as ever, he moves on to Sekondi in his father's old country to become a full-time fisherman and – a gratuitous gesture of goodwill intended by the author for the European reader – a Christian.

'...and reel to the brink of the grave
which awaits you '

Sodji was dead. Avlessi and her son could not get over it. They just could not believe their eyes. But the fact was there in all its poignant reality. What an event and what a tribulation!

Like the deceased, the mother was a fetishist. She had stayed at the convent [of the Thunder] with him and knew the precepts of their religion. Trying to control herself and biting her lips to keep from crying, she regained her composure and faced up to the situation. First she imposed silence upon her children and bade them to be sparing in the manifestations of their grief. Then, with her torso bared in compliance with the rule of the convent, she ran to announce the news to the chief fetish priest of the village. He sent out messages to his followers, who gathered at once. Just as the women had done for the ceremony of the twins, they went out to the forest again to collect certain plants with their left hand to put them on the dead body. Religious songs and dances followed. Then a gunshot sounded to indicate the end of the fetishist practices and the beginning of the funeral rites in accordance with the usual custom.

The sun was disappearing, setting the whole of the west on fire. On the opposite horizon big black clouds leaped on top of each other as if distracted by an unexpected disaster. In an oblique plunge some drops of rain thudded down on the miserable countryside. A heat as oppressive as the fumes from a furnace weighed down on the village. Like an army in discord the group of clouds broke up, their concerted action and their unforeseen anger having come to a brutal compromise. A second gunshot, this time fired by Dansou, greeted their dispersion and announced to the whole of Séva the great terrestrial drama which had its strange repercussions up to the clouds. Weeping, which one might have thought was touched off by the report, echoed the gunshot. Every chest panted in unison, convulsively heaving irrepressible sighs. Soon the vast courtyard of the dead man was too small to hold the crowd of sympathizers and onlookers. With some difficulty those who were courageous enough cleared a way for themselves through the dense crowd, and got through to the mighty one whose life had just been snuffed out like a flame.

'How strong death is and how it laughs at our skilful schemes,' wondered those whom Sodji had cured, attended to, and even brought back to life when they had been suffering from swooning-fits or epilepsy. 'We are lost,' others murmured, who wept for themselves while weeping for the dead man.

Still others, who were sorry that they would no longer be able to make use of the old man's services or that they had not always been kind to him, added, 'Why must it always be the best that have to leave first?'

Tears flowed abundantly. Shouts tore the motionless air. And consternation struck all souls.

After the great excitement of the first hours, the visitors gradually withdrew. Soon only some relatives and helpful neighbours, actively engaged in putting up a shed, were left in the yard. Messengers were sent out to announce the bad news to everybody in the village. The relatives living in other places were not forgotten, notably Têko, the dead man's senior brother. Helped by Aholou, Botsoé, and some friends of the house, Dansou, the son of the fetish,* refraining from crying like everybody else, faced up to the problems incumbent on him and gave precise orders as if he had been making preparations for funerals all his life. He ordered a coffin at Porto-Seguro and several cases of *sodabi* from the distilleries in the bush at Vogan.

At about ten o'clock in the evening, the dead body was carried into the inner yard and put face downwards on the ground. The workers, running with sweat, had almost finished the construction of the *apatam*. One of them, acting as a mouthpiece for all the others, intoned the funeral song composed by Dansou. Everybody answered him in chorus starting with the following passage:

*The son of the snake god, reputed to have given fertility to Dansou's mother, Avlessi.

> To weep a whole night
> Without a single drop of liquor
> Is not a good thing at a funeral.
> So bring on the drinks, slaughter the animals,
> Too bad for the man who has died.
> The living must make merry.

Nobody was afraid that this would be considered begging. They sang to spur each other on in their work. The only thing was that in their songs they casually slipped in a reference to the hankerings of their thirsty throats. And, quite accidentally, the song was addressed to its own author. Dansou was flattered and scandalized at the same time. Unable to condemn the song he himself had created and to impose silence, he hummed its sequel to console himself. It went like this:

> The words one speaks in the house of the dead
> Have always filled me with pity for the dead.
> May those who are still able to enjoy life
> Enjoy it as long as they can
> For everything ends the day you stop living ...
> Then putting you at the head of the procession
> Of people staggering drunkenly,
> They will start shouting like animals
> And reel to the brink of the grave which awaits you.

In a dolorously tragic way Dansou realized once more the rightness of the ideas he had once had, and appreciated in his heart the boldness of his thinking. He also understood what his friends were trying to say by their allusions. Anxious above anything else to have a funeral worthy of his father, surrounded by the necessary extravagance, he brought five bottles of spirits, which the fifteen men present drained like exhausted siphons. Then began a wake that lasted till dawn. At daybreak work on the corpse was started. Amagan and Kodjo, real giants, who specialized in macabre brutalities, took on Sassi, a real virago, as an assistant to wash and trim the body. We use the word 'brutalities' with particular good reason, and we hope that the reader will soon understand us and will not bear us a grudge for not having used a euphemism.

While the house began to fill up again with people and the

tears were mixed with the songs, the two strong fellows and their sinister helper down beside the dead man sipped the liquor Dansou offered them. Soon basins of boiling water were carried into the small private yard, and also soap and sponges. Amagan and Kodjo undressed the stiffened body and placed it on three stools, one under his head, another under his back, and a third under his feet. Then began the bath, or rather the cooking, to judge from the high temperature of the water. The body was soaked and then rubbed powerfully for more than three quarters of an hour. The supply of boiling water was assured by women who did their best. When the corpse was considered sufficiently scoured, the cleansing of the inside followed. This consisted of applying pressure on the abdomen in order to empty it completely. Then they grabbed the stiff members and straightening their spines, sneering, they broke the knee, elbow, and shoulder joints. Dead people had to be supple when arriving at the place of their ancestors. And that was the way he became, better and even more supple than an acrobat. It made one want to die abroad, even from the panther's fang, rather than have to deliver one's body to such unsympathetic heavyweights. Fortunately, the display of their strength did nothing to disturb their victim's last sleep.

Finally old Sodji was shaved to make him look younger before his departure on the great journey. Then the martyred body was rinsed with cold water. Sassi wiped it and covered it with garments bearing the emblems of the Thunder. With rags and cotton the eyes were bandaged and the orifices plugged. A length of white linen which served as a shroud was rolled around the corpse, which was then laid in the beautiful coffin from Porto-Seguro. Coins, banknotes, and *gree-grees* were put next to him as viaticum. A well-sharpened razor was shining in his hands, for the dead man had to kill the sorcerer or the poisoner who had perhaps brought him death. Then the coffin was nailed up and carried into the large courtyard where a tremendous crowd was waiting. Weeping broke out everywhere, brought on by deafening explosions.

18

Ferdinand Oyono

The Medal

Writing about African music in his novel, *Le Fils du fétiche* (1955) David Ananou concluded that 'the African, too, is capable of making all sciences his own and of penetrating the subtleties of metaphysics and knowledge, provided that he allows himself to be guided by those who have a more precise idea about things than himself.' After this kind of pandering to the benign complacency of not always enlightened colonial despots, which was common in earlier French African writing, the work of two young Cameroonians, Mongo Beti and Ferdinand Oyono, seemed almost revolutionary in the tepid literary scene of the 1950s.

Oyono first assaulted the French public with *Une Vie de boy* (1956) a taboo-wrecking tale of blood and sperm, savagely caricaturing the colonial parade. It was followed up by *Le Vieux Nègre et la Médaille* which, a trifle more subdued, deals with the illusory greatness and lightning decline of a gentle Uncle Tom. A fool to his countrymen and a tool to the colonial administration, old Meka has donated his land to the missionaries and the blood of his sons to the greater glory of France. In his finest hour, decorated and carried high by the ritual of Franco-African fraternity on that fateful 14 July, he becomes to his wife among the watching crowd a Judas who has sold his children.

The time spent in the chalk-circle of the chosen, which here separates farce from tragedy, and the humiliations that follow, prepare Meka the medallist to reassess the role of *colonisateur* and *colonisé* and prompt his question: 'Do they want us to stop being ourselves?'

The Medal

It was hot. Meka began to wonder whether his heart was thumping in his feet. He had put on his shoes at the top of the hill from where one could see Mr Fouconi's office. He had almost not felt them when he had reported to the commandant. Meka marched back to his place under the flag as if he were 'the king of Doum'. He had not even deigned to cast a glance at the native chiefs, whom he had recognized by their red escutcheons.

'Some more people who are going to burst with envy,' he said to himself. 'I loathe them! I loathe them!'

Then he had put his heels together as he had seen the soldiers do when a white man walked past them. When the white man walked past Meka, he would smile at him and then point him out to his fellow-whites with his finger. Meka would then hear a confused rumble of voices from amidst the Europeans. But he remained standing frozen at attention. He felt as tough as a piece of wood.

The first thing that had tired him was his stiff neck. Meka began looking around him again. Now that he felt his heart thumping in his feet he began to wonder apprehensively whether he would be able to hold out in the circle they had drawn for him, until the arrival of the great chief of the whites. He looked at his shoes; they appeared even more inflated to him now than they had in the morning when he had emptied them of the sand that he always put in them at night. He tried to move a foot, clenched his fists, and kept from breathing. For some seconds he felt an infinite calm. Then he tried to shift his whole weight on to his right foot, which was hurting less. His left foot gave him a little respite but he no longer knew what was going on in his right foot. It felt as if the needle Ela had given him was piercing his small toe, going up through his ankle and on to the thigh, and was stuck in his spine. This needle itself had multiplied into a myriad needles which were now tingling all over his body. Meka was drenched with sweat.

'Fortunately I didn't put on socks,' he said to himself.

He tried to imagine a more searing pain than the one he was suffering. But he said to himself, 'So what? I'm a man. My ancestors left me the way I am. They are bound to see me in the place where I'm now ... Let's try not to make them ashamed of themselves. I was circumcised with a knife and the sorcerer spat pepper on my wounds and yet I didn't weep ...'

He clenched his teeth a bit more grimly. 'I didn't cry,' he thought. 'I've never cried in my life. A man, a real one I mean, never cries ...'

Meka was one of them, a man, and a real one. Was he not the son of the great Meka who had put up a long resistance against the first whites? What? Was he now going to cry right in front of them and in front of his fellow tribesmen who had known his father or had heard others talk about him?

A changed Meka looked over towards the whites. He stretched out one foot, set the other one sideways, went through this action the other way round, and then put his heels together again. He turned around and smiled at his countrymen as if he wanted to reassure them. He crossed his hands behind his back and waited. It seemed to him that he was not feeling his shoes any more. He looked at the flag flying over his head, looked at the whites and the soldiers, and then stiffened his neck.

'Even if he arrived in the night, I would wait,' he told himself. 'Even if he arrived tomorrow, in a year, or at the end of the world ...'

Suddenly a frown crossed his face, which took on an ominous expression. It seemed to him that his abdomen weighed him down. He felt it coming from far away, from very far away, the urgent need to pass water.

Mr Fouconi stood in the first row of the Europeans from Doum, between Birdneck the police chief, and his deputy, a young man with round curves, a heavy growth of black hair, and a wide pelvis, whom the blacks had nicknamed 'de sideman what dey look like woman'.

Mr Fouconi stepped forward, descended a step, and came out into the yard. His deputy joined him immediately. They chatted for a while a few paces away from Meka. Mr Fouconi looked at him and then smiled. Meka answered with the biggest smile he could muster. The two whites then went off to discuss something with the leader of the soldiers. Finally Mr Fouconi, still followed by his deputy, returned to the group of whites.

'What if I walked away?' Meka thought. His feet were on fire. 'What if I just walked away?'

He asked himself this question several times, fidgeted with his shoulders, then picking up all his courage suddenly passed his palm over his face that was bathed in sweat. He looked around as if trying to find somebody giving him a sign that his performance had been appreciated. He wiggled, made another vague gesture, and even wanted to whistle. He constrained himself once more and passed his palm over his lips. He wondered how he could occupy his thoughts so as to forget the urge he felt getting stronger, and the heat of the fiery furnace consuming his feet.

He would have given everything just to be behind his hut, under the umbrella tree where he squatted down every morning after prayer. He closed his eyes.

'Almighty God,' he prayed silently, 'you alone who sees everything that goes on in the heart of man, who sees that my dearest wish at this moment when I am expecting the medal and the chief of the whites, alone in this circle between two worlds'– he opened his eyes, looked in front and behind him and then closed them again – 'between two worlds, oh, my God, which you made entirely different, my dearest and greatest wish is to take off these shoes and to piss ... yes, to piss ... I am only a poor sinner, and I don't deserve it that you should listen to me, but I pray to you to help me in this situation which I've never before in my life been through, in the name of Jesus Christ our Lord. Amen ... I mentally make the sign of the cross.'

He opened his eyes and ran his tongue over his lips. He felt relieved.

It was half past ten. Mr Fouconi was starting to get nervous. The High Commissioner was an hour late. He was expected for

the saluting of the flag. Mr Fouconi went to the group of local
civil servants, then to that of the chiefs. He passed by Meka
again.

'It's hot, isn't it?' he said.

'Yes, yes,' said Meka. That was all the French he knew. Mr
Fouconi was joined by Birdneck and the deputy. The whites
started to walk up and down in front of Meka.

'They are lucky not to suffer in their shoes,' he said bitterly
to himself. 'They're wearing topees and they're young. And I, a
poor man advanced in years, am forced to let my head fry in the
sun like an egg.'

The Europeans walked past him again. The whiteness of their
suits hurt his eyes. He closed them but his ears were at the same
time martyred by the grating of the pebbles crushed underfoot
by the heavy tread of the whites.

Meka did not know what hurt him most, his feet, his abdomen,
the heat, or his teeth. If at that moment somebody had asked him
how his body was doing, he would not have lied, as he usually
did, by answering that pain was tormenting him all through. He
was sorry that he had not dropped in at Mami Titi's bar. 'There
I could at least have taken something to help me not to feel this
pain,' he thought.

He looked over to the shopping centre. At the same moment
the sound of a bugle alerted everybody. Meka saw a big black
car with a little tri-coloured flag travelling at a brisk speed towards the courtyard where he was. The car pulled up in front
of Mr Fouconi and his deputy. The commandant of Doum
opened one of the doors, and two colossal whites got out. Meka
wondered which one of the two might be the big chief they were
waiting for.

The two whites, followed by Mr Fouconi and his deputy,
paced up and down in front of the soldiers. Then Mr Fouconi led
them to the veranda of his office where the whites of Doum were
waiting for them.

Some moments later Mr Fouconi introduced the group of
native civil servants to them, then the group of chiefs, with some
of whom they shook hands. When Meka saw them coming towards him, he thought a knife's blade was cutting through his

bowels. He clenched his teeth and tensed his muscles as he did when confronting some danger. Mr Fouconi pointed him out with his chin and turned back to his chiefs, talking to them all the while. Meka wondered whether they had guessed his urge. He blinked and rolled his fists into a ball. When Mr Fouconi fell silent, the two whites held out a soft hand to him, one after the other, and he pressed them like wet laundry. Then they went back to their countrymen.

Meka could not stand it anymore. It was so hot that he raised his eyes to make sure that the sun was still in the sky and not right on his back.

Why were they waiting to give him the medal? How could they keep a man his age standing up for one hour? Could they have lost or forgotten the medal he was expecting? The thought frightened him. What would he tell his friends, especially those in whose eyes he had assumed a certain importance? Oh, these whites! Nothing was easy with them. Although instead of walking they would run, they acted in the slow manner of tortoises when they had promised you something. They were really taking their time now over there on the other side of the courtyard, what with their endless introductions and greetings. Meka shook his head and looked at his feet. He suppressed a little hiccough. 'My feet are swollen! My feet are all swollen up!' he said in panic.

He crossed his hands over his abdomen and immediately felt much better. He hurriedly joined his heels together when he saw the two strange whites, Mr Fouconi, his deputy, and Mr Pipiniakis coming towards him. He welded his arms to his thighs as tightly as he could, raised his head once more, and then did not stir again. He saw Mr Pipiniakis taking up a position beside him. Mr Fouconi and the others stayed a few paces in front of them. The bugle sounded and a drumroll started. One of the two fat white men stepped up to Mr Pipiniakis.

'The big chief, that's him,' Meka said to himself. But he was at a loss for anything or anyone to compare him with. The one thing that had struck him was the voluminous bag under his chin which partly concealed the knot of his tie.

The big chief of the whites talked to Mr Pipiniakis, who stayed motionless like a statue, as if he were shouting at a deaf man. When he had finished, he took a medal from a small box, which Mr Fouconi's deputy held out to him, and stuck it on Mr Pipiniakis's chest. Meka then saw the big chief of the whites seize the Greek by the shoulders and put his cheeks against his. Every movement he made caused the bag under his chin to tremble. It looked like an old breast the colour of laterite.

Now it was Meka's turn. The big chief of the whites began mouthing in front of him. According to whether he opened or shut his lips, his lower jaw went down or up again, puffing up and deflating the bag under his chin as it went. He took another medal from the little box and came talking towards Meka. Meka had time to note that it did not resemble the one the Greek had got.

The chief of the whites reached up to his shoulder. Meka looked down at him the moment he stuck the medal on his chest. Meka felt his hot breath through his khaki jacket. The chief of the whites was sweating like a wrestler. One would have thought that rain had fallen on his back. A large wet spot stretched from his shoulders to his buttocks. Meka wondered full of anxiety whether he would stick his moist crop on each of his shoulders as he had done with Mr Pipiniakis. He heaved a sigh of relief when the chief of the whites, having fastened the medal, stepped back a few paces and held out his hand. Meka wrapped his hand around it as if it were wet cotton.

He took a sneaking look down at his chest. There was the medal, pinned to his khaki jacket. He smiled, raised his head, and noticed that he was singing under his breath while his whole face was beating the rhythm. His torso undulated despite himself while his knees bent and unbent like springs. He was no longer suffering and did not even hear his joints creaking. The heat, his urge, the pain he had felt in his feet, all had disappeared as if by magic. He looked at his medal again. He felt his neck growing longer. Yes, his head rose and kept rising like the tower of Babel, taking the sky by storm. His forehead was touching the clouds. His long arms rose imperceptibly like the wings of a bird ready to fly away . . .

19

Mongo Beti

Saving Souls in Tala Land

In Mongo Beti's work, the spiteful laughter and irreverence towards colonial institutions which he shares with his compatriot Oyono is tempered with a rare poetic sensibility.

In all of Beti's novels a raw youth is confronted with the vagaries of adult life and the complexities of the changing African scene. The story-teller, or rather journal-writer, in *Le Pauvre Christ de Bomba* is fifteen-year-old Denis, an altar-boy, whose eyes are forever focused on his master, the Rev. Father Drumont, whom he identifies with Christ. The Father is an energetic salesman for the kingdom of God, but a man of profound kindness under his gruff authoritarian shell. Thus the bond of affection which unites priest and altar-boy endures even when its religious basis – a child-like faith on the one hand, and a high sense of mission on the other – slowly but inexorably crumbles away.

Saving Souls in Tala Land

At about four o'clock in the afternoon there was an urgent call for the Reverend Father Superior, who had just about finished hearing his faithful in confession. A man working in his field had had an accident. He had been working furiously on a tree with his axe. As the tree happened to be caught at the top in the strong lianas of the nearby bush, it did not fall away in the opposite direction to the man but crashed into the ground, dragging the man along as it went and piercing and crushing his body below his stomach. His brothers and all the other villagers had not been able to pull him out by the time we – the Reverend Father Superior, the local catechist, and myself – arrived on the scene. The Reverend Father Superior said that since it was difficult to get him out, they should just leave him there until he had heard him in confession. The man was articulating with great difficulty. He had at one time been baptized but had later lived a disorderly life. The Reverend Father Superior made him swear to renounce his disorderly matrimonial habits. The man also promised that, no matter how, his savings would be used to pay his outstanding church-rate. The Reverend Father Superior then made a point of hearing him in confession, and we therefore moved off a short distance. The villagers seemed quite impressed by the scene. The R.F.S. had squatted down near the dying man's ear. The tree had buried itself in the ground, horribly mutilating the man's body; he was not even twitching any more as he had done when we arrived.

I was happy with the idea that this event might bring the villagers back to the straight path. And perhaps if the people mended their ways, the R.F.S. would not give up this beautiful country.

The man died just as the R.F.S. was giving him absolution.

What a blessing! This man who would never have dreamt of going to confession, who would have died without the sacraments, whose soul would have appeared before God in the worst possible state had the R.F.S. not happened to be around at the moment the accident occurred, lo and behold, he will henceforth be among the chosen! But how many other people will be given this kind of chance? And the tree had miraculously enough pierced him just below his belly. This goes to show that man is always punished in that part of his body which was the instrument of his sin! The R.F.S. will not fail to point out all these co-incidences in his sermon to the faithful tomorrow.

The R.F.S. helped them to get the corpse free. It was not an easy job. Some villagers wanted to cut the tree again with an axe thus risking an even more horrible accident. The R.F.S. ordered them to set the bush on fire. As the bush was consumed by the flames, the lianas gave way under the weight of the tree, and the tree fell full length, freeing the body of the unfortunate Joseph ... Joseph Garba. That was his name as I learned later on. Poor man! His wife, or rather his concubine, who had been forbidden to go near the corpse, uttered piercing cries in the village, which fraught with their total despair reached us, who were still so far away in the forest.

Because of this death the whole village, all the parts of it without exception, was gloomy this evening when we came to visit it. While we were walking on the bushtrack, which here [...] develops into a street, the R.F.S. explained to us that people sometimes need accidents like the one this afternoon in order to realize the vanity and fickleness of the things of this world.

The first place we entered was the chief's house, a nice brick house covered with corrugated iron sheets. On the spacious veranda stood an impressive number of comfortable easy-chairs. I think the chief likes a quiet and easy life, which doesn't make him any different from other chiefs. It seems that the chief is an old friend of the R.F.S.'s; to be more precise, they have known each other ever since the R.F.S. first came to Bomba. It even appears that at a time which is now quite remote they used to visit each other a great deal. But this evening the chief was absent. He had not come running to meet his friend but had preferred to abscond, leaving an enormous billy-goat for us, which had been tied to one of the ornamental trees planted in front of his house. One of the chief's men was expecting us. While the R.F.S. listened to what the man had to say, I saw his face take on an expression of discouragement which it grieved me to see. One would have thought that he would have liked to have a little chat with the chief, to talk to him about the horrible accident we had witnessed; for the case of the chief and that of the man who died this afternoon have many things in common, according to what I have just learned. The chief was once a Christian, and a very good one at that. He used to come to Bomba every Sunday to attend mass and to ask the R.F.S.'s advice on everything. Unfortunately his first wife had not given him any children. He must have opened his heart to the R.F.S. about this, and the Father must have advised him to be patient and to resort to prayer. But when the event did not come about, the inevitable happened. The chief took a second wife, and it was the first time since his baptism that he had taken a decision without consulting the R.F.S. After that he didn't show up anymore at the Bomba Mission. Then, having developed a taste for polygamy, the chief took several wives in a row even though his second wife bore him a child every other year and the first excuse he had used for his polygamy had lost its validity altogether. But in spite of all that the chief, with an assurance that made the R.F.S. wince, never ceased protesting his devotion to and his orthodox belief in the Catholic religion. He was full of regret for not being allowed the sacraments, and he would send his wives to the R.F.S. to present their newly born for baptism. And in so doing he was acting like a great number of other people in these parts who, if it were announced to them that they could consider themselves good Christians notwithstanding their polygamous status, would prostrate themselves on the ground, beside themselves with gratitude toward the Eternal God, and would not be able to work off their happiness about this event in a full week's celebrations. And yet in some way the R.F.S. is convinced – maybe because he has a sixth sense; from day to day I am getting more proof that this is so – of the chief's basic goodness, and he has never given up hope that he will one day bring this prodigal son back to the fold, the son who was already cherished above all others long before he left his father's house. But this evening, like all the other times for more than seven years that the R.F.S. has been coming to Timbo, the chief had stolen away, he had slipped between his fingers like an eel.

The catechist untied the billy-goat, and we left. What a pity, really! I have no doubts whatsoever that with the arguments placed at his disposal tonight by that horrible accident the R.F.S. would have managed to reach the infidel's heart. And if the big chief had realized his sins, set free his fifteen wives as if he had opened the door of a well-stocked chicken coop, and knelt down in front of the R.F.S. begging to be absolved, how easily could this have tipped the scales which they use in this land, in this village, to compare God and Satan, the Eternal and the Temporal, the narrow uncomfortable path bristling with thorns which leads to true happiness and the wide and lovely smelling road strewn with flowers whose gentle downwards slope leads to pleasure! We were walking along the gloomy huts made even more dismal by the squalling of the babies, who seemed to be aware of what had happened. The R.F.S. said,

'I don't give up hope that I shall convert him one day. Why not? After all, I've succeeded with others . . .'

This means he won't abandon Tala land! I have known for sure that he would not give up, considering his usual perseverance. And yet there's something strange about it, where did he get this sudden idea just a while ago to drop everything, this unexpected discouragement – a man like him who never gets discouraged?

> Whatever you do,
> Even if it's beyond you,
> Never give up,
> Work twice as hard . . .

'I won't give up hope . . . After all, I've succeeded with others.' Zachary, whom I've told all this, claims that the R.F.S. has really performed such feats, but in times immemorial! . . . We entered some more huts before returning to the presbytery. In addition to the goat from the chief, we were offered chickens and some pounds of cocoa and groundnuts. Obviously, this is a pretty poor show. As Zachary says, 'We're not on the main road here.'*

The R.F.S. hardly ate anything. Zachary, who was present at the meal, took on an annoyed expression and asked him, 'Father, don't you like my cooking anymore?'

Of course, the R.F.S. protested that he did. This Zachary is a real hypocrite. It wasn't he at all who had prepared the meal but some kids, no longer those of the local catechist, who only has very young ones, but kids who have come from nobody knows where, who have handled the R.F.S.'s food and maybe left germs there. My God, how unhappy I am! To watch Zachary's hypocritical doings every day and not be able to tell the R.F.S. anything about them! And I am so scared to make any remark to Zachary. He would just tell me as he does so often, 'No, really, who d'you think you are? The son of the R.F.S.? Oh, not that I doubt that he does have kids but they certainly don't have your colour, young fellow . . .'

After the meal, the R.F.S. started work with the catechist, asking him lots of questions. Yes, I followed their conversation as long as I could, and then I went to bed. Besides, Zachary had quite exasperated me, butting into the conversation when nobody had asked him to. For example, the R.F.S. asked the local catechist the following question,

'Why in your opinion are people turning away from religion the way they are? Why did they in your opinion come in great masses at the beginning?'

The catechist answered, 'Well, Father, formerly we were poor, and doesn't the Kingdom of Heaven belong to the poor? There's nothing surprising in our people getting converted to God's religion in those days. But nowadays, Father, just come to think of it, they have got incredible amounts of money by selling their cocoa to the Greeks; they are rich. Tell me, isn't it easier for a camel to pass through the eye of a needle than for a rich man to go to Heaven? . . .'

*Africans living near the main road were so hard pressed by forced labour and the brutality of the *tirailleurs* that they fervently turned to the Christian missionaries for help and were more generous in their offerings to them.

Then suddenly Zachary started speaking, interrupting the words full of wisdom of the catechist.

'Nonsense,' he said, 'you're not getting it at all, man. Now let me tell you exactly how matters stand, Father. Well, here goes. The first of our people who were in such a hurry to get religion, *your* religion, I mean, came to it like to a . . . revelation, that's it, a revelation, a kind of school where your secret, the secret of your power, would be revealed to them, the power of your aeroplanes, of your railways, what do I know . . . the secret of your mystery if you know what I mean. Instead of all that, you started to tell them about God, the soul, life everlasting, etc. Do you imagine that they didn't know all that long before you came here? I say, they were under the impression that you were hiding something from them. Later on they realized that money could buy them a lot of things, for example, gramophones, cars, and one day maybe even aeroplanes. There you are! They give up religion, they start running the other way, after money, I mean. This is the plain truth, Father; whatever else people tell you is a lot of nonsense . . .'

When he was talking like that, he took on an air of importance. I was boiling with indignation listening to this empty illiterate talk, this blablabla as Father Le Guen, the new curate, would say . . . I felt sweat trickling down my forehead, along my nose, down my cheeks, and forming into droplets at the point of my chin, getting all heated up with anger as I was. I would have liked to give him some good slaps. . . . The strange thing was that the R.F.S. listened to him attentively.

20

Sékou Touré

**Speech Delivered on the Occasion of
President de Gaulle's Arrival at
Conakry, 25 August 1958**

The generation born in the early 1920s reached maturity during the Second World War, and the Africans who had contributed to the Allied victory were destined to be particularly militant in the struggle for independence. Among this group were the ideologist of Negro history, Cheikh Anta Diop; the poet-politician Fodéba Kéita; the trade-unionist turned novelist, Sembène Ousmane; and the trade-unionist turned political leader, Sékou Touré.

An intransigent advocate of African independence, Sékou Touré led the only territory in French-speaking Africa which issued a resounding 'no', in the 1958 plebiscite, to the offer of mere autonomy within a new 'French Community'.

Speech Delivered on the Occasion of President de Gaulle's Arrival at Conakry, 25 August 1958

Mr President of the Government of the French Republic,

There are moments in the lives of nations and peoples which seem to determine a decisive part of their destiny or which, at any rate, are inscribed in the book of history in capital letters, with legends growing up around them, marking in a particular way the culminating points on the diagram of the arduous evolution of mankind, the pinnacles which express so many victories of man over himself, so many conquests of society over its natural environment.

Mr President, you are coming to Africa with the double privilege of belonging to a glorious legend which exalts the victory of freedom over bondage, and of being the first Head of the Government of the French Republic to step on the soil of Guinea. Your presence in our midst symbolizes not only the 'Resistance' which saw the triumph of reason over force and the victory of good over evil, but it represents also, and I can even say above all, a new stage, another decisive period, a new phase of evolution. How could the African people be insensitive to these omens – a people which lives daily in the hope of seeing its dignity recognized and which intensifies more and more its wish to be equal to the best.

You, Mr President, undoubtedly know the value of this people better than anybody else, because you were its judge and witness in the most trying hours France has ever known. That extraordinary period, at the end of which liberty was to rise again with renewed radiance and increased vigour, was marked by the people of Africa in a way all their own since in the course of the Second World War they rallied, without any apparent obligation, to the cause of the liberty of the peoples and of human dignity.

Throughout the vicissitudes of history each nation makes it way in accordance with its own lights, and acts in keeping with particular characteristics and its main aspirations, without the true motives of its actions being necessarily apparent.

Though the African mind has been initiated in the inexorable logic of means and ends as well as in the harsh discipline of everyday realities, it is constantly being attracted by the great necessities of human upliftment and emancipation. The evolution of African values is handicapped, not through any fault of those who moulded them, but because of the economic and political structures we inherited from the colonial régime with its lack of balance between its own realities and its aspirations for the future.

That is why we want to set these structures right, not by timorous and half-hearted reforms, but by starting from their very foundations so that the movement of our societies may follow the ascending line of constant evolution and perpetual improvement.

Progress is in fact a continuous creation, an uninterrupted development towards the better and for the best. By stages societies and nations enhance and consolidate their right to happiness and their claim to dignity, and they increase their contribution to the economic and cultural heritage of the whole world.

Black Africa does not differ in this respect from any other society or any other people. Following our own road, we intend to strive towards our happiness, and we shall do so with all the more will-power and determination as we know the length of the way we have to cover.

Guinea is not only that geographical entity delimited by the accident of history in accordance with the facts of French colonization, but it is also a living part of Africa, a piece of this continent which throbs, feels, acts, and thinks in relation to its singular destiny. But vast as our field of investigation may be, extensive as our field of action may be, it is insufficient in the light of our own requirements of evolution.

In response to these requirements we must enlist not only the whole of our own potential but also everything that constitutes universal achievements and universal knowledge, which develop and grow imperceptibly each day.

Amidst the spiritual disorder due to colonization, and amidst the profound contradictions dividing the world, we must silence all idealistic speculation in order to come to grips with real possibilities and efficacious means of immediate usefulness. We must try to ascertain exactly the conditions under which our people live so that we can bring them the rudiments of an indispensable evolution, without which the betterment to which they legitimately aspire cannot be achieved. If we did not put our hands to this task, we would not be justified in wishing to perform the functions we are charged with and we would have no right to the confidence of our people. Because we refrain from taking away the sovereignty of the people of Guinea for our own profit, we have to tell you bluntly, Mr President, what the demands of this people are, so that hand in hand with them the best means for their total emancipation may be found.

A poor nation has the one advantage that the risks its undertakings run are inconsiderable and the dangers it incurs are fewer. A poor man can aspire only to getting rich, and nothing is more natural than the wish to wipe out all inequalities and all injustices. This desire for equality and justice is all the more deeply rooted in us as we have been subjected more severely to injustice and inequality. However, logical analysis and an ever increasing knowledge of our own values, of our potential means, and of our real possibilities, keep us free from any complex and fear. We are solely preoccupied with our future and concerned with the happiness of our people. This happiness can assume multiple aspects and various characteristics depending on the nature of our aspirations, our desires, and our own estate. It may be a single thing as well as a bundle of a thousand things, all equally indispensable to its realization. As far as we are concerned, we have one prime and essential need: our dignity. But there is no dignity without freedom, for any subjection, any constraint imposed and undergone degrades him who is labouring under it, takes a part of his quality as a human being from him, and arbitrarily makes him into an inferior being. We prefer freedom in poverty to opulence in slavery. What holds true for one man is likewise true for societies and races. It is this concern with dignity, this overriding need for freedom which in France's darkest hours was to spark the noblest acts, the greatest sacrifices, and the most beautiful deeds of courage. Freedom is the privilege of every man, the natural right of every society or every nation, and the basis on which the States of Africa will associate themselves with the French Republic and with other States for the development of their common values and their common riches. [...]

21

High Life

This piece seemed worthwhile including for its stylistic interest. Use is made of Nigerian Pidgin and conversational exchanges. But the piece is not in true 'Pidgin', which would have made it practically incomprehensible to the European reader. The language is that of a barely educated primary school boy exulting in the new words he is discovering and the new world he is beginning to know.

High Life

In fact ehn, if you know how I was feeling that night, you will be very sorry for me. I was at Aba and it was New Year Day. Anybody who has stayed in Eastern Nigeria will know or will hear of Aba. When you hear republic, republic, you don't know what it is like until you go to Aba. Christ Jesus! I have not seen one town in this Nigeria where everybody is equal like Aba. Just imagine, the taxi drivers can knack* big grammar; the traders whack tough suit like big Minister. Then if you go to the hotel, you will see a young man who will come and buy beer, beer not tombo, for everybody in that hotel. Wonderful. And then when you think of fine babies, you can't beat Aba. If you want high society one, you will get; if you want proper teenager who sells in the chemist shop, you will also get. And sometimes, you will get them cheap because everything in Aba is cheap. Indeed in the market, if you take care, you can get very big thing at small price. This is some of the reason why I used to like Aba. And that is why I went there to spend New Year with my brother who lives in that town. Actually, this my brother loves me very much. His father's mother and the sister of my father. . . or rather. . . . What am I saying? . . . yes, his father's mother and my father's sister come from the same mother and father. Exactly. So as I was saying, I went to spend my New Year with him.

On that day, things were very hot, In the morning, I was reading one book which I brought with me from Onitsha. The name of the book was *How to make love without spending Money*. There are many such books like that in Onitsha market. And in fact if you see the big English they blow in that book, you will respect the writer. So that morning, I was jollying and I was very happy. My brother's wife, Alice, can cook very well and that morning,

*Take pleasure in speaking.

she prepared jealous* rice with plenty of fish for us. It is only on occasion like New Year or Christmas that we eat such food, otherwise it is always gari with soup. After we have finished eating, we all went to church at St Michael's. There are many churches in Aba, for example Salvation Army, Christ Army which people normally call Chraisiamin, Assembly of God Mission where people beat drum and dance, then there is Catholic and many other smaller ones like for example The Holy Spiritual Joyful Church of Mount Sion which is at our backyard. The pastor of this church is a trader in okrika-wake-up. I like that church because of its indigenity; for example, they sing like Nigerians. It is not like St Michael's where they translate English songs into Igbo. And the pastor does not pretend that God sent him from Heaven to come and look after the members of the Church. Anyway since my father, mother and everybody in our family goes to Anglican, I also go there even though I do not like it. There is one other reason why I go to St Michael's. There are always very many fine babies there. On that day, they were dressed in very fine cloths, from kente to tight-knee. I won't tell you a lie. I like women very much and when I saw them looking fine inside the church that day, I forgot about the prayer and the sermon very many times, but I had to pray for forgiveness again and again. When church broke, I told my brother not to wait for me because I will go to see some of our townspeople who were living in other parts of the town.

It was a very hot day and there were many people in the road. Some were singing and dancing and others were looking at those who were dancing. In one place, I saw some people in masquerade. That masquerade was very ugly but the man who was inside it was dancing very well. One time, he came to me, I was very afraid, to talk true, I wanted to run away but since there were many babies around, I was forced to wait. The masquerade begged me too for money as they always do. I pretended not to hear him. But he stood there until shame caught me. Then I put my hand into my pocket and was glad to find that I had only one one pound currency note. I brought it out so that he may see it

---

* He means of course Jollof rice, a variety of fried rice to which meat is sometimes added.

and go away because I had no change. But do you know what happened? No sooner he saw it than he snatched it away from me. God of mercy. My eyes began to turn. All the fine babies around me were laughing. To preserve my persy, I laughed too. That is what my master used to call laughing on the other side of your mouth. To lose one pound in such time of austerity is no joke at all. After some time, I left that place and went to the house of one of our townspeople that I knew very well.

When I got there, lo and behold, many other of our townspeople were congregated. There were more than forty people or even self, fifty people in that small room. All of them were eating stockfish and drinking tombo wine. When I saw this stockfish, I swallowed saliva because it was looking very very sweet. As soon as Adibe the owner of the house saw me he shouted:

'Hei, my brother, welcome. Where have you been all this time?' I told him that I am working at Onitsha.

'So those who work in Onitsha cannot come to Aba to see his brothers, eh? Is it so?'

'I have been very busy that is all.' This one seemed to angry Adibe very much. He turned to everybody who was in that room and said: 'Children of my mother, here is one of us who says he has no time to come and see us. You see what is wrong with our young men of nowadays? They spend all their money running after hotel woman and cannot keep even one penny to give their poor brothers at home. In our time, will we have do the same?'

'At all, at all,' everybody answered like choir in the church. I thought he was going to stop there. Not at all. Adibe was like tap for water. If you turn it, the water will continue to run till you turn it again. Exactly. So Adibe said again:

'Now you see, my brothers, all of us here are sitting on the floor of this house is it not so?' They all 'greed like choir in the church. 'Now if we ask this our young man to join us, do you think he will 'gree? Will he not say he is too big to sit on the ground?'

Believe me yours sincerely, I thought Adibe to be drunk. However, to satisfy all of them, I immediately sat on the ground. Then they passed the stockfish and tombo to me. Everything was very bitter in my mouth because all the time I was eating, I was thinking of my trouser which was dirtying. I had just dry-cleaned that trouser, and now, they were forcing me to sit on the ground with it. After some time, I took excuse because I wanted to go away. No sooner, than Idika jumped up and said we should go to his house. I did not want to go but I knew that our people will say that I was prouding that is why I did not want to go with Idika. So I followed him like a goat to his house. And do you know where his house is? At Amammongo which is farther away and which is one of the worst quarters in Aba. When I saw that Idika was walking still, I asked him whether we will not take taxi.

'My house is very near,' was what he told me. So I continued to follow him like a goat. After some time, I asked him again whether we will not take taxi. This time, he looked at me like a tiger and said:

'Why are you always asking for taxi, taxi? Did your father keep any taxi in this town? Or has your father who born you ever entered a taxi before? You young men of nowadays have very bug eye. Alright, we will enter taxi but you will pay for it.' When I remembered how I had lost one pound that morning and that I had no more money in my pocket, I shut my mouth like African Continental Bank on Saturday afternoon. I did not ask for taxi again, so we walked till we reached his house.

I did not know that such a house was still existing in Aba. Even the house we have at home is a hundred times better than the house where Idika was living at Aba. But I did not say anything for fear that Idika will think that I was prouding. Then Idika entered the room and brought some kola-nut. I ate that one. Then he entered the room again and brought one bottle of coco cream. Then he took some and gave me the remainder part of it. As for myself, it was very hard to drink that coco cream. I pretended that I like it very much but in actual fact, I was very annoyed. Why did Idika call me to such useless house and make me walk such long distance for only one glass of coco cream? I was still rolling this thing in my mind when one short man came in. His eyes were red like palm oil. From the way he was shouting and singing like bushman I knew he was drunk. He came into that room and the first thing he did was to belch one big belch – 'Etiee'. The whole house started smelling beer beer. I did not talk. Then he said:

'Happy New Year.' And I answered;

'Same to you.'

'What!' he shouted, 'why you curse me? What have I done to you that you are cursing me like that?'

'How did I curse you?' was my next question.

'You said "shame to you" when I told you "happy new year".'

'I did not say shame. I said "same to you".'

'Idika?' he called, 'do you hear this your brother? he has repeated it again. Shame to me. Is it so? Do you think I am a thief man or what?' If you see how this short man's muscles were standing like the wheel of truck, you will be very sorry for me. I was afraid. I looked at Idika but the stupid drunkard was asleep. God in Heaven! Immediately, the short man held my neck and threw me through the door into the street like a ball. I continued to run and did not stop till I reached one hotel near Park Road, which is very near the motor station. I decided to go in there because there were many people who were jollying. By that time, night was approaching. When I entered the hotel, they were playing one tough record called 'bottom Belly'. I started to dance it and while I was dancing, I saw David eating and giving me a beckon. I went nearer him and joined him to eat the cock which he was eating. Then he brought another cock plus some congo meat. We two finished them. Then he went and brought some bottles of beer. Christ Jesus. And this is a common trader! and my junior in the elementary school too. And he was now very rich. It is only then that I realized that it is better to be a trader than to work for the government or for white man as cook. David serviced me all kinds of chop and drink. When we had finished, he brought some leaves from his pocket and gave me some part of it. I did not know what it was so I asked him.

'It is called gay,' was his answer.

'What is gay?' I asked. He refused to tell me but asked me to smoke it very quickly. And so I began to smoke that thing which looked like okro leaf. I drew the smoke into my belly and ...

before I could twinkle one eye, my eyes began to turn. I began to see double. Every man in that hotel was two in my eyes. I looked at David and I saw two Davids – one original and one duplicate. Then as if by force, I began to hala like madman. I made very big pandemonium in that hotel. I continued to hala until the hotel proprietor came and pushed me out for my rascality. That one annoyed me very much but however, I did not care too much.

I went along Asa Road towards the market. It was getting to twelve and they used to say that there are ghosts in the market by that time. But I was not afraid because the gay removed all fear from my mind. So I continued to walk around the road whistling one loud song in my mouth. I was perambulating lackadaisically like sophisticated portable damsel when I saw a policeman. No sooner I greeted him than he said:

'My friend, why are you disturbing the peace?' Then I told him not to give me any moless.* Then he asked me if I had any bribe for him. 'What!' I shouted. 'Are you mad? If you think I will give you bribe, you are mistaken. You are victimized by a magnanimous hallucination.' Immediately, the constable gave me a blow with his stick – kpum – on my neck. Christ Jesus. When I opened my eyes, I was in the house of John Apollonius Levi, the leader of the Christ Amin church. I had been lying there for three days. That is what my brothers them told me. Terrible. Since that day I have not gone to Aba again.

*Not to annoy me.

22

Timothy Wangusa

How Fast We Are Moving

This piece by an East African implies much while displaying careful economy with words. In contrast with the previous piece, where the words sprawl in delighted abandon, this is a tight-lipped serious account. There is no overt preaching, but the moral lesson, in its ironic vein, is scarcely less vigorous for that.

How Fast We Are Moving

There they sit, perched on exalted stools, and their glory pervades the whole room. They lean delicately against the counter, wielding in their right hands the glass that delights. Occasionally they release through their nostrils thick clouds of smoke, that decorate the air as they ascend heavenwards in little beautiful spirals. The entire front wall is covered with shelves whose rich and varied contents proclaim the wonder of modern industry. Do not enter purposelessly, for you stand before the very scene of the highest form of civilized social intercourse.

From the dance hall next door more people come pouring in, every female conducted hither by some gallant who affectionately holds her hand. Everyone is having a marvellous time; it would have been madness to miss this. There are more people tonight; for some of those who came to the political rally have chosen to postpone home till tomorrow. And it is the Real Life Band playing – those jolly fellows! Under the inspiration of their music you pick up some conspicuous lady to measure the floor with. Very quickly she distinguishes herself by the beckoning way she swings her slim exasperating body under her tight dress. She wins your respect and admiration, with the result that you ask her to retire with you to the refreshments room, to cool herself off and quench the thirst she must be feeling. She is not surprised by your courtesy and generosity; for good things are always happening to her, and in a way she expects you to do what you are doing – just like the gentleman you are. In her mind she is even planning how to spend (and it must be wisely, her life upon it!) the gift she is soon to receive from you.

And so the two of you settle down in this second chamber, where other comrades-in-fun are already busy. Out goes a five pound note, as easily as if you did not care a bit for that piece of paper – perhaps you do not (especially as it is the end of tl month). The lady smiles pleasantly, meaning tonight it is not h turn to go thirsty. Steadily bottles disclaim their contents, ar you, the vessels that are being filled, in turn grow livelier and free

Here flows the River of Oblivion, kept permanently at hig water-mark by the efficient Progressive Bottling Company. Yo only have to drink enough of it and an ineffable sweetness com over you. Inside you change like litmus paper. That disagre ment with your colleague, that debt of John's, your wife's sil jealousy over your lady acquaintances and your secret items guilt – all these dissolve. This is the way to solve problems, ar a sweet one too, one that makes you feel, as the saying goe that the dead hurried too fast through life. To confirm whi your lady inclines towards you and says the expected thing.

And simultaneously the music breaks through and thrills yo And by lucky coincidence you catch those very words that yo so agree with:

> Africa! Africa! Africa!
> How fast we are moving!

Yes, look at progress everywhere: in science and technolog in education and thought; in industry and commerce; and the steadily rising standard of living.

But the lady expresses obvious impatience; you must take h out of here now – and you do so. And of course there is no earth ly reason why it should cross your mind just now that at th very time away in a quiet village an elderly man, the head of uncertain home in a frightened country, stays wakeful on a count of his daughter who lives in town.

'It has been a wonderful evening, darling, hasn't it?'

'Yes, very much. I doubt if tomorrow could be the same; do you think – ?'

Your trouble is that good things come to an end. You mu part, that you may return to your nagging wife, who will obviou ly be fretting by now. Soon your Mercedes is roaring on tl homeward road. You must not forget about that bridge und repair. And it is undesirable that you should bump into tho fellow citizens who seek their daily bread by night, before who doors fall down in obeisance.

23

Speedy Eric

How Mabel Learnt

One argument that sometimes seems unanswerable is that which castigates 'African' literature as a literature of export. In the three pieces that follow, Nigerian authors are writing for a home market. The booklets from which these extracts are taken are usually printed on cheap paper and sell for about 1s. 6d. Over three hundred titles are in print, and for an emerging, barely literate audience they constitute an important area of reading. Most are written at Onitsha in Eastern Nigeria and used to be sold in the market and on the ferry.

'Ferry' literature vacillates between dramatic, epistolary and narrative styles. All stories are 'moral'. Women are wicked and men have to be wary of the evil to which women expose them. Writers have recently begun to employ uninhibited sexual descriptions, and two such books have appeared. An extract from one is printed here. With few exceptions, the original 'mistakes' have been reproduced.

How Mabel Learnt

By about 2 p.m. a young man came into 'Pleasure Home' for lunch. Mabel was serving some other customers then, and had her back to the door. Then somebody said behind her 'Hey baby, you are getting sweeter as the day goes by.' When Mabel turned round, do you know whom she saw? No other than the young man who had pressed her on the wall yesterday.

He was smiling down at her. Her heart missed two beats. The man was tall and strongly built. His shoulders were broad and masculine.

Mabel was losing her head. She served the other customers quickly and turned to face him.

'What will you eat, please?' she asked him, trying to hide her desire as far as possible.

'You, especially,' the man replied looking very sincere. Some men nearby began to laugh. It was very amusing.

'But you cannot eat me,' Mabel said seriously. 'Please tell me quickly.'

'Okay, juicy baby if you won't allow me eat you, then give me some eba and meat stew,' he dipped his hand in his pocket and brought out two shillings. Privately Mabel was wishing to hold that young man in her arms. That was the very man who had made her toss and twist in bed last night. Yet she was pretending she did not know him. This kind of world. She took the man's money and went to the kitchen to collect his orders.

When she came back with the food she saw that the man was looking at her at a particular place around the waist. She was quite uneasy, then their eyes met. She blinked at him. He just smiled and took the food and started eating. Mabel went to a far corner of the dinning room and surveyed the young man for long.

At one time the man caught her looking at him. She threw

away her eyes immediately. The man smiled. Without any need for it, he cried, 'salt please'. Mabel raced down with the salt and hold it out to him.

But he held both the salt and Mabel's fingers. The girl for a minute looked at him, not struggling to free her fingers. He looked deep into her eyes, a look that seemed to spell intense hunger and desire.

Mabel who had long fallen for the man gave him the same amorous look.

Somebody called for water at the other end. Mabel freed herself and went to attend. But something had been registered between her and the man.

The young man finished his meal and went out of the passage. Mabel went out too, pretending she was heading for the kitchen. As she tried to pass the man he held her by the arm.

'What's wrong?' she asked the man softly, looking into his eyes.

'You, and nothing more,' the man said tremulously. He was about twenty one years or less. But he was full and complete and healthy looking. 'I don't understand you please,' she said trying to continue on her way. But his hand held her strongly.

'Please Mabel wont you give me a chance?' he pleaded. 'Good God! who told you my name?' she looked very crossed. But she so like the way he called her. 'I know you very well,' he said. 'Its' only you that don't know me. I come here everyday and I long and long for you,' he stopped.

But Mrs Helen called from the kitchen: 'Maabel! Ma-be-el!'

'Ma-ah,' she answered. 'Please I must go and answer,' she told the man trying to free her arm. The man clung to her. 'Tell me first that you will like me a little,' the man insisted.

'I cannot tell you like that. But who are you. You know my name but I don't know yours?' 'I am Gilbert Erick. Gil for short,' he said. 'Okay Gil, I shall see you tomorrow when you come back,' she said. Gilbert's heart was singing with joy.

'Promise you must,' he insisted. 'I promise it,' she said softly looking at the floor. Gilbert left her and she ran down to the kitchen. Gil also left the 'Pleasure Home' feeling very pleased. But his pleasure could not equal one quarter of Mabel's own.

When she appeared before her mother she was bright and smiling. Mrs Helen noticed it, being that Mabel was always looking very gloomy and dejected. Even she could not help commenting on it. 'You look cheerful this afternoon, Mabel,' her mother said, smiling too.

'Thank you for that mamma,' said Mabel! 'I think it is because no customer has called me a dirty girl today,' she lied. 'I am glad of that,' her mother said. 'Go to No. 4 stall in the market and buy some meat. Meat worth about fifteen shillings. Take this pound note.'

Mabel took the money and speed to the market. She kept on looking this way and that to see if she would find Gil, but she didn't. But on her way home somebody halted her 'Please are you not living at Pleasure Home hotel?' the man asked, a man of about twenty six or more. 'Yes I am,' Mabel replied.

'Please can you do me a little service?' 'Say it,' Mabel urged her, 'Kindly deliver this envelope to Margie who works for your mother,' he held out an envelope to her. She took it 'But who is it from?' she asked him.

'The sender's address is at the back,' he said. She turned the envelope and read the sender – Edie Uzor then she smiled. 'What's wrong' the boy asked: 'Nothing,' she said and ran away with the envelope. So that was Margie's boy friend? She decided to keep the letter till they were in bed.

Things went by slowly till about five o'clock in the evening. Customers began to crowd in. Margie and Mabel were absorbed in attending them. By about seven p.m. it became necessary to use Mabel's room again. She agreed grudgingly to the use of it. Three men were taken into the room to be served.

Nothing happened till they finished eating, then one of them did something exciting to Mabel.

When she was leaving the room the man walked faster before her and went up to the door. As Mabel approached him he raised his hand and switched off the light.

Before anybody could tell what was happening he caught Mabel by waist and pulled her to himself. Then he kissed her cheeks strongly. She screamed. He left her and again switched on the light laughing.

She glared at him 'I am sorry baby,' he pleaded, 'but I couldn't help myself; you look so juicy that my blood flows in the wrong direction.' The other men laughed at that.

Mabel in her embarrassment rushed out of the room. But she did not tell anybody what had happened; how could she?

But one thing was becoming clear to her in that single-day. That was this. She had something the men could like.

It was dangerous for her to think so. But she did, under the influence of the romantic touches she was getting. She began to feel wanted. You know that such a feeling can have a disastrous effect on anybody. When you feel so needed, you have to do one of two things. Either you give yourself, or bluff for ever those that yearn for you.

WE SHALL SEE WHAT MABEL DID IN HER OWN CASE. READ ON, DEAR.

By about twelve Mid-night Mrs Helen closed down and Mabel and Margie retired to their room. It had been a very busy day, especially in the second half of the day. But Mabel had never had a happier day.

Margie, however, surprised her, 'Hah Mabel, you know I saw you this afternoon.'

'Doing what?' Mabel asked, in surprise.

'Talking to your young man in the passage,' Margie said.

'What? So you saw? Where were you peeping from?' Mabel asked her.

'I was not peeping,' Margie said 'I saw you through the window in the kitchen. That window faces the passage, you know' Mabel laughed. 'But we did not do anything' 'I know,' Margie said.

'You were making a beginning. But I liked the way the young man held your arm and the way he pleaded with his eyes. Please do not refuse him.'

'Don't be silly.' Mabel scolded. 'By the way, do you know that I met your Edie today?'

'Rubbish,' said Margie, 'You say its' rubbish? Then look at this.' Mabel brought out the letter that she had received in the afternoon and handed it over to Margie.

Margie stared at the letter in wonder. 'When did you get this,

Mabel?' She asked. 'Aha! you believe me now?' Mabel asked. 'You see I couldn't believe you before.'

'I got it when I went to buy meat for mama,' she said.

Margie, with shaking hands opened the letter and read:

My Sweetest,

This is to tell you that I received your vital letter this morning. As my heart is now, I think I can go without food for a week and yet never care, as long as I know you are mine.

Please Margie, there is one thing I will beg of you. Kindly tell me the day I will come and take you to my home.

You know that the hotel is always full of people and we will not be able to make true love and do that thing I told you about.

Tomorrow I shall come to the hotel and if your heart is as true as mine, you shall follow me home.

I dream about you,

Your own,

Edie Uzor

'What have you read from your letter, Margie?' 'He is inviting me to come tomorrow evening,' Margie replied.

There was a long silence. Mabel broke it at last 'And you shall go?' Mabel asked her.

'If I get one important thing, I will go,' she answered.

'What is it?' Mabel asked anxiously.

'Do you want me to tell you?' 'Please do.'

'Well it is something I shall use if I am going to let him do the thing he wants with me,' Margie said. 'But what is that something?' Mabel asked. 'Bring wine before I tell you.'

'Do not tease me Margie, please tell me. I may need it one day,' Mabel was pleading.

'Okay if you want to know it, I will tell you that it is medicine in tablets. Are you alright?' Margie asked. 'But what is the name of the tablet?' Mabel asked.

That I must not tell you. If you want to have some, simply give me money tomorrow and I will buy for you.' 'How much is the cost?' Mabel asked. Margie told her.

'Alright when you are going to buy tomorrow I will give you money,' Mabel said.

Dear reader you watch for yourself how the only daughter of

Mrs Helen (or even the only child) is drifting slowly to her ruin.

This is the child on whom great amount of money and care is lavished. The child that Mrs Helen is expecting to marry one day and take the wealth of Ojina's family for the training of her children.

One may say that Margie was corrupting her but one thing is certain – she is predisposed for corruption. She had an unhealthy desire for sexual matters.

The first time she saw some people kissing, she tossed and tossed in her bed during the night.

Now she has decided to buy contraceptives to help her achieve her ends uninterruption.

But when they finished this conversation, Mabel had another thought which kept her awake for the greater part of the remaining night.

She thought of her Gil who had promised to come the following afternoon. She remembered how Gil had looked appealingly into her eyes. At once something stirred inside her. She felt some sweat gather around her body.

Again she began to toss in her bed. This time however she did not wake Margie. She just kept on wishing that morning had come and she would dress up well again in readiness for Gil. It was about three a.m. before she was quiet enough and had some sleep. But something crazy happened by about five in the morning.

May be some devilish desire came into Margie's head. She slipped out of her bed and in groped her way to Mabel's own bed. By groping too she found out that Mabel was lying on her back with her belly upwards and with legs thrown carelessly apart.

You know what Margie did? Cool down and hear. She mounted on top of Mabel exactly in the normal position and began to push and push.

Remember that Mabel had gone to bed thinking of man and sex. So maybe she thought it was in a dream and what she did was to throw her arms around Margie and hold her tight and push too. But after some minutes she felt that she couldn't be dreaming and more over she sensed that it was a woman's body that she was holding. She stopped pushing, but the body on top of her kept pushing and pushing.

She called in a low voice 'Margie' Margie framed a man's voice and said: 'Sweet Mabel'. But she could not deceive Mabel who shouted: 'if you don't come down now, I will bite you to pieces.'

'Wait, wait!' Margie said going on with her business. But Mabel, with force, reared on the bed and dumped Margie on the floor.

She sat up and began to giggle. 'But why, Mabel, you were enjoying it at the beginning?' Margie said.

'Because I thought that it was just a dream,' Mabel said. 'But let me tell you the THING IS SWEETER than this' Margie said. 'It doesn't matter, but don't disturb my sleep any more, you hear?' Mabel warned and went back to sleep.

24

Miller O. Albert

Rosemary and the Taxi Driver

The author of 'High Life' was a university graduate in English, but his uninhibited gamble with language in no way seems overdone. If the Onitsha author of this piece seems to be straining for effect, this is because his aim is quite different from the writer of 'High Life'. In 'Rosemary and the Taxi Driver' he is seeking to impress a semi-literate audience with his virtuosity in English. This is not an exercise in an odd style, but a serious attempt to write good prose. The effects are sometimes startling.

Rosemary and the Taxi Driver

'If there was a prize to be awarded for falling in love at first blush, Rosemary should be given the richest golden medal.' She has been chasing around the romantic seaport of Lagos, with her flareful flush of romance. Her voilet gown with vibrant colours and heavenly patterns vested below her knees. She wore a dazzling gold necklace, shiny ear rings and a botanical veil, stained all over with jet colours.

It was in the moth of April, while the dry season was nearly over. 'The season that sparks off love, kisses and romance. Wasn't it wonderful? The long carefree days had gone.' It was time for love to roar on the air, and equally, the time for Rosemary to travel on a journey from Lagos to the East.

The sun flickered over her canon-ball-head, with the hairs on her forehead, heightened like onboard type of shaving. She resoluted to follow the train at the earliest declining hour of the day. At down, She got ready to march with all the guts of the times, besides her romantic love. She sang many love poems to them, while they twist, wiggle waggle and utter many love incantations, worthy of marring all the lively zests of any woman folk.

She was in her maiden form and had remained untampered, since her generate days. Even to meddle with her zestful glamour of beauty, nobody had ever succeeded. The grim enthusiasm of her ardent lust was bubbling on her romantic face, and her youth-full glances of shyness. She had got all the zests of the West and mettled her senses, to bolster up alertly, to crack love, romance and joke, up to their highest mediocre of acme. It was a day for love maniacs to come and a day for Rosemary to travel too.

Reaching the town station on April ten, Rosemary delved into an undisturbed romance, with her boy friend, who was sobering, with mournful bunch of derangement, sending love expressions with quakeful Arctic chill, over her love conscious nerves. He tossed her, to stop crying for her departure and urged her to beat her heart throbs and vibrating mind, quite at its intensive urgent, with the incidence. He tossed her, managing to serene her temper; cleaning with affection, all the bitter tears of love, which were journeying down her retroussed put-nose.

After it was just at mid-night the train could be notice rumbling through the land, making its harsh, grimy noises. Rosemary grimaced, twisting herself into a startled look. The youngs at heart there, all delved into a wonderful tremor for fear it was a moment to have each person clutched to a shock proof. It was a day for the saints to sing of love, blessed stars started to shine intensively overhead in the broad-day light and also a day for Rosemary to travel.

She had packed all her suit cases like sardines and noisted her headtie on her onboards shaving, allowing it a bit loose, to fly goodbye, waving hilariously to her dearly beloved, who took all the rigours of unprecedented impression, to escort her with pretty tough smiles of flamboyant gestures, to the station.

'Lagos is a beautiful town,' She said. 'Could rather get lost there, than to dream of Elfland. Would bend, kiss, wiggle at stage shows, of High life or give the highest jazz strokes of at least five pounds each. Highlife I know, Bonsue I know, but which shall I dance with brief happiness in the East? I know I'm Rosemary. Mary, is the last tail of it, Yes! But I will one day, add one "R" after a letter, from the last spelling, to make it a vital gut that's Yes the much sought after treasure, "Marry".'

Soon she entered into the train, rolling the sleeves of her gown, getting ready for any strange enventuality. All the mask faced odd boys were soaring on the air, for her cheerful romance because of her saucy red lips. The character they presented, became very chicky to happiness and some, were savouring insubordination, mostly the odd concemitant type, of immoral stimulation, which provoked the impetus of glaring at sexual menance, below the belt, leading to excessive giving back of daily toping and night time tipples of dry gin and Whiskey.

Rosemary was as active as quick silver. Bitter phenomenon of love commotions, had come her way since yesterday.

Quick steps to love, was taking breed, but she resoluted to shun it till a most suitable paragon of being, presents the most ardent glamour of flamboyant gestures. The frowning of her face, could portray her sliding tackles, which she kept in a store for African highlife. The key-notes, which the orchestra boys clangour, hurts her feeling of patience. She gestriculated within a moment, recording quickly steps occurring in her mind, as a great annal and reinvigorative general of classical Africa.

The beats were highly clamouring melodiously, making airy sounds over the sky, winding, round, the tympanum of every star highlife beater. It made many glamour of beauties shudder frantically. No doubt of Rosemary. She perceived the necessary vital guts about it too, pulling force as if she was glamouring briskly in a stage show 'Yeh!'

She was enjoying the slow gallops of the train, when she perceived a philosophy in herself which compelled her to taste all the life flavours of the beautiful town of Enugu. She could oh board a tinker omnibus the same day she alighted from the train to Onitsha; but faculties not remedying themselves, she resoluted to divide her journey in order to trace out one to marry, or to fall in love and gulp in all the broths nature packed into it, like parcels of sand.

The man she cloistered at first flush of her sight was a romantic virile odd, who introduced himself Okoro. After they made a nice little smile, they raged a torrential down pour of speeches, each trying to exhaust the querulous tone God had suffered to give out, free of charge to every individual. Soon they felt an impression of bigness in themselves, glaring at nature as super love maker.

This taxi driving dwart of a beauty, fell a heavenly victim to many sophisticated things of his expectation. He had committed many 'Why saints come' crimes of life, with unprecedented suave stratagems. He is noticed more on moral defamation than on tidy clearing off of indifference behaviours. He presents suave nonentities, each time he feels like marrying success, with a mahatma type of power. He laughs more as a freak, than as a human being, looking like crime offender, with illicit practical glances, evident in his hefty stature, timing the day with

unrecorded imshaps. He had shattered many plans and still it bub-
bles in his evil mind the more to present the highest catastrophe,
ever recorded.

After watching if any of his girl customers was on the guide,
he rendered a submissive character of:

'Hello, who goes there?'

Rosemary drifted to him, loving him and loving him and loving
too the more. She flashed her romantic eyes, bending down for
shamefulness. A little of a time, she made her character to be

'How is it?'

'It is quite well.'

'How far you're going driver? Your car's I know must be of
the sort I always ride of a time ago, you remember?' She touched
him on the chin.

'I do' He replied. 'What a ride, you want?' 'Are you still just
in the West African English, brought by the journalists? O
chuckle you to laugh.' Just within the veldt.' He replied, putting
his hands inside his pocket and bluffing arrongantly, boistering
eye signal of inviolable romance.

They delved into torrential down pour of speeches, making
their devilish introduction.

The love now brewing, with active hotness, was blasty and
could rather throw off each with the little idea they've got about
themselves.

Okoro, the taxi driver got a tanner trouser and touch adam
coats and glared at himself as the chap of the day. Soon he left
the taxi minor and took Rosemary home, to cool down.

The house Rosemary was put on their arrival was savouring
something of the old and Okoro having got informations about
his brother on tour, made way with her, into his brother's room
with Rosemary. Before their arrival, Okoro did the game of removing the pictures hoisted over the air which were all his
brother's pictures. He did that without time because something
of the lot he like best was down. He didn't want Rosemary to
feel that he wasn't the owner of the little end.

A little time, he took permission to go and get back his senior
uncle, but not knowing that he was going to carry the dirty
minor he kept in the taxi park, outside the railway station. On

his way back, he washed out the annotations terming the car a
taxi.

When he reached his brother's house, where he kept Rosemary he gave a nasty clangouring blasts of the minor horn. She
rushed out and welcomed him. She rushed, twisting her eye
brows and knitting it a bit, to show the zests of the West.

They ate the little bread and suasage Okoro brought from his
brother's electrolux. Rosemary was lost in arena of love adventure. They loved each other and satisfied with their talents at the
sametime. In fact, it could have been the best love so far, if it
wasn't meddled with malice and pugnacity.

The day for the owner of the house to re-occupy his little end
of no regret was come, just a day for the dumb and deaf, to have a
brisk enjoyment. Rosemary was planning to head to Osha;
but hadn't been to any toping society since her stay off in the
East.

She impressed Okoro, to give her enough subsidy, to foot the
tipple. Though it was stated, for the deaf and dumb, still she
was compelled to witness it.

Towards the down of the day, Okoro got ready to go out with
Rosemary for the dance.

The arrangement being to stop a tinker omnibus on the way,
after the night tipple, so that she could float down, a magpie to
Onitsha.

There was no chance for Okoro to hoist up the decorations in
his brother's house which he turned down, incase Rosemary
should recognise what was brewing. Actually, it was too tough a
play, to tell Rosemary to go out, while they were in the midst of
burning speech. He didn't want to be suspected, and had not lay
such impression so pompous, before, and ought not leat it go, at
this terrible moment. When it was just at the nick of a time, he
hurriedly put Rosemary's suit cases inside the minor, and
hurriedly ordered her to get in, in good faith. She soon got ready
and rubbed her pancake, feeling just on the lead. She raised her
black hairs, to suit her apex nose. A curtly smile bubbled on the
air, favouring Okoro. But there was no time, to blast romantic
flares. He dudged the love smiles.

Soon he kicked the taxi and went back, after half way to hoist

on the pictures he turned down when he was at the worst in-
stincts. He was shuddering at every hiss of a sound. Before he
could finish remedying the crime he committed, his brother, the
faithful owner of the house came in, standing at the corridor,
guessing that something of the sort which he doesn't want was
wrong. He soon sighed and got depressed. After many odd
remarks, the full automobile of his spirit, compelled him to leave
everything, threatening him with pretty tough smiles, of tremor

After his liberation, he trotted off with his craggy legs, jumping into the minor with a mad stampede, hoping to finish the
speedometre, within an active time.

25

Okenwa Olisa

Lumumba's Last Days

Four Onitsha novels have been written about Lumumba's death. They mix fake bits of biography with the sensational details relayed in the popular press. The piece reproduced here seemed worthwhile printing, since there is no attempt in it to see Lumumba as anything else other than an Ibo. The unintentional parallels may well become horribly clearer in time.

Lumumba's Last Days

Mrs Pauline Lumumba's Secret,
Letter to Mr Patrice Lumumba,
IN KATANGA PRISON

Pauline Lumumba,
14 New Court Road,
Leopoldville,
Congo.
10th January, 1961.

My Dear Husband,
    YOU ARE IN SUFFER

Oh! my dear sweetheart and husband, I have been informed that with regard to the worst condition you are kept in the Kantanga Prison. I have been informed that you sleep on the plank, bad food, dirty water are provided to you. What a miserable condition!

I have also heard that you are tied behind your back, heavily being suffered, for no just reason, I further heard that your Doctor has been prevented by the Katanga authorities, from visiting you. What an authocratic Government of President Tshombe.

I, and our three children have been weeping day in day out, knowing not what to do. To see you is certainly impossible. My life and the lives of our three children are in danger. These had been repeatedly threatened by President Kassavubu's supporters. We have ran away from the African quarters to a secret place. However, the United Nations is giving us some protection, but I have no confidence in the United Nations (Congo Operation) because of its indirect support to President Kassavubu.

This evening, I will be appealing to the Red Cross Society representative in Leopoldville, requesting him to pay a visit to you. I hope when he comes, he will deliver some message from me to you, and appeal to the United Nations to take measures in respect of the unlawful state, president Tshombe's Government keeps you. In fact, I am afraid of your life, but however, 'man no die, inogo rotten.'

I hope to hear from you at your earliest possibility. With love and best wishes. And may God save your life, from the hands of your bitter enemies.

Your affectionate wife,
PAULINE LUMUMBA

Mr Patrice Lumumba Replies his wife – PAULINE LUMUMBA.

Patrice Lumumba,
Katanga Prison,
15th January, 1961.

My dear wife,

DON'T CRY TOO MUCH

I have got your letter, and have to thank you for it. All the informations which had reached to you with regards to my conditions in the jail were reliable, but please worry and lament less, it should not pain you too much.

One of my greatest sorrows is your own condition in Leopoldville. I know that President Kassavubu's supporters will come to attack you and our three children but I hope that the God of Africa will protect you.

One of my supporters who secretly visited me yesterday told me that all our properties in Leopoldville had been damaged and some burnt with fire. Do not worry about all these. Just hide yourself and send our Children to Egypt to ensure their protection of lives.

There is no need crying day in day out with our three children. Don't allow the children to be too unhappy. I have told you to send them to Cairo-Egypt where they will be saved and weepless.

As you know, you will never trust the protection of the United Nations. When the Congo crisis started, I invited United Nations to come and intervene. The U.N. arrived and teamed up against me. As you know, they are indirectly supporting President Kassavubu.

Last two weeks, I sent a lengthly letter to the Secretary-General of the United Nations complaining to him about violation of the 'Congolese prison law' by the Katanga prison authorities. The Congolese prison law, paragraph 8 does not allow the prison authorities to hold an accused more than a week in cell. An accused should be brought to court within this one week for trial. I have been held over one month in the cell but the Secretary-General after receiving this my complaint, never protest.

I am not prepared any longer to appeal to the Secretary General to secure my release. Let the worst happen to me. If I die, it is a good death hence I have won Independence for the Republic of Congo. What again I have! I have tried. I beg to close, you have heard all I have told you, Send our children to Egypt, and please don't cry too much, there is God.

With love and best wishes.

Your dear husband,
PATRICE LUMUMBA,
Prime Minister.

Mrs Pauline Lumumba, replies – PATRICE LUMUMBA.

Pauline Lumumba,
14 New Court Road,
Leopoldville,
Congo.
17 January 1961.

My dear husband,

Yours dated the 15th instant was received today, thank you too much. All said in the letter were noted. My dear husband, I am dreaming much nowadays, and I am afraid and restless in mind. Thinking and sorrows have made me very tiny. Oh! God what have you done? Nothing. You are being suffered because you love your Country.

I dreamt yesterday night that the tallest Iroko tree in Leopoldville fell and the country was shaken. Oh! I am afraid of your

life, I am afraid! I am afraid of your life. May God save you.
I have seen the Representative of the Red-Cross Society in
Leopoldville, and he told me the story of how he visited Katanga
to see you. He had told me that when he landed at Katanga that
he was refused to visit you, by the Katanga prison authorities.
In this respect, I will protest to the United Nations Chief
representative in Leopoldville.

My hus, I repeat that I am afraid of your life, my dreams
frighten me, but let the Almighty do his mind.

Please take heart, let's see the mind of the Almighty Father.
I beg to close. With love and best wishes,

> Your affectionate wife,
> PAULINE LUMUMBA,

(The day the above letter reached Katanga, that Lumumba was
murdered. He never read the letter)

HOW LUMUMBA WAS KILLED

According to grave allegation, the legitimate Prime Minister
of the Congo Republic, Mr Patrice Lumumba, and his two close
associates, Mr Mpolo and Mr Okito, were murdered on the
18th of January, 1961, outside the dangerous Katanga prison.

They were ordered to kneel and pray, the allegation continued,
as they were kneeling down and praying, a Belgian Officer
commanded an African soldier to shoot them. Then the African
soldier fire Mr Okito and Mr Mpolo, both former Ministers of
Lumumba's government. He refused to shoot Mr Patrice
Lumumba. He got afraid, because he know that Mr Patrice
Lumumba was too great, important, and right in the gratest
political battle.

But what happened when the African army refused to kill
Lumumba, after he had executed his two faithful Ministers?
Then the wicked and ungodly Belgian Officer, shot Mr Lumum-
ba to death with his rifle, the allegation further stated 'Thou
enemy of the Belgians, I kill you', the Officer might said to
Lumumba. The whole world was shaking, everybody in Africa
weeping, when the sadest news of his death was broken to us.
What a sorrowful incident! People began to lament for Lumum-

ba's death, his followers, supporters, lovers and sympathizers began to mourn. Demonstrations against the murder of the hero – Mr Lumumba took place at many places of the world. Properties were damaged during demonstrations and the Police arrested some demonstrators at certain countries.

Many world figures paid unqualified tributes to the memory of Mr Patrice Lumumba. Certainly, Mr Lumumba was a patriot, a hero, the greatest lover of the Republic of Congo. The Congolese history would never be interesting, correct and readable, without Lumumba's name will be decorated and his activities stated carefully.

The earlier announcement by the illegal Katanga Government that Mr Patrice Lumumba and his two associates, Okito and Mpolo, escaped from Katanga jail with a spotted car which drove them away, was the greatest lie of the year. The Katanga authorities were playing a childish trick. They were deceiving themselves not knowing that the world opinion was against them. It was highly provocated to hear from one notorious Katanga Minister, that the bodies of Patrice Lumumba and his two Ministers 'were buried where they were found' and that the burial place 'was not important'.

Lumumba was not a person to be buried any place or anyhow. To bury him in the bush with his associates was a serious crime, unforgivable one.

An inquiry into the murder of Mr Patrice Lumumba and his two Ministers had been set up. Let me see how the puppet President Tshombe, Kassavubu, Mobutu could be free from the report. They have the gravest questions to answer in connexion with the murder of Mr Patrice Lumumba, and his two associates, Mr Okito and Mr Mpolo.

Mr Patrice Lumumba was suffered, given all types of maltreatments in the prisons, but the courageous man never one day asked for mercy. The more the prison authorities became harder on him the more he spoke against them. He had no fear and was not afraid of death.

Hon. Patrice Lumumba told the notorious President Tshombe, in Katanga prison when he, President Tshombe seriously slapped him, 'Look here, puppet Tshombe, traitor Tshombe, wicked Tshombe, dangerous Tshombe, you can slap me as you like, you can beat me as you like, you can kick me as a football, and can also starve me for one month. In short, you can suffer me as you like, you are in position to do so now. I will never ask you to be merciful on me.'

'What I would care to inform you is that the evil that men do lives after them. So you can be doing as you like.'

26

Sembène Ousmane

Strike

At first a fisherman in his native Casamance, then a soldier in World War II, a docker, trade-union organizer and writer, Sembène Ousmane has come up the hard way both in life and in literature. His first novel was a clumsy near-remake of Wright's *Native Son* set in Paris and the Marseilles docks; in his latest stories, *Vehi-Ciosane et Le Mandat* (1966), he displays a depth of vision and a sureness of touch unexcelled within the compass of African social writing.

Ousmane is particularly concerned with the African working-class, whose chronicler and exhorter he considers himself to be. But while in his latest novel, *L'Harmattan*, he endeavours to show an abstract but representative African country in a given historical situation, he confined himself to his native Sénégal in his previous *Les Bouts de bois de Dieu* – from which the present extract is taken – focusing on the historical railway strike of 1947-8.

Strike

The sun was setting slowly. On the motionless locomotives and carriages, the silent workshops and sheds, the white villas and the mud-houses, the huts and hovels a bluish shadow settled discreetly. A bugle call drifted across from the police barracks.

Thus the railway strike settled in at Thiès. An unlimited strike which for many people all along the line was an occasion to suffer but for many also an occasion to think. When the smoke stopped drifting over the savannah, they realized that an age had run its course, the age the old people would speak of, the age when Africa was a vegetable garden. Now the machine ruled over their country. By stopping its march for the whole length of a thousand miles they became conscious of their power, but they also grew conscious of their dependence. The machine was in fact making new men out of them. It did not belong to them, it was they who belonged to it. In stopping it taught them this lesson.

Days went by and nights went by. There was no news except that which each hour brought into each home, and it was always the same: the provisions had run out, the savings were drained, there was no money in the house. People would go and ask for credit, but the answer they got from the merchant was always the same, 'You owe me so much already anyway. And what about me? I won't even be able to pay my next bill. Why don't you take other people's advice? Why don't you resume work?'

So the machine was put to use a bit more; mopeds and bicycles were taken to the money-lender, watches likewise; sumptuous boubous which were worn only on big occasions came next. Hunger had come to stay; men, women and children began to grow thin. But they held out. They met more frequently, the strike-leaders increased their activity, and everyone swore not to yield.

Sembène Ousmane

Days went by and nights went by. And then to everybody's surprise trains were seen rolling again. The locomotives were driven by engineers who had come from Europe, soldiers and sailors were turned into stationmasters and railroad workers. The area in front of each station was converted into a stronghold surrounded by barbed wire. Behind it armed sentries mounted the guard day and night. Now it was fear that took up its abode among them. The strikers themselves felt an ill-defined fear, an awed surprise at this force they had set in motion, and they were not sure whether to nurture it with hope or destroy it with resignation. The whites, on the other hand, were obsessed with numbers. How could their small minority feel safe among this sombre mass? Those of the two races who had before maintained good and friendly relations avoided each other. White women no longer went to the market without being escorted by a policeman. It even happened that black women refused to sell their wares to them.

Days went by and nights went by. In this country, the men have several wives, and doubtless this was the reason why at the beginning they hardly appreciated the help they were getting from them. But soon they here also discovered a new facet of the time to come. When a man returned from a meeting with his head hanging down and his pockets empty, what he saw first was the kitchen without fire, the mortars overturned, bowls and calabashes empty and piled on top of each other. Then he would go into the arms of a wife, no matter if it was the first or the third one. And the women, confronted with these hunched shoulders, these dragging feet, were getting conscious that something was about to change for them, too.

But if they felt closer to the lives of their men, what about their children then? In this country they are numerous and people hardly are in the habit of counting their children. But now they were running about aimlessly in the courtyards or hanging on to their mothers' loincloths with their bones protruding, their eyes hollow, and that constant question which broke your heart: 'Mother, are we going to eat today?' Then the women got together in fours or tens, their babies hanging on their backs, the bigger kids running behind or in front of them, and they said, 'Let's go and see So-and-so, maybe she still has a little millet left,' and the pilgrimage proceeded from house to house. Very often Madam So-and-so would say, 'Oh, I have nothing left; I'll join you.' She would clasp a baby against her flaccid breast and come along to swell their procession. Sometimes they would arrive at a house where the woman still had some water left; she would pass a calabash around but would say, 'Don't drink all of it.'

The days were sad and the nights were sad. The miaowing of the cat made you shiver.

One morning, a woman got up, firmly wrapped her loincloth around her waist and said,

'Today I shall bring you something to eat.'

And the men understood that this age which produced new men also brought forth new women.

27

Castro Soromenho

Chief Xa-Mucuari's Grievance

Castro Soromenho, a white Portuguese, takes us into the sultry heat of the Angolan *sertão*, where a handful of whites – traders and petty officials – languish in the little town of Camaxilo amidst a mass of downtrodden blacks as yet unaware of their power.

Brazil looms afar as a possible alternative to Angolan degradation, with the promise of racial harmony and eventual social justice for all. Joachim Américo, the ex-revolutionary from across the Atlantic, is a misfit in the eyes of his fellow-whites: 'He could not get adjusted to colonial life and was considered a bad official who was too soft on the Negroes.' After a clash with Jaime Silva, the secretary of the local administration, over the latter's brutal treatment of a young mulatto, Américo leaves the stagnant town. A first gust of rebellion blows. João Calado, the disinherited mulatto, kills a guard, robs the public coffers, and sets the administration building on fire. He vanishes without a trace and leaves the town dying its own slow death.

Castro Soromenho's realism is poles apart from the exoticism of Pierre Loti. He disentangles the social, economic and historical factors corrupting Camaxilo and the surrounding tribal lands.

Chief Xa-Mucuari's Grievance

Francisco Bernardo spat, raised his hands and shook them several times.

'This dog will never die,' Anacleto shouted, getting up.

But it was only after a long silence that Bernardo spoke. 'You'll see, our turn will come first. An old Negro never dies. This Xa-Mucuari . . .'

'There are two more of them coming,' Anacleto remarked, sitting down again on the front step.

With deerskins draped around their waists the blacks were coming up the street. As soon as they noticed the two old men, they slipped off into the bushes, in the direction of Pancario's shop.

'Yeah, they're really Xa-Mucuari's men,' Bernardo said. He stood up to watch them through the leaves of the creeper. 'And they've seen us too, the swine.'

Just as the old settlers knew almost all the natives, so the old Negroes knew very well the names of the whites and also a great deal about their lives. In days gone by, they had gossiped over the counter for a long time, once business had been concluded. They had lived through the wars and the time before the wars, the slavery period and the ivory period, and then rubber. The number of those who had brought their loads of rubber and old ivory tusks to Bernardo's and Anacleto's stores had been considerable. At that time they had taken away from the shop all they wanted as an instalment on future business transactions. If they did not ask for credit themselves, it was the trader who would broach the subject, trying his best to tempt them so that they would be obliged to do business with him. 'The black man always pays,' – that was common knowledge – 'maybe he'll be late, but pay he will, and if he dies, not one of his relatives will disclaim the debt he leaves behind or refuse to accept it as his own.'

At that time the *soba** Xa-Mucuari had been a great friend of Bernardo's and Anacleto's. These two had come from Luanda well before the whites of the rubber boom and had helped him in the war against the *soba* Xa-Cungo. It was to them his men had sold all their wares. And Xa-Mucuari's men had only done business in the other stores when Bernardo and Anacleto happened to be short of cloth. They would, however, first apologize to them out of respect for the friendship their *soba* bore the traders. But since then many years had elapsed. During that period rubber was not yet being exploited; it was the time when Xa-Mucuari had sold them ivory, which he bartered for slaves in the Bula-Matari. Then had come the whites' big rush for rubber. Bernardo and Anacleto had also practised this trade and had managed to get rich. But there was a lot of gambling going on in those days. The flow of gold had attracted mulatto women from Malange to Camaxilo, and they had wasted most of their fortunes. Then, in an attempt to compete with their rivals, they had rushed headlong into business ventures that were not sound and had lost all they had left. They had come to the point where they were giving the blacks more money than their rubber was worth. The natives had taken advantage of the cut-throat competition between the traders and had exploited them as best they could, demanding large presents from them. They would give up one store for another, running after the *cambola-dores*.† Only Xa-Mucuari's men had remained faithful to the two traders. These had helped their *soba* to wage war against Xa-Cungo and in return they had received all the rubber of the defeated chief and Xa-Mucuari's friendship. Their *soba* had kept the slaves and the skull of the chief whom he had killed with his own hands.

But now not one of Xa-Mucuari's men, even among those who had been born after the wars with the whites, came near their door. And when they could not help doing so, being under

---

*Chief.
† Traders' agents in charge of attracting customers.

the orders of the *capitas*★ and the native soldiers who guarded them while they were working on the road-gang, they turned their heads and spat on the ground. The settlers would become enraged and shout insults at them but the men never answered for fear of the soldiers' whip, for a Negro is not allowed to raise his voice against a white man. They would withdraw into a silent rage and mentally heap insults on them. But in the evening, around the fires in the village, they would laugh uproariously while watching one of their number aping the settlers. Only their *soba*, Xa-Mucuari, would remain dead silent; his eyes would harden and his mouth become distorted.

★

The *soba* Xa-Mucuari had never forgiven the two settlers for having led the military column against his village and for having pointed out to the lieutenant in charge his old father, who was then led off to Camaxilo as a prisoner and poisoned there. He himself was already the *soba*, his father being very old, and that he was not fettered and imprisoned was only because he had fled in time. And these two whites to whom he had always granted free access to his village and whom he had charged less than the other traders, despite his father's warning that 'whites will never be the black man's friend', these two whites had taken part in the assault on the *senzala*† by the soldiery and had laughed at the screams of the women being hunted down by strange Negroes and rutting whites. Later, when he was hiding in the bush, Xa-Mucuari had learned that Francisco Bernardo had dragged one of his wives into a thicket and had taken her by force.

The Luanda chief had stayed in the bush for many long years, drinking the stagnant water of the swamps and feeding on roots in the torrid land of the Cuilo, which the natives, in their flight before the soldiers, were leaving by the thousands. He had always avoided walking near the *senzalas* on the river banks, for in those days of crime and treason the *sobas* had not even been able to trust the blacks. Many had used the opportunity to take revenge for the punishments to which the chiefs with their

★Helpers of the *cipayes* (local soldiers or 'sepoys'); they also serve as liaison agents with the local authorities.

†Village.

habitual cruelty had subjected them. Only after the soldiers' departure had he returned to his lands, and the whites who had moved in after them to collect taxes had not wanted to hear anything of these old stories; they had pardoned all the *sobas* who had come to pay tribute to them. He had found only a few people in the village, and of all his wives, only the *muata-muari* – his first – had been waiting for him. She was the only one the soldiers had not wanted to violate; her breasts, which for a long time had been hanging down listlessly, were spent like squeezed-out papaw fruits, and her belly fell down in folds. Her age was somewhat above his, but she had hardly recognized him, so old had he grown. The woman had told him the sad story of his people; she told him all about the requisitions made by the soldiers whom the settlers of Camaxilo had guided to the village.

His tribe was scattered. Many of his best men had emigrated, while others were living in distant villages under new *sobas* and had developed other ambitions. The old chief had spent several days cursing his unfaithful people and had then ordered the drums to be beaten to invite all his men to return to their village. But they had already adopted other lands and had laughed off his threats. They had sent him word that instead of trying to re-call them by beating the drum, he would do better to dance to his own music, for never would they return to a land which he himself had forsaken out of fear of the whites. And Xa-Mucuari had gone to weep over his lost people near the tombs of the old *sobas* who had been luckier than himself, and had died without knowing the whites, or the blacks coming from afar to join the whites in making war against the brothers of their own race.

Since that day, the old man left his village only once a year at the approach of the civil servant who came to count the population for tax purposes. He did not want to see even the shadow of the stranger. He would hide in the forest and return to the village only when the white man was far from his lands. As far as the authorities were concerned, Xa-Mucuari was always ill or on a journey, and when his people did not carry out the orders of the administration, he never answered a summons personally but had himself represented by an old slave who was ready to receive all the strokes of the cane meant for his master.

This slave finally passed for Xa-Mucuari and introduced himself to the authorities under that name. Xa-Mucuari would have nobody mention the whites to him, nor the new *sobas* appointed by the military and later by civilians, to whom taxes had soon to be paid, causing a number of rebellions. To these *sobas*, some of whom had been his slaves, he attributed all the misfortunes that had befallen his tribe, which had once been rich and powerful but was now divided into numerous small clans, each with its own *soba* imposed by the whites of the government, and all incapable of reorganizing themselves to wage war against the foreigners. He hated all those who had sold themselves to the whites to become *sobas*, who had supplied them with as many people as they wanted for the army, for forced labour, for the diamond mines that had just been discovered; and who in addition to all that, let them have all the tax money. Some would even take their own wives to the whites and feel very flattered when they slept with them.

The fate of the Negroes had changed. The white man had now become the master of the land. The traders no longer paid any gratuity to the *sobas* in exchange for their permission to trade with their 'sons', and they moved about freely as if the land belonged to them, as if they were born there and the blacks were mere strangers. And all the time they threatened to complain to the whites in the government. They were the masters of everything. A *soba* of the old days was now worth just as little as one of his slaves.

'Luandaland is lost,' the old Negroes, who had been through the wars, would say. And like Xa-Mucuari, they smoked *liamba** to forget their humiliation and to find in their dreams the past glory of a destiny which had betrayed them.

This whole world of memories welled up from Xa-Mucuari's past when his men mocked the two settlers. The old chief withdrew within himself; his face closed up and his eyes glittered with anger. And in those nights people knew that he was getting drunk on palm-wine and *liamba* tobacco.

*

The sun passed over the valley, glided over the plateau in the

* Indian hemp.

heights of the sky, and sank in the distance, on a level with the earth, setting formations of clouds aflame on the horizon. The two old settlers were still talking; the doors of their stores, thrown open to the flies, showed the empty shelves.

'It's been a good day, for Pancario I mean,' Bernardo said.

'For him one day is as good as another,' Anacleto rolled himself a cigarette and then added, 'The bell is due to ring soon now.'

The night was darkening in the valley and the villages were filling up with shadow. And soon the bell of the District Office building began to ring. This meant the end of work for the blacks, and for the traders closing time.

Anacleto returned home and Bernardo rose from his couch on which he used to spend his days. A cap protected his bald head against the flies. He dragged himself along the veranda and called one of his sons to help him close the shop. 'Tell your mother to have the coffee brought here,' he ordered his son when they had finished. And he returned to his couch and sat down on it with a deep sigh.

A song drifted across from the distance, from uptown Camaxilo, and reached the black night of the valley, from where it echoed back to the lower village and towards the distant skies above the plateau, where castles of clouds blazed in the setting sun.

28

Casey Motsisi

Riot

West African writers have criticized black South African writers for much the same reasons that they have attacked writers belonging to the *négritude* movement in French. They have held that the South African writer's obsession with race has tended to obscure his other interests. They have argued that South African writers, like earlier French African writers, have tended to sacrifice art on the altar of didacticism.

On the other hand, South African writers are responding to the pressure of a uniquely hideous situation. For them to deny a concern with race, with equality and social justice, would not only be to surrender the self-imposed burden of writer as reformer, but would mean a denial of their own everyday experience. In a special sense this is what Ezekiel Mphahlele meant when he spoke of black writers doing 'violence' to English. The violence is not in the language alone but in the entire area of experience which South African writers chart.

Riot

Maria Mbatha looked at the clock on the kitchen dresser. The clock had stopped. But she knew instinctively that it was very late at night and her eyes were heavy with sleep. She yawned as she continued to rock the young boy she was carrying in her arms to sleep.

But the boy kept staring unblinkingly into the dim-lit room with big, sleepless eyes. They both listened to the noisy silence of the room.

'Ma,' the young boy said softly.

'Yes, my son.' Her mind was still blank.

'Ma, I want water.'

'Water.' She repeated the word like a child learning a new word at school.

'Ma, I want water, water, water,' he rattled.

'Shut up, you're making noise. Why don't you wait for your mother to come and give you water?'

'I want water, I want water. Put me down. I want water.'

The palm of her hand came down hard on the young boy's buttocks. He did not cry. He started kicking his feet up and down.

'Next time I will make you feel the *sjambok*, Boetikie,' she vowed after the young boy's fist had caught her smartly on the chin.

'I want water. Put me down. I want water . . .'

Maria, still holding the young boy in one hand, stood up and gave him a mug full of water. 'You just wet the blankets tonight and see what happens to you tomorrow,' she said as she watched him gulp the water greedily.

'Ma, I'm hungry,' Boetikie said after finishing the water.

'You must be mad. You had food during the day. You think

I'm here to work for you as if you are a European?' She carried him over to the bed and tucked him in.

'I don't want to sleep. I want food. I'm hungry.'

'Shut up now. Don't act like a lunatic. One of these days I will kill you, Boetikie, God in Heaven hears me.'

Boetikie pulled the blanket and covered his head. Maria stood looking at the covered heap for a while. She shook her head and went outside.

Outside, Western Township lay sleeping restlessly under an overcast sky. Usually, at this late hour on Sundays, Western Township, like most African townships, would be alive with drunken revellers staggering home from shebeens and 'midnite parties'.

But tonight, like the past few Sundays, Western was quiet. Yet one could not fail to miss the undercurrent of restlessness that throbbed through the belly of the township. When will it ever end? 'I hate this boycott,' Maria cursed softly, bitterly, and went back into the room.

Boetikie was snoring nasally. She felt relieved that he was asleep. How this child gets on my nerves! But there was no anger or bitterness in her thoughts. Boetikie was all she had in the world. Her husband had been killed during a faction fight between 'Russians' in neighbouring Newclare.

Nana, their only daughter, was married and was now staying in Port Elizabeth. Boetikie was Nana's child but Maria had to look after him because the man who married Nana did not want the child to live with them.

Maria went to the stove and pulled out the ashtin. There was a bottle in it. She took it out, poured some of the liquid into a glass and gulped it down. Her face contorted into a mask of agony as the brandy burned her throat and warmed her stomach. She sat on a chair and placed the brandy on the table. She stared at the half-empty bottle, hating it and loving it at the same time. She wondered what her husband would have said if he had caught her drinking.

Maria squeezed her head with both hands. Her head was bursting with pain. She felt as though parts of it were falling away in pieces. She seized the bottle and poured herself another tot.

After gulping it down she felt the pain filtering out of her head, leaving a delicious sensation that was a mixture of dare and bravado.

Suddenly the world became a wonderful and beautiful thing and she began to mumble a song. She was now falling in love with the world she had hated so passionately a few hours ago. She thought of the long walk she would have to make the following day to fetch the bundle of washing in town. For tomorrow would be Monday – 'Washing Day'. Although she was not feeling tired, she told herself that she would not go to town. 'To hell with the boycott and the washing!'

It felt comforting to be able to say that. It made her feel like a person, a human being who has a right to live her own life the way she wanted to live it.

'*Azikhwelwa!*' she shouted. 'We won't board the buses,' she interpreted for herself. Just like at the meetings. She laughed and poured herself another shot. Then another. And yet another. After a while followed blissful unconsciousness.

She fell asleep on the table, holding the bottle in one hand, the glass in the other.

A slight breeze trickled through a crack in one of the panes of the window behind Maria's back. The flame of the cigarette-high candle that was stuck in a saucer flickered for a moment, as if struggling to hold its own against the breeze. But the breeze licked it off the wick and muffled it in its coldness. The room was now in semi-darkness.

Maria's body rose and fell rhythmically with her heavy breathing. As it rose, it seemed to swell with all the pride and joy that had filled the brief years when she had her husband and the crowning glory she felt when she gave birth to their only child, Nana. She had seen her grow into a fine woman.

And as it fell, it was as if all her forty-five years of frustration were weighing heavily down on her plump body, battling to drain the life out of her.

Maria slept, her mind steeped in the uncaring abandon of the drunk.

Peaceful. No thoughts; no dreams; no hopes nor fears of tomorrow. Bottle-kind of peace, but peace all the same. And the

Casey Motsisi

township also slept, nestled uneasily between the inflammable Sophiatown to the north and the lusty Newclare to the south. On the east was Coronationville, prim and pretentious. And on the west, Nature, grim and sad, licking at the scars, *dongas*, inflicted on her by man with the sharp spades of civilization.

Morning crept stealthily into Maria's room, like a policeman stalking a dangerous, armed *tsotsi*. Maria felt the nursemaid of the mind silently drawing the curtains of sleep away from her eyes. Slowly, she drifted back into wakefulness, but her eyes refused to open. Her head throbbed with a clanging pain.

She knew the pain. A hangover. A hangover coupled with the effects of drinking heavily on an empty stomach. She rubbed her eyes and realized that the door was slightly open. She remembered that she had not locked it last night. The thought that she had slept without locking the door sent a shiver of fright through her spine.

Then she felt someone shaking her rudely on the shoulder.

'Come on, woman. Don't waste my time. I'm arresting you.'

She looked up. Beside her stood a khaki-clad, hefty man. The Law! And in one hand The Law held a bottle of brandy and in the other The Law held a glass. Maria recognized them as her own.

Maria stood up. She was an inch or two taller than The Law. She looked at The Law, feeling sick and scared; cringing and confused.

'Come, woman, let's go,' The Law commanded authoritatively.

'Please, father policeman,' Maria pleaded. 'Don't arrest me, I have to go to work . . . . and I . . . . please, father policeman . . .'

But Maria knew that it was no use trying to plead with The Law. She had always regarded the police as sub-humans, people without compassion and feeling. People who only found untold joy out of life by arresting, bullying and manhandling others. She heard other policemen shouting and cursing outside. The police were everywhere. It was a raid.

She heard a woman protesting and recognized the voice. It was Ma Sello, her next-door neighbour. 'Don't hit my son like that! I will bring you before the court.'

238

'He has no pass and he's cheeky. These educated *tsotsis*! He says I have no right to ask him for a pass when he's in bed. Who does he think he is? I'll knock the education out of his head, I vow by my mother.'

Maria had resigned herself to the worst. She could not even believe her ears when the policeman gave her back the bottle of brandy and told her to hide it. 'Quickly, woman, hide it before I change my mind.'

Maria snatched the bottle and shoved it into the ashtin of the stove. 'I don't know when I'll become a Sergeant, doing such stupid things,' she heard the policeman mumble as he went out of the house. He banged the door so hard the house rattled with the impact.

The noise woke up Boetikie with a start. Maria, although she could not say why, was crying softly.

'Ma, you're crying.'

'Yes, my son,' she sniffed.

'Why, Ma?'

'Oh, sheddup!'

When Maria came back from town in the afternoon, carrying a bundle of soiled washing on her head, she was still bitter at the experience she had had at the bus stop. Because she was tired from walking all the way to town, she had boarded the Corona-ionville bus as these buses were not affected by the fare increase which sparked off the Bus Boycott.

A young Coloured boy had constantly bumped her and called her all sorts of names to unsettle her. But Maria had managed to keep cool.

She met Ma Sello outside. 'Ma Sello, did you send Boetikie to the shop?' she asked.

'No,' said Ma Sello. 'But I saw him running with Ma Batho's on towards Sophiatown. There's a fight there, you know. The people are stoning the buses and trams and cars. I understand that one of the buses from town – and it was empty, mark you – ran over an old man who was crossing the main road. That's why the people are stoning the buses.'

Ma Sello had hardly finished her narrative and Maria was dashing full throttle in the direction of Sophiatown.

Fear exploded in every pore of her body. She stumbled, fell and scrambled to her feet again, all the while calling Boetikie's name.

A few yards away from the trellis that divided Sophiatown from Western Township, she realized the full impact of the riot. There was screaming and shouting. People of all shapes and sizes were scampering up and down the streets.

And the police, from nearby Newlands Police Station, fired their guns and pistols above the heads of the milling mob.

Maria had seen Sophiatown many a time in an ugly mood. But today Sophiatown looked like a city at war. There were people lying wounded or dead along the tram rails and the main street.

A policeman, leading two children, a boy and a girl, by the hands, crossed over into Western Township through an opening in the trellis.

Maria realized that the boy was Boetikie. With a shout of joy and relief, she ran towards the policeman. 'Save my child, save my child!' she shouted hysterically.

Just at the moment, a group of women and young *tsotsis* who had been witnessing the little war from a safe distance, mobbed the policeman.

'What are you doing to our children, you government dog?' one of the women shrieked. In a moment the women were upon him, clawing at him, tearing his khaki uniform and battering his head with stones held firmly in their hands. He fell and everybody disappeared.

As Maria pulled Boetikie away she saw the face of the policeman. Something knotted inside her as if to squeeze all the water from her system and bring it out silently through her eyes.

When she reached home the shooting had lulled. A spasmodic 'boom' here and there after long intervals.

That night, Maria and Boetikie went to bed without having supper. She did not feel hungry and even Boetikie had not asked for food. It took her a long time to fall asleep. She just lay in the darkness of the locked and bolted room and listened to the whine of ambulances that made the dark room even more foreboding.

And she thought of a policeman whose body was perhaps still

lying cold and stoned and punctured along the trellis. She choked and wept.

... Only that same morning that policeman had been alive. That same policeman had been in her room asking her to hide the bottle of brandy. If he had arrested her, she thought, then she would not be remembering his young, pinkish face lying dead and uncared for along the trellis that divides Western Township from Sophiatown ...

29

Aké Loba

Kocoumbo and the Stowaway

Kocoumbo, the village boy, is going to Paris from Kwamo, the Kwamo that has meant working in the sun-parched fields, hunting the wild boar (after first tossing an egg against a tree to propitiate the gods of the forest), dancing with beautiful, bare-breasted Alouma at night, listening to the wise counsel of the old ones. Kwamo is a self-enclosed universe where the spirits of the ancestors live through daily experiences.

And Paris, where overgrown Kocoumbo hoped to meet the likes of his hero Victor Hugo, far from being a city of light which can be conquered with a smile, appears dreary and desolate to the forlorn African, devoid of human companionship, a house of death 'without a breath or a murmur'.

How the young peasant catapulted from Kwamo to Paris struggles and yet finally makes good is the story which Aké Loba tells.

Kocoumbo and the Stowaway

Ten days after their departure, when washing himself, Kocoumbo noticed with pleasurable excitement that his callouses were making away and that the resin spots were disappearing from his hands. He told himself that his palms would soon be as smooth as Nadan's. The thought of Nadan occupied his mind for a moment. Since he had embarked, he had not seen him any more, except once on the deck from a distance. What was he doing? Was he still going around with that elegant-looking young man? Maybe he would visit him down here in the hold . . . Kocoumbo kept turning his fingers this way and that. They were really getting clean. But he could not derive any pride from this fact. Had his father not told him many times that hands were made to work and that hair did not grow on one's palms? Still, educated people had smooth hands and he could not help feeling some satisfaction at edging up to them a bit more closely in this manner. Education held such a fascination for him . . .

Kocoumbo turned the tap off. He had decided to read some Victor Hugo. For the last ten days now he had done nothing but talk. It would be better if he did something for his education. A man whose hands were losing their roughness must not waste a second in bringing them at once into contact with books. It seemed to him that they would get softer and smoother at their touch.

He walked over to his hammock with a firm step and unhooked a small chain with a cork tied on to its end. The young man looked around him and since nobody was paying any attention, he brought two small keys out of the hollow cork. They were the keys to his trunk, which as a true, wary farmer he had thus camouflaged.

He bent down and pulled out the trunk. It prevented his

hammock from hanging down completely, which greatly incon-
venienced him when sleeping but had the advantage that he
could feel it with his hands from time to time.

The young man slipped his hand under his belongings and
gingerly took out a small book covered with very clean wrapping
paper. Then, having shoved the trunk back into place, he sat
down in his hammock, at peace with himself, his buttocks glued
to the precious planks. He opened the book and became engros-
sed in the reading of *Oceano Nox*.

A voice coming from near the ladder dragged him out of his
visions of storm and strife. 'Hey you chaps, I've just been to the
Third Class. It's great up there. It's no longer a ship but the
governor's palace.'

'Well, then it's like paradise. I once went inside the governor's
palace. Really, boys, I'm telling you, it's the true paradise described in the Bible.'

'But in Paris you'll see better things than that, take my word
for it,' somebody said in a shrill voice. 'The governor's palace
would be a chicken coop in France.'

'What do *you* know about it?'

'If you ask questions like that, it just goes to show you're not
clever. Look at the beauty of the governor's house in the bush.
Mind you, he's just a simple governor. But back home in France
they have the President of the Republic with all his ministers . . .'

'What are the ministers like? How do you recognize them?'
a jeering voice asked.

'They're tall, man, very tall.'

'Tall?'

'That's what I'm saying. Didn't you see de Gaulle when he
was canvassing for volunteers?'

'Are we allowed to go up into the Third Class?' somebody
broke in.

'Of course, I told you, I've just been there. You should've
seen it. It's as beautiful as an expatriate's villa.' The young man
who brought this piece of news gave a whistle of admiration.

'Tell us about it!'

'In the first place,' the narrator went on with his description,
'there are bars exactly like those in town, smoking and recreation

rooms. As for the bedrooms, they each have a wash basin and a mirror. They are called cabins.'

'You're exaggerating!' somebody shouted.

'Not at all. You only say that because you're not in a position to enjoy it. Europeans know something about travelling, man.'

'When I get my medical degree, I'll travel First Class,' a tiny chap with lively eyes, whose ancestors must have been pygmies, said in an exuberant tone of voice.

'Oh, you, Désiré, you always have to appear big, but what else would you expect? Isn't that so, boys?'

The little fellow did not seem worried by the allusion and joined in the laughter of his companions, jumping down from a bale to the ground with the suppleness of a liana.

'I forgot to tell you,' the fellow who had seen the marvels of the Third Class said, 'that up there I was taken for a stowaway. It seems there's one aboard, and the police are looking for him. I had to show my papers.'

At that moment the door of the hold opened and two men entered.

'Gentlemen, I'm the security officer of this ship. My assistant and I will carry out an inspection, for there's a stowaway on this boat.'

Silence fell.

'Let everybody go to his place along the passage.' The security officer went from one person to the next, staring him in the face and checking him against a file his assistant held out to him. Then the two men investigated the five empty hammocks. The assistant wrote something in a notebook, and taking some numbered labels from his pocket pinned them on all the berths while the security officer called out the names of the passengers one by one.

'The stowaway is a crook. He's robbed his employer and escaped. We've just been notified that he's hiding on our boat. If you notice any suspicious character, report to the police post. It is open any time of the day or night. We should also like to point out that the management is not responsible for the loss of any property not entrusted to its care.'

The term 'stowaway' had had a funny sound in Kocoumbo's ears. It seemed to him that there was in fact somebody who did not act like the others in the hold. But this whole performance and especially the security officer's booming voice got him a little mixed up.

He heard a voice whispering from behind the bales, 'Ask him what the stowaway looks like.' His eyes tried to pierce the shadows between the boxes, he saw an eye, and the voice mumbled again, 'Ask him what he looks like.'

Kocoumbo raised his arm and snapped his fingers. Only the legs of the security officer could still be seen on the ladder, and his assistant had also started going up. The last man turned around and asked, 'What's the matter?'

'What does the stowaway look like?' Kocoumbo questioned him.

'Good man!' the security officer exclaimed, quickly climbing down the ladder again. 'Who asked this question?'

'Me,' Kocoumbo replied.

'Here you see a young man with initiative,' the security officer went on. 'Are you a student?'

Kocoumbo hesitated but since everybody was looking at him, he articulated proudly, 'Yes, sir.'

'Congratulations. That's very good. ... He's of small size, has a narrow face, a very flat nose, and his lower lip is more protruding and thicker than his upper lip.'

'Has he a lot of hair, ask him that,' the voice behind the boxes begged.

'Has he a lot of hair?' Kocoumbo asked obediently, flushed with the officer's compliments.

'You're getting better and better. You'd make an excellent detective. Yes, he has a lot of hair. I think, sir, you now have all the information necessary to help us. I only have to thank you.'

Kocoumbo felt very cheerful. Up till then, he had thought in a confused way that to be recognized as a student you had to bear a special mark. What kind of a mark? Maybe a way of expressing yourself which would at once single you out for attention. Was it possible that a white man had admitted this quality in him without raising any objection? He felt a sense of contentment so close to rapture that a big smile spread over his lips. His arms relaxed along his body. He opened his mouth, closed it again, took a fountain pen from his back pocket, sat down and wrote the word 'student' in block letters on the first page of Victor Hugo's poetic works, just under his name. A pleasurable emotion swelled his chest. He got up and pulled out his trunk, which had OUDJO KOCOUMBO splashed in bold letters on its lid. He bent down to add beside it: *student*. A scruple made him hesitate and he started to look up a small dictionary. He finally made up his mind to draw in a firm hand: *student in Paris*.

30

Alex la Guma

Death in the City

At first sight there seems to be great deal in common between this piece, from Alex la Guma's novel *A Walk in the Night* (Ibadan, 1962), and Casey Motsisi's 'Riot'. Both writers are interested in the imaginative treatment of violence. But where there is a tone of justified complaint about 'Riot', the anti-hero of the la Guma is as much victim as accomplice. He is not at the other end, preserving tenements of order, but very much part of the disorder itself. In large measure the agitated, nervous quality of the writing manages to convey this.

Death in the City

The air outside caught him suddenly in its cool grasp, making his skin prickle; and the glare of street-lights and windows made his head reel, so that he had to stand still for a moment to let the spinning of his brain subside. The spell of dizziness settled slowly, his head swinging gently back to normal like a merry-go-round slowing down and finally stopping. On each side of him the lights and neon signs stretched away with the blaze and glitter of a string of cheap, gaudy jewellery. A man brushed past him and went into the pub, the doors flap-flapping and the murmur of voices from inside had the sound of surf breaking on a beach. A slight breeze had sprung up over the city, moving the hanging signs, and scuttling bits of paper were grey ghosts in the yellow electric light along the street. There were people up and down, walking, looking into the shop-windows or waiting aimlessly.

Michael Adonis pulled up the zipper of his leather coat and dug his hands into the slanted pockets and crossed the street. The courage of liquor made his thoughts brave. He thought, 'To hell with them. I'm not scared of them. Of Scofield and the law and the whole effing lot of them. Bastards. To hell with them.' He was also feeling a little morose and the bravery gave way to self-pity, like an advert on the screen being replaced by another slide.

He turned down another street, away from the artificial glare of Hanover, between stretches of damp, battered houses with their broken-ribs of front-railings; cracked walls and high tenements that rose like the left-overs of a bombed area in the twilight; vacant lots and weed-grown patches where houses had once stood; and deep doorways resembling the entrances to deserted castles. There were children playing in the street, darting

Alex la Guma

among the overflowing dustbins and shooting at each other with wooden guns. In some of the doorways people sat or stood, murmuring idly in the fast-fading light like wasted ghosts in a plague-ridden city.

Foxy and the two youths in tropical suits stood in the lamplight on a corner down the street. They were smoking and one of them spun the end of his cigarette into the street. They watched Michael Adonis cross the street, but did not move from where they stood or say anything.

Michael Adonis turned into the entrance of a tall narrow tenement where he lived. Once, long ago, it had had a certain kind of dignity, almost beauty, but now the decorative Victorian plaster around the wide doorway was chipped and broken and blackened with generations of grime. The floor of the entrance was flagged with white and black slabs in the pattern of a draught-board, but the tramp of untold feet and the accumulation of dust and grease and ash had blurred the squares so that now it had taken on the appearance of a kind of loathsome skin disease. A row of dustbins lined one side of the entrance and exhaled the smell of rotten fruit, stale food, stagnant water and general decay. A cat, the colour of dishwater, was trying to paw the remains of a fish-head from one of the bins.

Michael Adonis paused in the entrance on the way to the stairs and watched the cat. It tugged and wrestled with the head which was weighed down by a pile of rubbish, a broken bottle and an old boot. He watched it and then reaching out with a foot upset the pile of rubbish on to the floor, freeing the fish-head. The cat pulled it from the bin and it came away with a tangle of entrails. The cat began to drag it towards the doorway, leaving a damp brown trail across the floor.

'Playing with cats?'

Michael Adonis looked around and up at the girl who had come down the stairs and was standing at the bend in the staircase.

'I'd rather play with you,' he said, grinning at her. 'Hullo, Hazel.'

'You reckon.'

She came down and stood on the first step, smiling at him and showing the gap in the top row of her teeth. She had a heavy

254

mouth, smeared blood-red with greasy lipstick, so that it looked stark as a wound in her dark face. Her coarse wiry hair was tied at the back with a scrap of soiled ribbon in the parody of a pony-tail, and under the blouse and skirt her body was insignificant except for her small, jutting breasts. She was wearing new yellow leather flat-heeled pumps that gave the impression of something expensive abandoned on a junk heap.

Michael Adonis thought, knockers like apples, and said, 'Where you off to, *bokkie*?'

'Bioscope. And who's your *bokkie*?' She peered at him, her eyes sceptical.

'Okay. Don't be like that. What's showing?'

'What's it now again? *Love Me Tonight*. At the Metro.'

'That's a nonsense piece. I went to the Lawn last night. *The Gunfighter*.'

'No what. That isn't nice. They tell me the boy dies at the end.'

'Ah, you girls just like them kissing plays.'

He reached into the pocket of the leather coat and got out the cigarettes, shook two loose and offered the packet to the girl. His hand shook a little and she looked at him, smiling, and saying, 'You've got a nice *dop in*, hey?'

'I got troubles,' he replied, scowling at her.

'You drowning your sorrows?'

'Maybe.' The mention of sorrows brought back the sense of persecution again and he surrendered himself to it, enjoying the deep self-pity for a while, thinking, I'll get even with them, the sonsabitches. They'll see.

The girl had taken a cigarette and he put the other between his lips, feeling for matches. He struck a light and held it to her cigarette, the flame wobbling between his fingers, and then lit his own.

The girl said, 'Well, I'm going to blow now.'

'Hell, wait a little longer. It's still early.'

'No, *jong*. I haven't booked.'

She edged past him, smiling, holding the cigarette between her lips with one hand in an exaggerated pose. He made a grab at her arm, but she skipped out of his reach, laughing, and darted out through the wide doorway, leaving him staring at it with a feeling of abandonment.

He said, aloud, 'Ah, hell,' and cursed, climbing the stairs and nursing the foetus of hatred inside his belly.

The staircase was worn and blackened, the old oak banister loose and scarred. Naked bulbs wherever the light sockets were in working order cast a pallid glare over parts of the interior, lighting up the big patches of damp and mildew, and the maps of denuded sections on the walls. Somewhere upstairs a radio was playing Latin-American music, bongos and maracas throbbing softly through the smells of ancient cooking, urine, damp-rot and stale tobacco. A baby wailed with the tortured sound of gripe and malnutrition and a man's voice rose in hysterical laughter. Foot-steps thudded and water rushed down a pipe in a muted roar.

From each landing a dim corridor lined with doors tunnelled towards a latrine that stood like a sentry box at its end, the floor in front of it soggy with spilled water. Michael Adonis climbed to the top floor, and cigarettes and liquor made him pant a little. The radio was playing below him now, a crooner singing of lavender and shady avenues, and the child cried again and again.

The latrine at the end of the corridor opened and a man clawed his way out of it and began making his way towards one of the doors, holding on to the wall all the way and breathing hard with the sound of a saw cutting into wood. He was old and unsteady on his legs and hampered by his sagging trousers. His shirt was out dangling around him like a night-gown. He made his way slowly along the wall, like a great crab, breathing stertorously.

Michael Adonis stood at the head of the stairs and watched him for awhile, and then strolled forward. The old man heard his footsteps and looked up.

'Why, hallo, there, Michael, my boy,' the old man said in English, his voice high and cracked and breathless with age. In the light of the bulb in the ceiling his face looked yellowish-blue. The purple-veined, greyish skin had loosened all over it and sagged in blotched, puffy folds. With his sagging lower eyelids, revealing bloodshot rims, and the big, bulbous, red-veined nose that had once been aquiline, his face had the expression of a decrepit bloodhound. His head was almost bald, and wisps of

dirty grey hair clung to the bony, pinkish skull like scrub clinging to eroded rock.

'How are you, Michael boy?'

'Okay,' Michael Adonis answered, staring sullenly at the old
man.

This old man, who was an Irishman and who was dying of
alcoholism, diabetes and old age, had once been an actor. He had
performed in the theatres of Great Britain, South Africa and
Australia, and had served in two wars. Now he was a deserted,
abandoned ruin, destroyed by alcohol and something neither he
nor Michael Adonis understood, waiting for death, trapped at
the top of an old tenement, after the sweep of human affairs had
passed over him and left him broken and helpless as wreckage
disintegrating on a hostile beach.

'Give us a hand, Michael boy,' the old man panted. 'Give us a
hand.'

'What's the matter?' Michael Adonis asked. 'You got to the
can, you ought to be able to get back.'

'That's not polite, Michael. You're in a bad mood. Tell you
what, we'll sit down in my room and have a drink. You'd like a
drink, wouldn't you? I've got a bottle left. Old age pension yesterday.'

'I don't want to drink your wine,' Michael Adonis said. 'I got
money to buy my own booze with.'

'Who's talking about money?' the old man wheezed. 'Money's all the trouble in the world. Come on Michael boy. Come on.
Give your uncle a hand.'

'Youse not my uncle either,' Michael Adonis said, but took
the stick-thin arm and eased the old man ungently over to a doorway. 'I haven' got no white uncles.'

'Thanks. What's the difference? My wife, God bless her soul,
was a Coloured Lady. A fine one, too,' the old man said, reaching for the knob and opening the door. He was partly drunk
and smelled of cheap wine, sweat, vomit and bad breath.

The room was as hot and airless as a newly opened tomb, and
there was an old iron bed against one wall, covered with un-
washed bedding, and next to it a backless chair that served as a
table on which stood a chipped ashtray full of cigarette butts and

burnt matches, and a thick tumbler, sticky with the dregs o heavy red wine. A battered cupboard stood in a corner with cracked, fly-spotted mirror over it, and a small stack of dog eared books gathering dust. In another corner an accumulatior of empty wine bottles stood like packed skittles.

The old man struggled over to the bed and sank down on it clawing at his sunken chest with bony, purple-nailed fingers anc waited for his breath to come back.

Michael Adonis slouched over to the window and stared out through a gap in the dusty colourless curtain and the grimy panes. Beyond, the roofs of the city were sprawled in a jumble of dark, untidy patterns dotted with the scattered smudged blobs of yellow. Hanover Street made a crooked strip of misty light across the patch of District Six, and far off the cranes along the sea front stood starkly against the sky.

He turned away from the window, anger mixing with headi- ness of the liquor he had consumed and curdling into a sour knot of smouldering violence inside him. The old man was pouring wine into the sticky glass, the neck of the bottle rattling against the rim so that the red sloshed about and wet his knuckled fin- gers.

'There you are, Michael me boy,' he cackled, breathing hoar- sely. 'Nothing like a bit of port to warm the cockles of your heart.'

He held the glass up, his hand shaking, slopping the liquor, and Michael Adonis took it from him with a sudden burst of viciousness and tossed the wine down, then flinging the glass back into the old man's lap. The thick, sweet wine nauseated him and he choked and fought to control his stomach, glaring at the wreck on the bed, until the wine settled and there was a new heat throbbing in his head.

'A bad mood,' the old man quavered, and poured himself a glassful. He drank it, the wine trickling down his stubbly chin, and gasped. He cocked his head at Michael Adonis and said: 'You shouldn't get cross over nothin'. What's the matter with you?'

'Aw, go to buggery.'

'Now, now, that's no way to talk. We've all got our troubles.'

258

'Ya. Bloody troubles *you* got.'

'God bless my soul. I've got my troubles, too,' the old man said, with a sudden whine in his voice. 'Here I am and nobody to look after an old man.' Tears of remorse gathered in his pale, red-rimmed eyes, and he knuckled them with a tangled skein of dirty cord that was his hand. 'Look at me. I used to be something in my days. God bless my soul, I used to be something.'

Michael Adonis lit a cigarette and stood there looking at the old man through the spiral of smoke. He said: 'What the hell you crying about. You old white bastard, you got nothing to worry about.'

'Worry? Worry?' the old man whined. 'We all got something to worry about.' He mustered himself for a moment and shook a dried twig of a finger at Michael Adonis. 'We all got our cross to bear. What's my white got to do with it? Here I am, in shit street, and does my white help? I used to be an actor. God bless my soul, I toured England and Australia with Dame Clara Bright. A great lady. A great actress she was.' He began to weep, the tears spilling over the sagging rims of his eyes and he reached for the bottle again. 'We're like Hamlet's father's ghost. I played the ghost of Hamlet's father once. London it was.'

'You look like a blerry ghost, you spook,' Michael Adonis said bitterly. He jerked the bottle from the old man's hand and tipped it to his mouth and took a long swallow, gagging and then belching as he took the neck from his lips. His head spun and he wanted to retch.

The old man said: 'Don't finish the lot, boy. Leave some for old Uncle Doughty.' He reached frantically for the bottle, but Michael Adonis held it out of his reach, grinning and feeling pleasantly malicious.

'Want a dop, Uncle Doughty?'

'Oh, come on, man. Don't torment your old dad.'

'You old spook.'

'Give us a drink, give us a drink, sonny boy.'

'What was that you were saying about ghosts? I like ghost stories.' Michael Adonis grinned at him, feeling drunk. He waggled the bottle in front of the decayed ancient face with

259

its purple veins, yellow teeth and slack mouth, and watched the tears gather again in the liquid eyes.

'I'll tell you what,' the old man whined hopefully. 'I'll recite for you. You should hear me. I used to be something in my days.' He cleared his throat of a knot of phlegm, choked and swallowed. He started: 'I ... I am thy father's spirit; doomed for a certain term to walk the night ...' He lost track, then mustered himself, waving his skeleton arms in dramatic gestures, and started again. 'I am thy father's spirit, doomed for a certain time to walk the night ... and ... and for the day confined to fast in fires, till the foul crimes done in my days of natures's ... nature was burnt and purged away ... But ...' He broke off and grinned at Michael Adonis, and then eyed the bottle. 'That's us, us, Michael, my boy. Just ghosts, doomed to walk the night. Shakespeare.'

'Bull,' Michael Adonis said, and took another swallow at the bottle. 'Who's a blerry ghost?' He scowled at the old man through a haze of red that swam in front of his eyes like thick oozing paint, distorting the ancient face staring up at him.

'Michael, my boy. Spare a drop for your old uncle.'

'You old bastard,' Michael Adonis said angrily. 'Can't a boy have a bloody piss without getting kicked in the backside by a lot of effing law?'

'Now, now, Michael. I don't know what you're talking about, God bless my soul. You take care of that old port, my boy.'

The old man tried to get up and Michael Adonis said, 'Take your effing port,' and struck out at the bony, blotched, sprouting skull, holding the bottle by the neck so that the wine splashed over his hand. The old man made a small, honking, animal noise and dropped back on the bed.

31

D. N. Malinwa

Everything Under the Sun

There is usually a certain reticence amongst Africans towards the issue of homosexuality. The wicked colonialist, living in isolation without wife or children, is widely accredited with having introduced homosexuality on the continent. But in West Africa, it would seem that relationships which would normally be termed 'homosexual' in a Western context are very much taken for granted. It seemed worthwhile to include this piece by a young Tanzanian writer. What we liked about it was the simplicity, the absence of condemnation, the regard for the relationship on its own terms.

Everything Under the Sun

'I do not like to make things hard for you,' Meta said to Welimo, 'but when you act like this I do not know what is going to happen. You do not like nothing I do for you anyhow.'

The two boys, Meta and Welimo, shared a room over the south of Uhura Street. Meta had a job, but Welimo, who was twenty-four, seldom could find work. They were both down to their last few shillings.

'I told you a man was coming up here to offer me a job,' Welimo said.

'You cannot wait for a man to come offering you a job,' Meta said. He laughed. 'What kind of a man would that be anyhow.'

Welimo laughed too because he knew Meta did not believe anything he said.

'This man did promise me,' Welimo explained, and Meta snorted.

'Do not pick your nose like that,' Meta said to Welimo. 'What if the man sees you picking.'

Welimo said the man would not care.

'What does this man do?' Meta wondered.

'He said he had a nice line of goods I could sell for him and make good money,' Welimo replied.

'Good money selling,' Meta laughed. 'My advice to you is go out and look for a job, any job, and not wait for no old man to come to teach you to sell.'

'Well, nobody else wants to hire me due to my face,' Welimo said.

'What is wrong with your face?' Meta wanted to know. 'Outside of you picking your nose all the time, you have as good a face as anybody's.'

'I cannot look people in the eye is what,' Welimo told him.

Meta got up and walked around the small room.

'Like I told you,' Meta began the same speech he always gave when Welimo was out of work, 'I would do anything for you on account of your brother. He saved my life in the estate and I ain't never going to forget that.'

Welimo made his little expression of boredom which was to pinch the bridge of his nose.

'But you got to work sometimes!' Meta exploded. 'I do not get enough for two.'

Welimo grimaced, and did not let go the bridge of his nose because he knew this irritated Meta almost as much as his picking did, but Meta could not criticize him for just holding his nose, and that made him all the angrier.

'And you stay out of them arcades too,' Meta said to Welimo. 'Spending the money looking at them pictures,' Meta began. 'For the love of . . .' Suddenly Meta stopped short.

'For the love of what?' Welimo jumped him. He knew the reason that Meta did not finish the sentence with a swear word was he went now to the Jesus Saves Mission every night, and since he had got religion he had quit being quite so friendly to Welimo as before, cooler and more distant, and he talked, like today, about how good work is for everybody.

'That old man at the trucking office should have never told you had a low,' Meta returned to this difficulty of Welimo's finding work.

But this remark did not touch Welimo today.

'Meta,' Welimo said, 'I do not care about it.'

'You do not care!' Meta flared up.

'That is right,' Welimo said, and he got up and took out a piece of cigarette from his pants cuff, and lit a match to the stub. 'I do not believe in love,' Welimo said.

'Did you get that butt off the street?' Meta wanted to know, his protective manner making his voice soft again.

'I ain't answering that question,' Welimo told him.

'Welimo, why don't you be nice to me like you used to be,' Meta said.

'Why don't I be nice to you!' Welimo exclaimed with savagery.

Suddenly frightened, when Welimo suddenly acted too excited.

'You leave me alone,' Welimo said. 'I ain't interferin' with your life and don't you interfere with mine. The little life I have, that is.' He grunted.

'I owe something to you and that is why I cannot just let you be any old way you feel like being,' Meta replied.

'You always say you owe me on account of my brother saved your life just before he got himself blowed up.'

'Welimo, you be careful,' Meta warned, and his head twitched as he spoke.

'I am glad he is gone,' Welimo said but without the emotion he usually expressed when he spoke of his brother. He had talked against his brother so long in times past in order to get Meta riled up that it had lost nearly all meaning for both of them. 'Yes sir, I do not care,' Welimo repeated.

Meta opened his eyes wide then and looking straight at Welimo twisted his lips, trying not to let the swear words come out, and said: 'All right, Welimo,' after a long struggle.

'And if religion is going to make you close with your money,' Welimo began looking at Meta's mouth, 'close and mean, too, then I can clear out of here. I do not need you, Meta.'

'What put the idea into your head religion made me close with my money?' Meta said, and he turned very pale.

'You need me here, but you do not want to pay what it takes to keep me,' Welimo said.

Meta trembling walked over to Welimo very close and stared at him.

Welimo watched him, ready.

Meta said, 'You can stay here as long as you ever want to. And no questions asked.' Having said this, Meta turned away, a glassy look on his face, and stared at the cracked calcimine of their wall.

'On account of my old brother I can stay!' Welimo yelled.

'All right then!' Meta shouted back, but fear on his face. Then softening with a strange weakness he said, 'No, Welimo, that is not it either,' and he went over and put his arm on Welimo's shoulder.

'Do not touch me,' Welimo said. 'I do not want none of that brother love. Keep your distance.'

'You behave,' Meta said, struggling with his emotion.

'Ever since you give up women and drinking you been picking on me,' Welimo said. 'I do the best I can.'

Welimo waited for Meta to say something.

'And you think picking on me all the time makes you get a star in heaven, I suppose,' Welimo said weakly.

Meta, who was not listening, walked the length of the cramped little room. Because of the heat of the night and the heat of the discussion, he took off his shirt. On his chest was tattooed a crouched black panther, and on his right arm above his elbow a large unfolding flower.

'I did want to do right by you,' but immediately he had spoken, a scared look passed over his face.

Welimo suddenly went white. He moved over to the window.

'I cannot do no more for you!' Meta cried, alarmed but helpless at his own emotion. 'It ain't in me to do no more for you! Can't you see that, Welimo. Only so much, no more.'

When there was no answer from Welimo, Meta said, 'Do you hear what I say?'

Welimo did not speak.

'Fact is,' Meta began again, as though explaining now to himself, 'I do not seem to care about nothing. I just want somehow to sit and not move or do nothing. I do not know what it is.'

'You never did give a straw if I lived or died, Meta,' Welimo said, and he just managed to control his angry tears.

Meta was silent, as on the evenings when alone in the dark, while Welimo was out looking for a job, he had tried to figure out what he should do in his trouble.

'Fact is,' Welimo now whirled from the window, his eyes brimming with tears, 'it is all the other way around. I do not need you except for money, but you need me to tell you who you are.'

'What?' Meta said, thunderstruck.

'You know goddam well what,' Welimo said, and he wiped

the tears off his face with his fist. 'On account of you do not know who you are that's why.'

'You little crumb,' Meta began, and he moved threateningly, but then half remembering his nights at the Mission, he walked around the room, muttering.

'Where are my cigarettes?' Meta said suddenly. 'Did you take them?'

'I thought you swore off when you got religion,' Welimo said.

'Yeah,' Meta said in the tone of voice more like his old self, and he went up to Welimo, who was smoking another butt.

'Give me your smoke,' he said to Welimo.

Welimo passed it to him, staring.

'I do not think you heard what I said about leaving,' Welimo told Meta.

'I heard you,' Meta said.

'Well, I am going to leave you, Meta. God damn you.'

Meta just nodded from where he now sat on a crate they used as a chair. He groaned a little like the smoke was disagreeable for him.

'Like I say, Meta,' and Welimo's face was dry of tears now. 'It may be hard for me to earn money, but I know who I am. I may be dumb, but I am all together.'

'Welimo,' Meta said, sucking on the cigarette furiously. 'I did not mean for you to go. After all, there is a lot between us.'

Meta's fingers moved nervously over the last tiny fragment of the cigarette.

'Do you have any more smokes in your pants cuff or any-where?' Meta asked, as though he were the younger and the weaker of the two now.

'I have, but I do not think I should give any to a religious man,' Welimo replied. Meta tightened his mouth. Welimo handed him another of the butts.

'What are you going to offer me, if I do decide to stay,' Welimo said suddenly. 'On account of this time I am not going to stay if you do not give me an offer.' Meta stood up suddenly, dropping his cigarette, the smoke coming out of his mouth as though he had all gone to smoke inside himself.

'What am I going to offer you?' Meta said like a man in a dream. 'What?' he said sleepily.

Then waving arms, Meta cried, 'All right: Get out!' And suddenly letting go at last he struck Welimo across the mouth, bringing some blood. 'Now you git,' he said. 'Git out.'

Meta panted, walking around the room. 'You been bleedin' me white for a year. That is the reason I am the way I am. I am bled white.'

Welimo went mechanically to the bureau, took out a shirt, a pair of shorts, a toothbrush, his straight razor, and a small red box. He put these in a small bag such as an athlete might carry to his gym. He walked over to the door and went out.

Below on the sidewalk, directly under the room where he and Meta had lived together a year, Welimo stood waiting for the streetcar. He knew Meta was looking down on him. He did not have to wait long.

'Welimo,' Meta's voice came from the window. 'You get back here, Welimo, goddam you.' Meta hearing the first of his profanity let loose at last, swore a lot more then, as though he had found his mind again in swearing. A streetcar stopped at that moment.

'Do not get on that car, Welimo,' Meta cried. 'Goddam it.' Welimo affected impatience.

'You wait now, goddam you,' Meta said, putting on his rose-coloured shirt.

'Welimo,' Meta began when he was on the street beside his friend. 'Let us go somewhere and talk this over ... See how I am,' he pointed to his trembling arm.

'There ain't nowhere to go since you give up drinking,' Welimo told him.

Meta took Welimo's bag for him.

'Well if it makes you unhappy, I will drink with you,' Meta said.

'I do not mind being unhappy,' Welimo said, 'It is you that minds, Meta.'

'I want you to forgive me, Welimo,' Meta said, putting his hand on Welimo's arm.

Welimo allowed Meta's arm to rest there.

'Well, Meta,' Welimo said coldly.

'You see,' Meta began, pulling Welimo gently along with him as they walked toward a tavern. 'You see, I do not know what it is, Welimo, but you know everything.'

Welimo watched him.

They went into the tavern and although they usually sat at the bar, today they chose a table. They ordered beer.

'You see, Welimo, I have lied to you, I think, and you are right. Of course your brother did save my life, but you saved it again. I mean you saved it more. You saved me,' and he stretched out his trembling arm at Welimo.

Meta seeing the impassive look on Welimo's face did not care whether anybody heard him or not, he said: 'You are all I have got, Welimo.'

Welimo was going to say all right now, but Meta went on speaking frantically and fluently as he had never spoken before. 'You know ever since the war, I have been like I am ... And Welimo, I need you that is why ... I know you do not need me,' he nodded like an old man now. 'But I do not care now. I ain't proud no more about it.'

Meta stopped talking and a globule of spit rested thickly on his mouth.

'I am cured of being proud,' Welimo finally said, folding his arms and compressing his mouth.

'All right?' Meta said, perhaps not quite sure what it was Welimo meant. 'You can do anything you want, Welimo. All I need is to know you won't really run out. No matter what I might some day say or do, you stay, Welimo.'

'Then I do not want to hear no more about me getting just any old job,' Welimo said, drinking a swallow of beer.

'All right,' Meta said. 'All right, all right.'

'And you quit going to that old Mission and listening to that religious talk.'

Meta nodded again.

'And there ain't no reason we should give up drinking and all the rest of it at night.'

Meta agreed.

'Or women,' Welimo said, and he fumbled now with the

button of his shirt. It was such a very hot night his hand almost unconsciously pushed back the last button which had held his shirt together, exposing the section of his chest on which rested the tattooed drawing of a crouched black panther, the identical of Meta's.

'And I do not want to hear no more about me going to work at all for awhile,' Welimo was emphatic.

'All right, then,' Welimo took Meta's hand.

32

Amos Tutuola

Remember the Day After Tomorrow

Nigerian students doing African literature are frequently embarrassed by Tutuola's grammar. In a way they are right to be; he is very much the upstart crow in a continent where, unfortunately, the creator of literature in English is someone who has first imbibed the mellifluous sounds of 'approved' literature in the Honours degree syllabus.

Mercifully Tutuola was saved from this. He belongs to the generation of traditional artists. He knows how to tell a story, to amuse, to instruct. But he writes novels. His problem of shaping the traditional legends and tales has therefore not been an easy one, for he is not an anthropologist but the creator of a new kind of novel. The Yoruba cosmogony is re-created in his first novel, *The Palm Wine Drinkard*. One says re-created since, as he has pointed out to the editors of this anthology, the details are all there. But he has centred his story on a contemporary, who re-enacts the legends and the myths, and emerges at the end as a person, not an anonymous figure from folklore. This is Tutuola's most impressive contribution; in him the individual is refashioned from the anonymous figures of folklore land.

Remember the Day After Tomorrow

'Remember the day after tomorrow, my sons.' That was how the father, when he was alive, used to warn his two sons, Yaya and Shita, whenever they offended one who was older than them. But alas, the two boys did not understand what their old and weary father meant by that and they did not remember to ask the meaning of this proverb from him until he died.

'Perhaps, Remember the day after tomorrow is the name of our eldest brother who was born and had left our father for another town before we were born?' Yaya suggested one day to his young brother, Shita.

'And probably our father is just reminding us not to forget him!' Shita supported his brother, because both of them were puzzled about this warning.

At last, the two brothers put in minds that Remember the day after tomorrow was the name of their eldest brother who was born and had left their father for another town before they were born. But unfortunately, after a few years that their father had started to warn them like that continuously, he died and two months later their old mother died as well. Then these two boys began to take care of themselves but not as satisfactorily as when their father and mother were alive.

Their father and mother had hunchbacks before they died and so for Yaya and Shita. So for their strange hunchbacks the rest people in their town used to call them 'Hunchback family'.

After a year that their father and mother died, a strange man came to them in their father's house. The name of the strange man was Totofioko. Totofioko was an expert trickster and kidnapper of children. He was overhearing whenever the father of the two boys was warning them – 'Remember the day after tomorrow, my children.' He noticed as well that everyone of them had a hunch on the back. So, one day, he put a flat stone on his back in such a perfect way that the stone seemed exactly a real hunch when he wore big garments. After that he held a big suit case, a very costly umbrella, he put on costly shoes and then came to Yaya and Shita in their father's house and he met them as they sat down in the sitting room.

'Hello, my two junior brothers! (Totofioko entered the room and put down the costly umbrella, suit case, etc. which he held) I am very sorry to tell you now that this is the first time I ever came home since when both of you were born!' Totofioko explained to the two boys loudly and with a joyful voice immediately he entered the sitting room.

'Hello sir! Welcome sir! Please have a seat sir!' Yaya and Shita received Totofioko with great respect especially when they saw the costly garments which he wore and the costly suit case and umbrella in his hand.

'This is the cold water, sir!' Shita ran to the pot of water and brought the cold water. He knelt down with great respect as he was giving him the water.

Then Totofioko drank the water and rested for a few minutes. He asked from them as if he had not yet heard of the death of their father and mother – 'Where is your father?'

'Father? Our father had died over a year now,' Yaya and Shita explained at a time with sorrow.

'Could you remember that your father, before he died, was warning you that you must not forget – "Remember the day after tomorrow?"' Totofioko asked with grief.

'Oh, yes, our father used to warn us always before he died that we must remember – "Remember the day after tomorrow" and he told us also that "Remember the day after tomorrow" was coming home soon!' Shita hastily explained.

'Was that so? Good!' Totofioko asked and then paused for a few moments as he was raising his head up and down in a slow motion as if he was thinking seriously about the father's death.

'I confess to both of you now that I am your eldest brother, whose name your father, before he died, was mentioning to you always. And my name is "Remember the day after tomorrow" and I am before you today (Totofioko stood up and posed himself before the two boys for a few minutes and then sat back). I was born and went to another town before both of you were born, therefore both of you are my junior brothers because your father was my father as well. So I come to stay with you and I shall be taking great care of you as well as our father did before he died. Even to make it clearer to you that I am your eldest brother the first born of our father, look at my hunchback, how it resembles that of your own (Totofioko stood up and showed them his own false hunchback and then sat back). Of course, it is bigger than your own, and that must be so, because I am older than you!' Totofioko, with his trick, persuaded the two boys in such a way that they admitted at the same time that he was their eldest brother.

'Hah-a-a! this is our eldest brother whose name is "Remember the day after tomorrow".' Yaya and Shita embraced Totofioko with gladness for they admitted that he was their eldest brother.

'By the way, where is your mother who is my mother as well?' Totofioko asked loudly with trick.

'She died just a few months after our father's death,' the two boys replied with sorrow.

'Hoo-hoo-hoo!' Totofioko, with his trick, having heard like that from the town boys. He covered the head with both palms and wept bitterly for a few minutes. But he did all this just to deceive the two boys.

'Hah! Stop weeping, brother! What are you doing all that for! Stop that, sir!' the two boys caressed Totofioko until he stopped to weep. Then he stood up. He walked up and down the house. He peeped to every room just to know the kind of property which were inside them.

'I am glad, all the property in the rooms are precious enough to be carried away to my town,' Totofioko thought in his mind before he came back to the sitting room where the boys were preparing food. He and the boys ate it together.

After a few days that Totofioko was with them as their brother, one morning, he told them, 'Yes, as both of you aware that only the eldest brother or the eldest person in the family used to be in charge of all the property of their dead father, etc.

Therefore, I want you to gather all of our father's property together and bring them before me now. But instead to share them now, I shall keep them in one of the rooms. I shall lock up the room and keep the key for myself!' Totofioko deceived the two boys.

'You are quite right to do so, sir! And you are the right person in our family to do that!' Yaya and Shita exclaimed with gladness. Then they gathered all of their father's and mother's property together and brought them to him. He put them in one of the rooms. He locked up the door of that room and kept the key in his pocket. Because in fact, it was the eldest person in the family had the right to keep the property of their dead father, etc.

In the mid-night, when Totofioko noticed that the boys had slept deeply, he opened the door of that room. He took out all of the property, he carried them to his own town which was far off and then he came back before daybreak. But the two boys did not aware that their inherited property had already gone to Totofioko's town.

Having spent a few days with them, he advised the two boys – 'I believe things are too dull in this town. So I shall take both of you to the town where I came to you. You will be working in that town and earning a large sum of money. I believe, in one year's time, every one of you will become a rich man. Out of your savings, you will marry beautiful ladies and after that you will come back to this town to enjoy your lives as you like!' Totofioko deceived Yaya and Shita just to take them to his town as well and sell them as slaves.

'Thank you, brother, for your useful advice. But who will be taking care of our property after we have gone away with you?' Yaya and Shita asked with surprise.

'Never mind about our property, my junior brothers, and you should not be afraid, there is no any thief who can break into the room to pack the property away. Now, look at this juju (Totofioko showed them one wrapped leaf) which I am going to hang on the main door now. Its work is to keep all thieves away from this house!' Totofioko stood up, he went to the main door and hung the wrapped leaf on the main door.

Then in the following morning, they followed Totofioko to

his town and on their presence, he sold all of their father's and mother's property to an auctioneer.

'Ah, these are our inherited property! Don't sell them to the auctioneer!' Yaya and Shita shouted greatly when it revealed to them that Totofioko had carried their property to his town and that he wanted to sell them.

'Shut up your mouths there! Or don't you know whom you are talking to?' Totofioko boomed on the two boys and also struck their mouths with a stick.

'Don't harsh to us like this! Please remember that you have confessed to us that you are our eldest brother whose name is – "Remember the day after tomorrow",' Yaya reminded him with due respect.

'Who is your brother! Tell me now! Who is your brother?' Totofioko shouted terribly on them. So terribly that Yaya and Shita could not talk out again.

'I am afraid, everything has changed now!' Shita whispered to Yaya.

In the following morning, Totofioko sold the poor boys to the slave buyer and it was that time it was revealed to Yaya and Shita that Totofioko was not their brother in any way but he was an expert trickster, deceiver, thief and kidnapper of children.

One morning, as Yaya and Shita were tilling the ground in the front of the house of the slave-buyer who brought them, Totofioko who had well dressed in costly garments, came to them and then he proudly told them – 'I am sorry that it is too late before you do understand that "Remember the day after tomorrow" is not the name of a person but it is a warning. And it should have been better for you if you have asked the meaning of it from your father before he died. So there would not a deceiver like myself who would be able to deceive you like this. And it is also a good practice for a young boy who does not understand a warning, proverb, etc. to ask for its full meaning before it it too late!' Totofioko explained to Yaya and Shita with pride and then hastily went away as they were weeping bitterly.

33

Edward Babatunde Horatio-Jones

Mourner's Progress

This piece by the Nigerian writer Edward Babatunde Horatio-Jones represents, we feel, the direction in which African literature is likely to travel – towards concern with the individual. Too much recent writing has been confused, blurring the distinctions between oral concerns with community and written self-interest in the creator. This has meant that, in large measure, African literature lacks the privacy that one has come to associate with other literatures. Throughout this piece, however, the 'I' stands out; the girl and the dead mother live on the farther side of the narrator's consciousness. The end is significant; the internal gropings of the 'I' temporarily agree to give way before the external rituals of 'them'.

Mourner's Progress

... The face of the bush changed and the sky clapped into a satanic torrent of heat that tapped the leaves on the trees. When we got to her house, I sat down and let my things drop beside me, it ebbed into spots of water and then like a mighty ocean the tide of perspiration on my brows settled on my wrinkled forehead, and then like on the bus, I tasted the salty water on my lips. My clothes were pasted to my body and the silk shirt felt funny on my back, I would have liked to have taken my clothes off immediately, I wanted to make sure of my surroundings by trying to feel things, she was in the kitchen and when she came back to me, her eyes lit into mine, I was taken aback with fear, I asked her her name, but she shoved my request off, and with a shrug of her lips oozed out a name that sounded like Laka ... it was simple, but for no reason in my particular state, I couldn't get myself to repeat the name immediately, maybe it was the shortness of the name and also the meaning, it carried all that is eerie in Africa, and then it was a name that could not be repeated without thinking of death, it was the first time that the word death meant something to me, (it was not fear but a kind of dread, something that only the African could understand, for the white man, living in a different world, would not be able to race with the fantastic myriads of the black mind.) Laka is a dreaded city which had played a fantastic role in our youth, everybody could feel it creeping on, and it is bound to arrive sometime or other, I was busy playing with the meaning of the word in my mind, and like she had always done, her little body appeared in front of me, she wanted to take my clothes off, in fact it was like a command which I didn't bother to question, when she asked me to take my clothes off, I was thinking about the funeral, her husky voice hushed my inquiring mind.

'Don't worry about anything,' she said.

I picked my head to look at her but her reclining back and my clothes dangled in her hands, and what was funny, my bow-tie was trailing on the ground attached to the sleeve of my shirt.

It must have been sometime after we were able to speak, as a matter of fact all the talking was done by me, not that I was forced to, but there are times when talking could mean a lot even though it might mean nothing to anybody, and she was there playing the part of a reluctant audience, I continued getting steam of my chest that way, my clothes had been unbearable, not that they were on my body but the fact that I knew they were mine and then drying somewhere, the fibre being sucked somewhere by some infernal steam, possibly the steam coming out of my chest, I would have to ask her to lend me a *boubou* to go to mother's funeral, but I have never worn one, and I couldn't figure my long arms slung in one of them, it would have been awful, and then it occurred to me how silly it would have been, I had never worn one of these gowns before; you can't go to your aunt's funeral anyhow in brown shoes so it dawned on me that it would be impossible to go to mother's funeral naked, as far as I know I wasn't going to put on any *boubou* ... and that's that, I decided. I wasn't aware of her absence, and when I opened my eyes, I was almost blinded by the steaming bowl of soup she held in front of my face, I couldn't complain because that came as a relief, I gulped everything down voluptuously, and then passed my tongue on the bones, I couldn't tell what sort of meat, one thing I knew was that it wasn't the usual beef of a cow, but why bother, Africa is full of a variety of carcasses, as I was still naked I couldn't wipe my hands, my handkerchief being left in my trousers pocket, but this didn't bother me at all as she fetched me a bowl of water into which she dipped both my hands and then wiped them in a linen, she handed me a bowl of palm-wine, and then watched me drink the calabash dry, yes ... it was no ordinary kind of palm-wine, it was the sweet type tapped from the trees that lined the Rokel across the Guinea. I licked my lips like a dog, and then sucked my teeth in contentment. It occurred to me that I wasn't the only one in the room, other voices than mine multiplied into the crevices of my environment, the fact of being naked made me take offence at my surroundings, it must have been a kind of forethought for her, she was always appearing and disappearing, just when I began to decipher myself. This time she caught me standing by the window; I was able to watch the clear sky, blue in patches and then with a vague grey shawl hung towards the West ... the West never interested me, I was brought up in the East, not that I didn't know the West, but I had no use for the type of people one would come across in that particular part of town, they could be good people but they never impressed me. The blue on the ceiling of the sky was still there, tender like the innocence of a baby; her hand pulled me back into the centre of the room ... my nudity was now taken as a common thing, and funny as it appeared, it never bothered me, her arm dropped to my penis, I made a click with my tongue which must have frightened her, she wanted to know if I was being hurt or rather to put it in her way of speaking ... I couldn't reply and then she wanted to know if I had ever been with a woman, she wasn't being personal. I expect women talk like that because Marie once asked me the same question. Yes ... I said. But she cut me short before the words could hardly touch the cool wind that was coming to us from the window.

'You don't have to say,' she said. 'The way you jumped when a woman touched you frightened me.' Then she looked into the winking stars that floated in the sky and the thumps of the distant drums drifted into the room, and then inaudibly dissolved into my erected nakedness. And then she told me that she had fetched me to her place for that ... but now she was looking straight into my eyes when she let me know that whatever intention she had, had been flayed away, I didn't bother because I knew very well it was just a ruse, and then she added, 'You are going to kill me, I could feel it.' She couldn't take her eyes off my person. I laughed. 'You shouldn't laugh ... you could kill a woman ... you could.' I took this as an insult, customarily insults never interested me. I ignored her for a while, and then she wanted to know if I would want my clothes now, but I didn't answer, and my entire self swayed under her bluff,

I was sort of trying to make up my mind whether I should ask her for my clothes, her hands fell again on my heavy shoulders, the boldness and the mystery that had shrouded her smothered into the ordinary weakness of age against youth, the sensibility of my body awoke in her a death ... if it must be; we lay on the bed for a while.

I could hear her voice, she whispered into my ears, but I couldn't make out what she was trying to say as that didn't interest me.

'You mustn't kill me yet ... ' she said, but this didn't bother me. Then she wanted to know if I was human, or if she had done the impossible in picking the devil himself, but I told her not to be superstitious, as I know too damn well myself that there was mystery about my being. I decided to continue but something which struck me, drove an iciness through me, I thought that she had died, I jumped down on to the floor and then watched her chest heaving, her eyes shone in the darkness, I picked my clothes as it was time I left. I fixed my bow-tie and then shoved my mourning band on ... smoothing the wrinkles on my sleeve.

'I want you to stay,' she said. I don't like jokers and they never meant anything to me, and what's more, I wasn't going to answer but something human forced me to open my mouth, I told her that even though I wouldn't think of that I still had something important to do. Yes, I said, there is a chance of your seeing me again, but this was as absurd as our relation and it was much more fleeting than the sound of my voice. This was a kind of condescension because mother had that funny habit of reminding me of her present state, her cold body lying there in my imagination was something pleasant to me, it was the ice-coldness of something wrapped in the essence of the absolute ... that is the breaking of the dark mask. If it had been my father then there wouldn't be the point of my going to the strain of thinking that he should be buried, she was the incarnation of all for me and the fact that she lay there was something wonderful, it soon came on me that my love for her was too deeply dyed to think of another delay, and the ideas of all these petty delays had been deliberate, for her to be with me in this world; well; and anyone else sharing the same sensation would invoke in me a kind of bloody anger. 'Yes' ... I said, brushing the creases off my sleeve; she was there lying cold, breathing with the wind, non-existent; left me in solitude with my eyes opened to the windows of the world and deaf to the clutches of time, and to my essence. For no just reason my ideas suddenly became catholic, I never thought much of those people, my logical existence was counted by me. Laka unfolded her legs and then the softness of the inside of her hand rustled on my face. She reechoed her desire to see me once more, I was rather reticent, but then she soon added that if she felt much better, she'd meet me in the Home by the afternoon and then she would accompany us to the cemetery. This was an impertinence that I wouldn't invite, I politely told her that it wouldn't be nice for her to come to mother's funeral, she buried her head on the pillows, but I soon added that the warden and my aunt would bother since it was a family affair, and as far as my decision goes, the fact that she didn't know my mother, it would be most impolite to come, she became adamant, she limped forward and asked me not to speak like that.

When I stepped on the verandah, she held on to my arm, I released her grip on me and then passed my arm on my sleeve as I kept on doing reflectively. The broken pavement on the pathway opened into the rugged bush-path; she stood on the porch and the stars lit her burnt-ebony face, her hands held out in the twilight of the night.

34

Ezekiel Mphahlele

A Ballad of Oyo

This piece by Ezekiel Mphahlele exhibits none of the racial concern that imbues so much of his other short stories and his autobiographical *Down Second Avenue*. It is also a 'curiosity' piece because the author, a South African, just about manages to reach beyond the surface of Nigerian life. He is so much an expatriate that he takes an obvious delight in showing off the superficialities – a Yoruba word in one case, in another the explanation of a name.

There are two voices here – that of a fairly straightforward writer of prose and that of someone exulting in the dialogue which he is re-capturing. (Incidentally, Yoruba market women do not speak Pidgin, but it seems churlish to push this.) The two voices are never merged, perhaps intentionally so. The commentator stands outside it all. Does this, one wonders, explode the theory that there is an underlying unity in African literature, or does it exhibit still another aspect of the variety?

A Ballad of Oyo

Ishola (also called Mama-Tunji because her first son was Tunji) found a tramp on her counter slab at Oyo's central market, where she took her stand each day to sell vegetables and fruit. Furiously she poked the grimy bundle with a broom to tell him a few things he had better hear: there are several other places where he could sleep; she sells food off this counter, not fire-wood – like him; so he thought to lie on a cool slab on a hot night, eh? – why does he not sleep under a running tap? And so on. With a sense of revulsion she washed the counter.

These days, when market day began, it also meant that Ishola was going to have to listen to her elder sister's endless prattling during which she spun words and words about the younger sister's being a fool to keep a useless husband like Balogun in food and clothing. Off and on, for three months, Ishola had tried to fight against the decision to tell Balogun to go look for another wife while she went her own way. Oh, why did her sister have to blabber like this? Did her sister think that she, Ishola, likes being kicked about by her man the way Balogun did? Her sister might well go on like this, but she could not divine the burning questions that churned inside Ishola.

That is right Ishola, her sister, who sold rice next to her, would say. You are everybody's fool are you not? Lie still like that and let him come and sit and play drums on you and go off and get drunk on palm wine come back and beat you scatter the children – children of his palm wine-stained blood (spitting) like a hawk landing among chicks then you have no one to blame, only your stupid head (pushing her other breast forcibly into her baby's mouth for emphasis). How long has he been giving you so much pain like this? How long are you going to try to clean a pig that goes back into the mud? You are going to eat grass very soon you will tell me and do not keep complaining to me about his ways if my advice means nothing to you.

And so goes the story of Ishola, Ishola who was called Mama-Tunji, a mother of three children. Slender, dark-and-smooth-skin with piercing eyes that must have seen through dark nights.

Day and night the women of Oyo walk the black road, the road of tarmac to and from the market. They can be seen walking riding the dawn, walking into sunrise; figures can be seen, slender as twilight; their feet feel every inch of the tarmac, but their wares press down on the head and the neck takes the strain, while the hip and legs propel the body forward. A woman here, a woman there in the drove has her arm raised in a loop, a loop of endurance, to support the load, while the other arm holds a suckling child in a loop, a loop of love. They must walk fast, almost in a trot, so that they may not feel the pain of the weight so much.

The week before the week before Mama-Jimi started for Oyo Market, her body feeling the seed of another child grow that had not yet begun to give her sweet torment, bitter ecstasy in the stomach. The night before her husband had told her he was going to the north to see his other wives. He would come back – when? When he was full of them and they of him, Mama-Jimi knew. When he should have made sure that the small trade each was doing went well he said.

Mama-Jimi looked at his shadow quivering on the wall in the light of the oil lamp as he stooped over her, and loneliness swept over her in a flood. They loved and they remained a promontory rising above the flood. And Mama-Tunji again took her place in the order of things: one of three wives giving all of her to one she loved and taking what was given by her man with a glad heart. Oyo will always be Oyo whatever happens to it the market will always be there, come rain, come blood, come malaria.

It was the week before only the week before when the rain caught the market women on the tarmac to market. The sky burst and the rain came down with power. It rumbled down the road in rivulets. Mama-Jimi felt the load inside became heavy knotting up beneath her navel. Her feet became heavy, the hips failed to twist. But she tried to push on. She could see the others away ahead through the grey of the rain. Mama-Jimi's thoughts were on the market of Oyo: she must reach it. For if she should fall, she thought, or feel sicker other women were there.

But the woman sagged and fell and dragged herself out of the road. She felt the blood oozing, warm and cold. A life was running out of her, she was sure of it. A life dead just as soon as born and sprouting in her ...

Two women found her body on the roadside: cold, wet.

Whispers bounced and rebounced at the market that Mama-Jimi was dead, dead, Mama-Jimi was gone, gone in the rain.

Did she know it was there? Ehe, she did she told me so. And her man gone to the north, a-ah? So it is said. Are they going to call him? They must. Only yesterday night we were together and she was glad she was going to give her man a second child.

To die when your people are far far away from you, a-ah! We are most of us strangers here. It is true.

This was a week before, and the market at Oyo jingles and buzzes and groans, but it goes on as it has done for many years before when the first Alafin came here.

You know what the market is like every morning, not so? Babbling tongues, angry tongues, silent tongues. Down there a woman was suckling a baby while she sold. Near to Ishola a woman was eating *gari* and *okaran* and gravy out of a coloured enamel bowl. Someone else next to her handled her sales for her. As the heat mounted a lad was pouring water on bunches of lettuce to keep them from wilting and thus refusing to be sold. But the lad seemed to be wilting himself, because as soon as he leaned back against a pole, sleep seized him and his head tilted back helplessly like a man having a shave in a barber's chair.

The mouth opened and the lettuce lost its importance for a while. Mostly *oyingbo* – white people – came to buy lettuce. On and off while he slept, someone sprinkled water on his face. This seldom jolted him out of his stupor. He merely ran his hand over his face, stared at the lettuce and then poured water on it. Some fat women opposite Ishola's counter were shouting and one seldom knew whether they were angry or simply zealous. They also splashed water over the pork they were selling so as to keep away blue flies that insisted on sitting on it. All the would-be buyers who stood at the pork counter fingered the pieces: they lifted them up, turned them round, put them back, picked them up again. There was no exchange of smiles here.

Ten shillings, said the pork woman who herself seemed to have been wallowing in grease.

Four shillings, suggested the customer.

Eight shillings last.

Five (taking it and putting it back as if disgusted).

Seven las' price.

With a long-drawn sound between the teeth to signify disgust, the customer left. The pork woman looked at her fellow-vendor, as if to say stupid customers!

Oyingbo women did not buy meat at these markets. They said they were appalled by the number of hands that clutched at it. They bought imported meat in the provision stores at prices fixed seemingly to annoy expatriates. One missionary woman had been known to bring a scale for the vendor to weigh the meat in order to get her money's worth. What! she had exclaimed, you don't weigh meat in this market? Ridiculous! The meat woman had looked baffled. The next time the missionary brought her own balance. This time *they* thought something was ridiculous, and they laughed to show it. Even after weighing a piece, she found that she still had to haggle and bargain. Enthusiasm had flagged on her part, and after this, she only came to the market to rescue some of the lettuce and parsley from continual drenching and to buy fruit.

So did the other white women. One of them turned round in answer to a shout from a vendor, Custamah, custamah! She approached Ishola's counter where there were heaps of carrots and tomatoes. She was smiling, as one is expected to do from behind a counter.

Nice car-*rot* madam,

How much?

Shilling (picking up a bunch)

Sixpence.

No madam, shilling (smiling)

Sixpence.

Ha-much madam wan' pay? (with no smile)

All right, seven pence.

Ni'pence.

Seven?

No 'gree madam (smiling)

The customer realized that she had come to the end of the road. She yielded, but not before saying Ninepence is too much for these.

A-ah madam. If not to say madam she buy for me many times I coul' 'ave took more moni for you.

Towards sunset Ishola packed up. She had made up her mind to go to Baba Dejo, the president of the court of the local authority. She firmly believed that the old man had taken a bribe. Either her father-in-law or Balogun himself, her delinquent husband could have offered it. This, she believed, must be the reason why the court could not hold a hearing of her case against her husband. Twice Ishola had asked him to hear her case. Each time the old man said something to delay it: The old fox, she thought. This time, she fixed simply on putting five pounds in front of the president. He cannot refuse so much money, Ishola thought. But go back to that animal of a husband, never – no more, he is going to kill me one of these days I do not want to die I do not want to die for nothing I want to work for my children I want to send them to school I do not want them to grow old on the market place and die counting money and finding none. Baba Dejo must take the money he must listen to my case and let the law tell Balogun to leave me alone with the children and go his way I will go mine I know his father has gone and bribed him to keep the matter out of the court and why? – because he does not want to lose his son's children and because – I do not know he is very fond of me he has always stood up for me against his son – yes he loves me but I am married to his son not to him and his love does not cure his son's self-made madness. Lijadu loves me and I want him let my heart burst into many pieces if he does not take me as his wife I want him because he has such a pure heart.

Ishola was thinking of the day Lijadu came to fetch her in his car and they went to Ijebude for that weekend of love and heartbreaks: heartbreaks because she was someone else's wife someone who did not care for her and even then had gone to Warri without telling her. Now Lijadu was ready to give Balogun the equivalent of the bride price he had paid to Ishola's parents and so release her to become his wife. Balogun and his father had refused Lijadu's money.

Just what irritates me so, Ishola thought. I could burst into a hundred parts so much it fills me with anger. So they want to stop me from leaving their useless son, useless like dry leaves falling from a tree. Just this makes me mad and I feel I want to stand in the middle of the road and shout so as everyone can hear me. That man! – live with him again? He beats me he leaves me no money he grows fat on my money he does not care for the children the children of his own blood from his very own hanging things . . .

I wonder how much the old man will want? The thought flashed across Ishola's mind, like a streak of lightning that rips across the milling clouds, illuminating the sky's commotion all the more.

If your father-in-law Mushin were not my friend, says the president of the court, Dejo, when Ishola tells him the business of her visit, I should not let you come and speak to me on a matter like this. It is to be spoken in court only.

You do not want me to bring it to court, sir.

I would do it if, if –

How much, sir?

Give me what you have, my daughter. He looks disdainful in the face as he says so. It does not please the young woman. He takes five pounds in paper money from her hand.

What is this I hear from your father-in-law, that you want to leave your husband? Ishola feels resentful at the thought that her case must have been chewed dead by these old men. But she presses the lid hard to keep her feelings from bubbling over. I beg that you listen, sir, she says. Balogun beats me he does not work he eats and sleeps he does not care for the children of his own-own blood, sir, he drinks too much palm wine this is too much I have had a long heart to carry him so far but this is the end of everything no no this is all I can carry.

Is he a man in bed?

Not when he is drunk and that is many times, sir. She was looking at the floor at this time.

Hm, that is bad, that is bad, my child, that is bad. What does he say when you talk to him about his ways?

Nothing, sir. He just listens, he listens and just listens, that is all.

A man has strange ways and strange thoughts.

There is silence.

So he drinks himself stupid. I know there are certain places in Oyo where you can hear the name of Balogun spoken as if he were something that smells very bad. So he drinks himself stupid until he is too flabby to do his work in bed, a-ah! How many children have you, by the way.

Three, sir,

The youngest is how old?

Two years, sir.

If a man gets too drunk to hoe a field another man will and he shall regret, he will see. He seems to be talking to himself: But a man who comes home only as a he-goat on heat, the old man continues, and not as a helper and father is useless. I will tell him that, I will tell Balogun that myself. Animals look for food for their mates and their brood, why cannot a man?

You have talked to him twice before, sir.

Oh yes oh yes I have my child I know.

Silence.

But your father-in-law Mushin loves you so much so much, my child.

I love him too but I am his son's wife, not his.

You speak the truth there.

Silence.

It would break his heart all the same. Look at it whichever

way you like. You fill a space left in his heart by the death of his wife and often defiled by the deeds of a worthless son.

Dejo's face is one deep shadow of gravity.

I do not like that boy Balogun not one little moment he goes on, but his father will weep because he holds you like his own-own daughter.

Ishola's head is full of noises and echoes of noises, for she has heard all this a few times before. She has determined her course and she shall not allow her tender sentiments to take her out of it, she mustn't, no, not now. Perhaps after, when tender feelings will be pointless. She still bears a little love for Balogun, but she wants her heart to be like a boulder so as not to give way.

Let me go and call my wife to talk with you more about this, Old Dejo says as he leaves the room. As he does so, he stretches out his hand to place a few crumpled notes of money in Ishola's hand, whispering Your heart is kind, my child, it is enough that you showed the heart to give, so take it back.

Ishola feels a warm and cold air sweep over and through her. She trembles a little and she feels as if something were dangling in space and must fall soon.

Old Dejo's wife enters, round-bellied: the very presence of life's huge expectation.

But – such an old man! Ishola thinks . . .

I can see it in her eyes Balogun I can see it in her eyes, Mushin said in his son's house one morning. Ishola is going to leave us.

She is at the market now, Papa. She loves me too much to do a foolish thing like that.

When are you going to wake up you useless boy. He gasped, as he had often done before. What kind of creature was given me for a son! What does your mother say from the other world to see you like this!

Balogun poured himself palm wine and drank and drank and drank.

I can see the blade of a cutlass coming to slash at my heart, the older man said, I can feel it coming.

Go and rest father, you are tired.

And Balogun walked out into the blazing shimmering sun, stopped to buy cigarettes at a small stall on the roadside and walked on, the very picture of aimlessness.

When are you going to stop fooling like this with Balogun I ask you? Ishola's sister said rasping out as she sat behind her counter. Her baby who was suckling looked up into her face with slight but mute concern in its eyes.

She does not know she does not know this woman she will never know she will never know what I am made of ...

I would never allow a man to come stinking of drink near me in the blankets (spitting). I told you long ago to go to court and each time you allow that old Dejo with his fat wife to talk you out of it. Are you a daughter of my father?

Oh what a tiresome tongue sister has ... You wait you, you just wait ...

Just a black drunken swine that is what he is. A swine is even better because it can look for rubbish to eat. Balogun does not know what people are he would not go a long way with me no he would not he does not know people. Eat sleep and lay a pile of dung eat sleep and lay a pile of dung while men of his age group are working: the woman who gave birth to that man! ...

Sister! Leave that poor woman to lie quiet in her grave!

I will but not that wine-bloated creature called Balogun.

Lijadu must not forget to send Mushin's money of the bride-price ...

That piece of pork? a customer asked.

Ten shillings.

Five.

Nine.

Six.

No 'gree.

Six and six.

No 'gree. Eight. Las' price.

Seven.

No 'gree.

And the market roar and chatter and laughter and exclamations and smells put together seemed to be a live symphony quite independent of the people milling around.

Black shit! Ishola's sister carried on ...

Ishola was out of Oyo in the evening, going towards Oshogbo with her three children. Lijadu would follow the next day and join them in a small village thirty miles out so as to make pursuit fruitless. Lijadu joined her at noon the next day, looking pale and blue and shaken.

What is it with you Lijadu? Why are you so pale? Are you sick?

Silence.

Lijadu what is it?

He sat on the ground and said Mushin has passed away. He passed away about midnight. One of the neighbours found him lying cold in the passage. People say they heard him cry the last time: Ishola, my grandchildren!

At break of day each morning you will see the women of Oyo with their baskets on their heads. You can see them on the black tarmac going to the market, their bodies twisting at the hip the strong hip. You can see their feet feel their way on the dark tarmac as they ride the dawn, riding into daylight. The figures are slender as twilight. You can see Ishola, too, because she came back, came back to us. She told us that when she heard of the death of her father-in-law she thought This is not good for my future life with Lijadu I will go back to that cripple ...

35

Luis Bernardo Honwana

The Old Woman

There are few African prose writers in Portuguese. The urgency of the poem recommends itself more to writers confronting colonialism and the poverty of plantation workers, the aggressions of Portuguese overseers and the dismay of the defeated. It seemed to us that the best writers in translation were Castro Soromenho, a Portuguese born in Africa and the only white writer represented in these pages, and Oscar Ribas, a blind mulatto who has not written a great deal. More recently short stories have begun to appear from a young writer, Luis Bernardo Honwana. Honwana differs in that his work has a larger and, we believe, more universal appeal. His world is that of youth experiencing the break-up of its innocence, the loss of youth representing the loss of faith in a world where all efforts crumble.

The Old Woman

I swear I never really lost consciousness, although just before falling down I experienced that slowing-down of sensations which, when it seizes us, restricts our capacity for self defence to those purely instinctive and stupidly slow gestures we all recognize in a groggy boxer. I think no one could estimate the tremendous effort I made in those long or perhaps brief moments to control my fists – brutally heavy before they regained movement, and floundering unbelievably after I raised them. Meanwhile, the blows I was receiving produced no corresponding physical sensation, because I was aware of them only through a fading echo slowly reverberating through my head. This cursed echo, and it alone, was responsible for my fall – for it confused me terribly, making me force myself to think of lifting my arm before I could lift it. I fell slowly, fully conscious that I was falling.

At first I felt a certain relief to be lying down, although the echo continued to fill my head. When I opened my eyes the buzzing started, and I was furious with myself for having fallen. The echo was affecting my sight so much that I wasn't at all sure what I saw, but afterwards when my eyes stopped trembling I became aware of the two darkly clad legs, stiff and tense, straddling my body, stretching way up, and converging on to the shining metal plaque of the belt. Above them, far above, close to the lamp on the ceiling, the face stared at me attentively, smiling with satisfaction. I closed my eyes again. I felt myself trembling, but the echo was easier to bear because it had ceased its disordered jumbling and resolved itself into a sort of regular throbbing. I only opened my eyes when I was sure he had gone away, fully satisfied with proving to everybody that he had hit me.

Luis Bernardo Honwana

I needed to go home. I think I already felt like going there even before I went into the bar, so really what had happened there wasn't the reason for my wanting so much to go home. I hadn't seen the old woman and the children for I don't know how long, because lately I'd been going home very late and leaving very early, but I still wasn't quite sure if I wanted to see them again. The old woman was so dull, and the children were such a nuisance with their constant squabbling and clamouring for attention. Of course this was nothing compared with what happened in the bar just now, and in all the other bars, restaurants, cinema foyers and those places where everybody eyed me strangely, as if they repudiated something in me – something queer, ridiculous, exotic: Heaven knows what else. They made me sick! And I having to restrain myself from exploding precisely for the sake of the wretched old woman and the snivelling kids!

That in the bar just now was really what had been happening all along. I didn't manage to hit the fellow because he was all the others, and it was exactly as such that he hit me. Let's face it – they're all the same. Even those who try to pretend that they are not like the others are only different on neutral ground, or only when they need me, because they too surround themselves with walls of taboos, and defend themselves with the same nauseous, nauseating stares against anyone who goes beyond those walls. And I should know!

I needed to go home. I would eat rice and peanut curry as they wanted me to, but not to fill my stomach. I needed to go home to fill my ears with screams, my eyes with misery and my conscience with rice and peanut curry.

Sitting on the straw mat, the old woman was quietly watching the children eat. Now and then one of them would get up and bring the aluminium plate for her to serve another helping. It was at one of those intervals that the old woman noticed me. She had the wooden spoon stretched out, filled with rice, and she was going to empty it on to the plate, when she seemed to remember something and turned towards the door. As soon as she saw me she glanced down to the bottom of the pot, and asked me if I wanted something to eat.

'I don't know yet whether I want to eat or not,' I replied.

She turned towards the fire, and waited some time with the ladle in the air, looking at the flames.

'Are you angry? Are you so angry that you can't eat, and don't even know whether you want to eat or not?'

'No, I'm not angry.'

The old woman thought for quite a long time, then muttered, 'Well, then that's all right, if you're not angry.'

While she was saying this she turned towards the child, so she asked him, as if this was more important to her than anything else:

'Quito! What's that you're chewing and chewing all the time, Quito?'

Before he could empty his mouth to reply, Khatidya yelled from the other end of the room:

'That Quito's chewing the meat he stole from my plate while I wasn't looking. It's mine, Mama! *Chi!* Quito, you're a thief!' And she turned to me, 'It's mine, I'm telling you, brother!'

Quito held out his hand to show what he had taken out of his mouth, and said indignantly,

'This meat, Kati, this here? It's the meat Mama gave me, I'm telling you.' And to me, 'Didn't she, brother?'

By this time they had already started a disgusting row, and the old woman took control.

'Shhh.'

They all stopped at once, except for Khatidya, who still whined,

'It's mine. It's mine, he stole it. *Chi!* Quito, you should be ashamed of yourself, I saw you.'

But the other children helped the old woman.

'Shhh.'

Khatidya turned to them, 'Shhh.' And they all started to hiss as loud as they could.

With the wooden spoon still raised, the old woman watched them all. Then the children got tired of their nonsense and began eating: and Quito put back the food he had spat out into his hand. Only then did the old woman put a spoonful of food on to Quito's plate. Before giving him curry she thought a while and served him spoonful after spoonful of rice. When the children went away, she asked me, distractedly,

'But is it true you don't know whether you want to eat or not?'

'Well, and supposing I did want to?' Heavens! This insistence was irritating me!

The old woman seemed to be upset. She gazed at the bottom of the pot and smiled at me apologetically.

'All that's left is *ucoco*!'

From the other end the children started to comment, '*Chi! Ucoco!*' Quito said, 'Shhh!' and they all hissed again. The old woman shouted at them and they went on eating.

'So why do you keep on asking me if I want to eat – anyway, what are you going to eat?'

'I'm not hungry,' the old woman replied.

'But there's no more food, isn't that it?'

'I'm not hungry, I'm not, really I'm not. But if you like I'll make some tea in a second. Would you like some?'

'I'm not hungry either.'

'Well, then I'll make some tea for the children in case they're still hungry after they've eaten.'

Then I could no longer resist the impulse to embrace the old woman. She remained quite still while I buried my head between her breasts. Laughing nervously, she protested,

'But you don't usually do this ...' And she continued to laugh until she had the courage to embrace me.

'My son ...'

I felt her rough fingers timidly caressing my face.

Then she kissed me and laughed a lot.

I heard the children laughing too.

'You're not usually like this! What's happened to you? My son ... my son ... Are you hungry? Shall I make you some tea?'

I hadn't heard that tone of voice for I don't know how long, and perhaps I didn't remember ever having heard it.

'Did they hit you? Tell me, my son, did they hit you? Who was it?'

'No, they didn't hit me.'

'But they did something to you, didn't they, my son? You're angry with them aren't you? ...'

I tried not to speak, but I had no time to think. 'They've destroyed everything ... they've stolen ... they don't want ...'

I felt her catch her breath and stiffen slightly. 'Don't you want to tell me? Don't you? Don't you?'

'It's no use.'

The children drew nearer, 'Tell us, tell us.'

'No, I won't, you'll have to grow up first ... Don't be a nuisance now.'

'Yes, my son, there's time, there's time ... Everything will change, everything will be better, and when they're grown up ...'

'They'll grow up all right ... They'll have to grow up in all this ...'

'Do you really not want to tell?'

'Tell us, tell us!' The children gathered around us on the straw mat.

No, I wouldn't tell them. It wasn't for this that I had come home. Anyway, I wouldn't be the one to destroy anything for them, whatever it was. All in good time someone would be charged with telling them the truth about the lie, about all those lies. They themselves would feel the bitterness of having to destroy the monument to Youth and Faith, built on the lie of a hope. No, I would not tell.

'My son ...'

I was startled to hear the old woman speak. 'My son, I don't quite understand what you're trying to say, really I don't understand. But you are trembling; either you're frightened or very angry or something like that, and what you're saying can't be good, because you're trembling, you're actually trembling! ...'

Perhaps the old woman was right, because it is very rare for her to be mistaken. But anyway this made no difference. I wouldn't tell, and that was that ... and even if I did, what would be the good? Yes, what good would it do seeing that the filth, the damned filth of it all would come to these children in other circumstances, with other details, and with other names.

'Eh, all of you, go to sleep, go on! Yes, sleep. What are you looking at? Go to sleep!'

But, who knows? and also, why not believe? Why not believe

in something really nice? Like perhaps, that the upbringing of the children would be different from mine, and would endow them with a tolerance of things, a tolerance that my emotional make-up could not endure. And for them, perhaps, how should I know? – perhaps time would create more understanding, more tenderness, yes, more humanity ... Because, perhaps, the old woman was right, there is time, time.

'My son, the children have gone.'

'Yes, I'll tell you, they did hit me.'

'Who was it? But is that all? You're trembling ...'

'Yes, this isn't everything, and it's not even anything. They made me small, and they succeeded in making me feel small. Yes, that's it. That is everything. And why? They don't even say it out loud. And everything falls on me, not as a slow soft erosion, for this no one feels, but it falls suddenly, with agonizing noises inside me, and falls, and falls ...'

'Well, I think it's better if I don't know about this at all, because I don't understand anything you say.'

We both became silent, in so close an embrace that I didn't even know if she was the one who was trembling. It was only at this moment that I saw the flames, although I had been looking at them a long time. The heat enveloped us pleasantly, and the flames twisted and turned in a strange ruby dance. I only stopped looking when the old woman talked in a way that made me realize that she had long been meditating on how to say something she eventually did not say. She only said, 'My son.'

Her fingers were rough, but her dark velvet embrace was soft and warm, and exuded the strong, pure fragrance of the good years of my faith.

36

Nazi Boni

The Meeting

Nazi Boni's 'Ancestor', an old chief narrating the story of his tribe, concentrates mainly on the period before the coming of the white man. His story, he claims, reaches back over a period of two hundred and eighty years. Near the end of the book, the time is 1888, when Captain Binger appeared in Bwamuland, Upper Volta, to hand the chief a treaty – 'a paper filled with cabalistic signs ... probably a talisman'. Then there is a sudden shift to the heroic uprising of the Bwawa in 1915. It was one of the many armed rebellions in French West Africa, another of which, among the Tuaregs, the Malian writer Fily Sissoko has described in *The Red Savannah*.

Boni's style is often pompous and incongruous. But the material sprawling through what looks like a rough sketch of a historical novel pregnant with footnotes, is fascinating. The main character is Térhé, a great lover and warrior and the leader of his age-group, who wrests the power over the tribe from his elders. There is also a weirder kind of hero, Kya the Killer, whose vocation is to slay stragglers from neighbouring tribes. When he gets killed in turn, Lowan, his satanic uncle, visits his fate vicariously on Térhé, whom he hates. To the Bwawa, Térhé's death 'is the death of our sun'.

The Meeting

That evening, Mb'woa P'hihoun, the Moon, which had been away on a journey for several days, had failed to keep her appointment with the stars. The night was black. The town was sunk in heavy sleep. People wrapped themselves in their blankets, trying to find protection from the mosquitoes, which filled the houses with their humming, while outside the chorus of frogs alternated with the hooting of the owls and the distant laughter of the blood-thirsty hyenas.

At a distance of two thousand paces from the town two hundred and fifty young men, sitting in a group on dead tree-trunks, were holding a discussion in low tones in the middle of a vast millet field. They had stealthily left their huts, dressed only in their old working shorts despite the low temperature. Any other way of dressing would have attracted attention to their departure and aroused suspicion. One by one they had silently crossed the low ground to meet on the plateau, in the solitude of the bush. Still everybody had his bow and his *fouhoun*, or quiver, with him. The men had to go armed under any circumstances so as to be able to counter any unforeseen attack.

As a result of a quick check it was found that the group was complete, and it seemed unlikely that anyone would come. A serious decision, which would bring about the most important event in the life of a young Bwanii, had to be taken. Though Terhé was the leader, it was up to B'êêni as the son of the priest in charge of Dô, the god of field cultivation, to open the debate.

'Friends, you know that our prosperity depends on our health, the fecundity of our women, and also the abundance of our harvests. Now, when Dô is contented, our granaries are full to overflowing with food and our wives are happy and do not try to shun us for the benefit of more fortunate competitors. This year threatens to be catastrophic. The excessive rainfalls have laid waste our fields. It has been claimed that the gods have decided to impose sanctions on Bwamuland because a woman was said to have cut deadwood in "Frog Valley", a sacred place reserved for the Power ruling over the waters. But the falseness of this allegation has just been confirmed.

'Some people, who are even more stupid than the others, are going about saying that two lovers forgot themselves in the bush, an act which is generally considered just as odious as adultery. But if that had been the case, we would rather be suffering from a protracted drought which would not come to an end until after the culprits had been found, exposed to public shame, and then stoned to death. But the penalties imposed on this act of lechery are so horrible that nobody dares commit it.

'In actual fact, Dô is dissatisfied and we have to find out why. There is no need for us to be present at the council meeting of the Elders to guess the real reason.

'The last group initiated to Dô has been in charge for ten years. That is too long. For ten years these seniors whom we call Pammas, that is, the "mighty ones", the detainers of Force, have been monopolizing all those responsibilities which are not incumbent on the Elders. They do not fulfil their obligations to the great god regularly. During each dry season they should organize ten racing competitions in accordance with the required rites but they can hardly manage seven. Besides, they act towards us, their juniors, their *bruwas*, like real tyrants. Whenever they feel like it they put on their leaf-mask, lock our wives and ourselves up in our houses, and smoke us like porcupines in a hollow baobab tree. They flog us with *xnignenna*, those flexible, tough, and painful whips which cut you right to the marrow. They do not even hesitate to use their clubs on us, just as if we were wild beasts. If they torture us, it's all right, but what about our wives, who are the daughters of other clans and come from villages that do not owe allegiance to our Dô? Is it right that they should subject them to the same treatment as ourselves? You have to admit that nobody could be more dishonest in his dealings than they are, for they want to intimidate the women in order to be able to court them. They are definitely going too far.

'Apart from that, whenever there is a big meal to round off communal work, they are always the ones who preside, who choose the best dishes for the Elders – of course nobody would object to that – and for themselves, and who contrive to humiliate us by offering us food that smells of rancid fat and slop that even a dog would refuse.

'To bring them to their senses, the leaders of the preceding group of initiates have driven them out of town twice and forced them to spend two days and two nights in the bush, but to no avail. There is no end to their bullying. Dô forbids any act of revenge. But some of them make us pay for what they claim was bad treatment meted out to them by our fathers, our uncles, or other close relatives of ours. Dô is a god of loyalty and justice; he cannot be happy with the present situation. Custom has made us their slaves but it also allows us to redeem ourselves. We could have been doing so for the last two years. We have preferred to wait because some of us seemed too young. Now we are in a position to request our initiation into the cult of Dô. This is my personal opinion. We must assert ourselves.'

'It is our duty to request our admission to the Dô cult,' Kâàgnounayi replied. 'As soon as the crops have been gathered in, we shall undergo the required endurance tests. If there is anybody who has the slightest apprehension, let him tell us now so that we can make arrangements to withdraw two candidates. You know that we cannot face the tests if we appear with an uneven number, at the risk of having the youngest member of the group "swallowed" by Dô.'

'We are men and not women,' Sunsuna said. 'The tests will last only seven days. Then we shall take the "Force" and become in turn the Pammas, the backbone of our community. To demand our advancement is at the same time to attain our own freedom.'

'As far as I'm concerned,' Terhé added, 'I think we have waited too long already. But after all this has not done us any harm. If we had demanded the "Force" two years earlier, our group would have been reduced by at least twenty-four men. But everybody must be aware of the difficulties ahead and must

311

therefore get inured to hardships. We will be subjected to a test in stoicism; we must learn how to be impassive martyrs. The slightest sign of weakness, the least sigh uttered under the harsh treatment we are going to receive at the hands of the outgoing group of initiates would be used by them as a pretext to disqualify us. On the other hand we must try to justify our pretensions by seizing every opportunity: communal labour, wrestling matches, hunting, races, dances, and war. We must clearly show our superiority to the Pammas. Only then can we win over the Elders and public opinion. In a few days' time Mb'woa P'hihoun, the Moon, will reappear, and then the whole of our town will be invited to cultivate the field of Kââgnounayi's parents-in-law at Wakara, as miraculously enough that particular plot of land is not flooded. We shall arrange to have an argument with the Pammas so that they will be forced to work alongside us from dawn to dusk without a single break, that means without eating or drinking. As they have no previous warning, they will not take any precautions. Some of them will almost certainly drop down in a faint under the onslaught of the heat, of thirst, hunger, or exhaustion. If no incident of this kind is reported on our side, we shall for the first time have supplied proof of our maturity. When the crucial moment comes, keep away from the *hanwa*.* Love sucks a man dry. I mention this especially for those who cannot control themselves.'

A cheerful murmur greeted this reflection. Some fellows noted for their sexual stamina became the butt of jokes but they retaliated by mischievously accusing others of having similar dispositions. All this was said in a playful mood.

'Every one of us,' Kââgnounayi insisted, 'must clearly state his opinion before we separate. Are you all ready and willing to face the tests in order to seize the "Force"?'

'Your question is pointless,' Yézouma replied. 'Nobody is afraid to state clearly what he thinks. We all agree unanimously.'

'Of course,' B'êêni concluded, 'the decision we have just taken must remain secret. We shall have a second meeting at the end of the rainy season.'

The group got up. *Swish! swish!* Two deer, which had been

* Women.

browsing in the millet at the edge of the field, fled in fright, making a whistling sound. Fire-flies were describing a maze-like pattern of luminous figures in the air, while on the heights of Diokny, four thousand paces away, Mb'woa Yere, the Lion, was roaring as if he wanted to denounce the young men's plot.

37

James Ngugi

Limits

James Ngugi is a Kenyan writer, exposed to problems that are different from those which the West African or the South African writers face. *Weep Not Child*, his first novel, described the impact of the forceful transition which a tribal society experienced. Under the impact of change the family of the young boy, through whom the action of the book is witnessed, disintegrates. There are certain stock themes – the wicked landowner, the corrupting influence of the town, colour prejudice. On one level the book is a gigantic praise poem to Kenyatta.

Public issues are also paramount in his second novel, *The River Between*, from which an extract is reproduced here. But in this novel the social conflict is tribal rather than racial, and the search for individuality begins. The piece shows Waiyaki battling with tribal commitments which seem to engulf the self. And somehow the clichés and the attitudinizing seem in keeping with the individual's first gropings towards understanding his role in the new society.

Limits

He could not sleep. Thin rays of the moon passed through the cracks in the wall into the hut and fell at various spots on the floor. It was no good staring blankly at the hazy darkness in which every object lost its clear edges. Waiyaki wanted to talk to someone. That was what oppressed him: the desire to share his hopes, his yearnings and longings with someone. His plans in education. The desire for assurance and release. Twice he had tried to tell his mother, to ask her something. But each time he stood in front of her and he heard her shaky voice, he found himself talking of irrelevant things. It was strange that the tremor in her voice should set doubts darting in his soul.

After all, what was the longing, what was the something for which he yearned? Did he know it himself? Yet the hopes and desires kept on haunting him. They had followed him all his life. Even as a boy grazing his father's cattle in the hills and plains, he had always wanted – what? Could he define it?

He did not want to think. But thoughts came and flooded his heart. Strange chapters of his life unfolded before him. His young sister who had died early was the only person with whom he had been intimate. He had loved her, if that sort of closeness could be called love. He thought he loved the hills and their people. But they did not give him that something he could get from her. Yet he had been very small, many seasons before his second birth. He wondered why he remembered that time, though vaguely. But she was dead. And death was the end of everything, on this earth. After you were buried, you turned into a spirit. Waiyaki wondered if his sister was a spirit. A young good spirit. Was she watching him? He turned round, rather frightened. He felt guilty.

Waiyaki was superstitious. He believed the things that the people of the ridges believed. Siriana Mission had done nothing effective to change this. His father had warned him against being contaminated by the ways of the white man. Yet he sometimes wondered. Was the education he was trying to spread in the ridges not a contamination?

He wanted to sleep. From side to side he wriggled on his bed, trying to close his eyes and shut away these thoughts that would not let him alone. He thought: There is something unexplainable in the coming of the white man. He had found no resistance in the hills. Now he had penetrated into the heart of the country, spreading his influence. This influence could be disruptive. Muthoni had died on the high altar of this disruption. She had died with courage probably still trying to resolve the conflict within herself in an attempt to reach the light. Since her death everything had gone from bad to worse, and probably conflicting calls and loyalties strove within the hearts of many. So all the confusion, because not many were like Muthoni in courage. Waiyaki wondered where he was. Was he trying to create order and bring light in the dark? Or was he part of the confusion himself?

The image of his sister, that of Muthoni and many others followed each other across his mind in quick succession; shadows that had no concrete form; shadows that came and went; sometimes merging, forming nothing. Then, for one moment, there was nothing. All his life became one white blur. But only for a second. Then came the mist, dark with no definition. The clear edges of life had gone. He lay still, a little frightened, not knowing what to think or how to find a way out.

The mist began to fade, slowly. The edges seemed to be forming. He could now see the outline of a definite shape coming into being through the thinning mist. Waiyaki waited for it to melt away into nothingness but it did not. The shape remained there, fixed, and he could not drive it away. He peered at it and for a time was fascinated by it. It was the shape of a woman and he could not make out who she was.

Even this too vanished. And still he could not sleep. It was no good sitting in bed, staring into the hazy darkness.

He got out of bed and it creaked as he stood up. He put on his clothes, quietly yet with a slight inner agitation, an excitement of a lover thinking of the impending meeting with his woman. He went out of the hut; he wanted to go to Makuyu to see Kamau, or any other person; a man maybe would understand him, a man to whom he could talk.

The moon was also awake. Her glare was hard and looked brittle. The whole ridge and everything wore a brilliant white. And all the little things that in the day appeared ordinary seemed now to be changed into an unearthliness that was both alluring and frightening. Waiyaki listened for voices on the ridge but he could only hear silence. As he moved across the ridge, through small bushes and trees, the silence and the moon's glare seemed to have combined into one mighty force that breathed and had life. Waiyaki wanted to feel at one with the whole creation, with the spirits of his sister and father. He hesitated. Then the oppression in him grew and the desire to talk with someone mounted. The brightness of the moon seemed now soft and tangible and he yielded to her magic. And Waiyaki thrust out his arms and wanted to hold the moon close to his breast because he was sure she was listening and he wanted her cold breath near him. Now his muscles and everything about his body seemed to vibrate with tautness.

Again he was restless and the yearning came back to him. It filled him and shook his whole being so that he felt something in him would burst. Yearning. Yearning. Was life all a yearning and no satisfaction? Was one to live, a strange hollowness pursuing one like a malignant beast that would not let one rest? Waiyaki could not know. Perhaps nobody could ever know. You had just to be. Waiyaki was made to serve the tribe, living day by day with no thoughts of self but always of others. But even this now seemed hopeless and unsatisfactory. He had now for many reasons been trying to drain himself dry, for the people. Yet this thing still pursued him.

Suddenly he thought he knew what he wanted. Freedom. He wanted to run, run hard, run anywhere. Or hover aimlessly, wandering everywhere like a spirit. Then he would have every-thing – every flower, every tree – or he could fly to the moon.

This seemed possible and Waiyaki raised up his eyes to the sky. His heart bled for her. But he could not run. And he could not fly.

38

Jonathan Kariara

The Initiation

Because the writer in Africa is very often a university graduate, this has frequently meant that he has been too conscious an advocate of the traditional way of life. He has not been able to enter fully into indigenous practices which it may be fashionable to accept, but which his Western education has encouraged him to deny. Some of this is present in the short story below – a fierce attempt to believe in rites, an unintentional give-away bordering closely on satire.

The Initiation

Mirashi sat brooding by the bamboo bed, quietly watching the rise and fall of his son's chest. His mouth was hard set; his look was anxious and strained. He was watching the sleeping youth, Mlaponi, his only son. The boy had been very sick; today was the fortieth day since he had undergone circumcision. Mlaponi slept quietly. The bed was woven with rope and bamboo poles. A blanket protected his body against the hardness. His head rested on a heap of rags and bark cloth put over the short tree trunk which raised the mat at one end. They were in an isolated hut of poles and grass thatch, about a hundred paces away from the main camp.

Under the blanket wrapped round him, one could feel the frail wasted body of Mlaponi. He had been tender and weak from birth and the past weeks had made him thinner. The boy reminded his father of the plucked doves he used to roast with other boys in the fields, with his thin chest and the ribs spreading out like bare boughs on a dry tree. His body was feverishly hot, just like one of those birds. His wound had not yet healed, and possibly would never heal. All the other candidates for the year's initiation had recovered within the usual six weeks. But Mlaponi had got worse every day. There was only another week to go. The camp would close down, and the candidates, fit in body, and mature in manhood, would return home to be respected as men of the tribe. It was a disgrace and an ill omen for a candidate to return home with the wound half healed. It predicted death in the family.

Mirashi was thinking of the day the boy was born. That was before his journey to Lindi, how many years was it? Twenty. He had gone to cook for Mr Allison. Mr Allison had gone back 'home', the name he always used when referring to his place of

birth. He had inherited two things from the white man, a new
religion and the desire to decide for himself. But he had not
been given the chance to decide for himself when he came back
to his birthplace. Mlaponi had to undergo initiation in the tribal
manner ... Mirashi wanted to be a Makua, an ageing member
of a venerable tribe. And why not? Who were his parents? Had
not his father's people been always Wamakua of Mpeta from
time immemorial? But he was different. And he knew it.
Mlaponi, however, had to undergo the ceremony. 'I, Mirashi,
desired it!' he insistently went on, showing his doubts even in
his insistence.

He was interrupted in these thoughts by the waking of his son.
Mlaponi was perspiring; he tossed about wailing fitfully. 'Father,
am I going to get well? Is there no help, Father?' he asked
repeatedly. When he was not asking these questions, he kept
looking accusingly at his father with eyes that spoke openly:
'You must know of a way of releasing me from this pain. You
must!' There the father sat, helpless with suffering, seeing no
way out, none but that suggested by the elders. Why must he
always come up against the elders? He had had great difficulty
persuading them to let Mlaponi be initiated, so sure were they
that Mlaponi was too weak and young. How hostile they had
been when he refused to accompany them to the communal
ceremony of planting herbs on the outskirts of the camp and on
the circumcision ground.

Was there no way out, indeed? He knew the answer too well.
Mirashi could not bear to reflect. He stepped out of the hut and
walked towards the camp. Like a hawk he surveyed the elders
grouped round evening fires, seeking out Omanya. The elders
watched him with apparent interest. There was a secret understanding among them, a tie that excluded Mirashi. Had they
not always said that somehow something would go wrong in
Mirashi's household? And had they not taken care to tell the
older relatives that Mirashi had proved obstinate?

It is not that they enjoyed the fact that their fears had been
realized; rather they pitifully patronized him. They had confirmed by consulting the witch-doctor that Mirashi's bad luck
had been brought about by the ill-will and magical practice of

Mlaponi's maternal aunt. They had advised Mirashi to accede to custom and make a supplication to the woman to ease the pain in the boy. But he had refused, becoming blind and dumb to any suggestion that he would ever ask help from the woman. How, humiliate himself before the woman who had thought her sister had not married well by marrying him. No! But now he began to feel he would have to go – to save the boy.

Presently Mirashi spotted Omanya in one of the groups and called him out. He asked him to look after Mlaponi, promising to come soon.

'But where are you going?' asked Omanya, surprised. 'Oh, nowhere,' Mirashi answered carelessly. He turned round, indifferent to the elders' stares and purposefully trod through the grass to the top of the hill. His eyes were fixed, seeing nothing. But he had his destination clearly in his mind, the tall baobab-tree near his house. He went on stiffly, feeling alone and tired.

At last he reached the tree and climbed it, branch by branch. He turned towards the woman's house and let out the plaint: 'Leave my son alone. Oh, leave him alone. He is not the one who has wronged you! Why don't you harm the one who is responsible for the wrongs done to you? Oh, let him come back home safely. Let him come and die in his mother's eyes! Spare my child; leave my son to me; spare him!!'

He came down the tree feeling ashamed. The shame almost drove him mad, so that he was running, shouting, 'It will never be repeated again.' He had hoped against hope that the sacrifice of his convictions and integrity would lead to the recovery of his son. But now, as he slowly made his way back, he knew he had only shamed himself. He reached the bottom of the valley and stopped. He realized that even at this moment, Mlaponi might be dead. This apprehension grew.

He was almost running now, to get back to the boy. At the top of the hill he stopped, breathless. Before him spread the blurred lights of the camp. He looked back to the village, to the baobab-tree, the scene of his shame. The fires in front of the houses in the village danced before his eyes, mockingly. And before him was always the pleading face of the boy, and the maddening question always in his ears – 'Is there no help, Father?'

'No, no help for you, Mlaponi; your ritual must be the agony of ritual carried to the extreme, even the agony of death. It is me you have got to save, from fear and pride, from wanting to graft the old to the new.' It dawned on him then; that his son had been weak all the time, that it was his pride that had forced his son to go through an ordeal for which he had lost his life. Already he felt his son was dead.

Wearily he began to descend. And then it was as though out of the silence a piercing cry was directed to his ears, the cry of a fox. 'It means death,' he told himself. He felt strangely calm, and relaxing his steps he walked easily as a countryman walks when enjoying a well-earned hour of ease. He went to one of the camp fires, and chose a seat among the elders. He sat easily among them, letting the warmth of the fire knit him into the group. He could even crack jokes about Kagasi, a young man of twenty-five who had the incurable habit of roasting sweet potatoes wherever he was, whenever there was a fire handy. Quiet little jokes which drove fear into the people so that several were already squirming in their seats and clearing imaginary obstructions in their throats. 'You know that the boy is dead,' Mirashi said quietly. They looked at him as if to say that they knew, but how could he know? He read this in their eyes and in a tired small voice which strived to be normal said, 'Oh yes, I know. Or is it not so?' tugging the shoulder of the man next to him in pathetic little movements. 'Ay, it is so,' said most of the neighbours.

'You must then help me to carry him to the village – no, not to the village. It would not be right. His wound never healed; it would bring ill-luck to the villagers. No, not to the village, but to the top of the hill, where we must dig a grave for him in the night, before the women wake to make their noises. And neighbours, you can come to my house on the third day from this, and you will find ready the beer and foods that our funeral rites dictate. I will not be home that day, but I am sure you will not miss me. I will see to there being enough beer.'

On the third day, in the village could be heard sounds of much rejoicing, a lot of noisy drumming and thick hoarse shouts of a people who have drunk freely from a beer-gourd. Mirashi had apparently fulfilled his promise to the people. But he was not among them. After the burial in the night he had gone home, ordered the feast that was to take place in three days and had immediately started on a journey to Lindi. He did not find Mr Allison in the growing mission, but that did not matter. A language already existed between Mirashi and these white men, a language that could handle day-to-day experiences, even death, with ease. The rites that had not been fulfilled in his village were fulfilled at Lindi, and so on the third day Mirashi was on his way home again, carrying a small wooden cross hidden in his clothes. He climbed to the top of the hill, stumbling a little over the newly turned clods at the graveside. He dug a small hole, inserted the cross at the head of the grave. He felt physically tired. Moving a few yards away he lay himself down on the warm grass to wait for the rejoicings in the village to stop. The ritual was over. The cross was not high; it could never be seen from the village. But it might be seen by a few who by chance might stray into the hills, perhaps by a shepherd looking after his sheep in the fields.

39

Sadru Kassam

The House

Davidson Nicol, the Sierra Leonean writer, has remarked that child-hood recollections constitute a large area in the experience of the African writer. Frequently these recollections sprawl, merely representing indulgence in a past that is intended to excite the curiosity of the foreign reader. In this piece it seemed to us that the recollections were organized into a passionate unit.

The House

It was an old-fashioned, double-storey wooden house, dark green warped in places with the paint peeling off, revealing a dull, weathered sickly grey of the wood. Long sharp blades of grass sprouted from crevices at joints as if to escape the dullness. The doors and windows were closed. Along the front eaves of the roof was a string of nests, mostly silent, like the house. The roof itself, of flattened kerosene tins, had gone rusty; and so had a drain-pipe winding between side windows. Adjoining the house were a few tall pawpaws, guavas and gum, and the usual scrub and grass, green and copious after the recent rains. There was a thicker growth of bush behind the house, but the rest of the surrounding land was grass with palm and mango trees scattered about irregularly. There were no other buildings nearby. About twenty yards at an angle in front of the house was a well to which women from far away huts came to draw water.

The house stood there, alone, brooding, abandoned.

I was then twelve, and my sister, Nargis, eight. Though we lived a good distance away near the main road, on our way to school we always went by the house since it was a short cut.

One early morning as we were walking past the building we heard a faint whine of a child come from the upper storey, followed quickly by a shooing of a female voice. We stopped, startled, and looked up, curious, even a little frightened.

The voice had stopped.

Nargis took my hand, and staring in the direction, asked whose voice it was.

'I don't know,' I replied, shaking my head and cocking my ears. 'Perhaps some people have come to live there.'

But I wasn't sure. I remembered the stories mother had told me of djins frequenting deserted houses. I wondered if the voice wasn't of a child of a djin. Or it could be, I thought, some homeless mother and her little one had stealthily entered the house; though I wondered how they could have done that with all the doors and windows closed.

Nothing happened for the next few days. The house stood there silent as ever, though more ghost-like now.

Then one afternoon as we were returning from school we noticed the figure of a small Indian girl beside the wall fumbling with a pail and a rope. She was slightly taller than Nargis and lean as a reed with elbows protruding through her clinging skin. She wore a long, crumpled, dirty frock, sleeveless and with the seams open. Her curly hair was faintly gold and done in two short plaits. We watched her tie the pail to the rope and lower it carefully down the well.

'Who's that?' Nargis asked loudly as we walked past the girl. She at once looked round, though continuing to draw water. There was no expression on her face. She stared at us blankly while her hands moved forward and backward like a bicycle pedal.

'I don't know,' I replied. 'Perhaps she lives in that house.'

We looked at the building.

There was a woman standing on the balcony of the upper storey, with her chin resting in her hand, the elbow upon the parapet. She had long black hair and a dark brown complexion. Her frock, long and dirty like that of the girl, had big oily splotches which showed clearly between the balusters. A small naked child (a boy, I think) was playing at her feet. There was also another older boy in oversize dirty clothes. All of them were looking in the direction of the well.

We walked on, now and then looking behind till the girl had disappeared.

As days went by we came to learn more about these people. The woman's husband, a plumber, had left the family and gone off to some remote place in Tanganyika. She had been allowed to live in the house while her relatives looked for him or found her a more suitable place. She lived by patching clothes that were occasionally brought to her and by selling sweetmeats.

In the morning on our way to school the whine of the child

would come our way. In the afternoon the girl would be at the well drawing water, though her mother would not always be on the balcony.

To me the girl was merely one of the many who came to the well to fetch water and went away. But to Nargis she seemed an object of great curiosity, as I believe Nargis was to her. They would stare at each other as if each were a being from another planet.

One afternoon as we slowed down near the well to watch her, Nargis whispered, 'Poor her! Don't they have a servant to do that work?' Then, as the girl was going away glancing at us suspiciously, Nargis could hold back no longer. She called out impudently, 'Hey girl! What's your name?'

The girl stopped, put down her pail and answered in a half-frightened voice, 'Amina.'

'Don't you go to school?' Nargis asked, staring harshly into her eyes, the way perhaps her teacher did.

'No,' the girl replied.

There was a silence.

Then the girl picked up the pail and went away, fast, spilling water on her frock and on the ground.

Some days later as Amina was returning to the house from the well she stopped, and looking round at us, called out aloud to Nargis:

'Hey girl!' she shouted. 'What's your name?'

'Nargis,' my sister replied.

'And you go to school, is it?'

'Yes.'

'And what's your mother's name?'

'Khatun.'

'And your father's?'

'Janmohamed.'

'What?'

'Janmohamed.'

'And your brother's?'

'Karim.'

'And your sister's?'

'I don't have a sister.'

'You don't have a sister, is it?' And she burst out laughing.

That was the start of it. They soon became friends. Every time we passed the house the two would stop and talk in whispers. Amina was the one who wanted to know the most, asking Nargis about her teachers and her studies and about our house and its furnishings. Nargis enjoyed replying to her. It made her feel big. Sometimes she would save her potato crisps or a toffee (from what she had bought with her recess money) which Amina would slip into her pocket and, smiling at her brothers watching from the balcony, go running away behind the house. One day Nargis pushed me aside and asked me to walk on, and then I observed her give the girl a ten-cent piece. I didn't like that and warned her I would report her to mother if she gave money like that.

Once I even heard her promise her an old frock of hers which she said was rotting.

On her part Amina brought Nargis (and me, too) pieces of cloyed sweetmeats or berries or a ripe pawpaw. Or sometimes she would offer us a dirty mugful of water and if Nargis refused she would in a motherly way call her a good girl and press her saying how hot the afternoon was and that if she didn't have water she would die. 'O.K., your wish then,' she would add when Nargis just wouldn't have it.

Only I seemed to stand in the way of their friendship.

One day, for instance, Amina asked me (I'm sure at the suggestion of Nargis) to allow her to return in the evening so that they could play together. But I refused, saying she had sums and reading to do, though I wasn't sure. (Looking back I wonder at the reason. Was I so cruel? Or jealous? Or did I feel my sister could not be allowed to play with someone so poor and dirty?)

On another occasion Nargis had a big load of books to carry home and I had refused (in revenge for something) to help her. But when we met Amina she immediately offered to help carry the books right up to our doorstep. Nargis pointed at me and told her, 'Ask him.' I, however, declined, saying I would help her myself. I think I didn't want her to be seen by mother (who would be waiting outside) and be called in and perhaps made to sit at the table for lunch with us.

One very hot afternoon the girl wasn't at the well. Nor were the woman or her children on the balcony. But the windows were open and we could hear a murmuring of female voices and an occasional shriek of the child.

Nargis insisted that we should go behind the house and find out about the girl. She had bought for Amina a pencil which, she said, she must give to her. But I refused.

The following morning a small open flame of light that I had often seen in the evening on my way back from games now flickered through an open side window. It was the first time the window had been open so early. We slowed down and watched closely for any movement inside. There was none. Just the flicker and a swaying dimness. We could see nothing else.

In the afternoon the girl wasn't at the well again. Nor was anyone on the balcony. The windows were closed. We walked past and looked at the side window through which a light had shone in the morning. It, too, was closed.

'Where have they gone?' Nargis asked in a weak, concerned voice. She couldn't understand it. Where indeed had everyone disappeared – the girl, the woman, the child, the brother? Her face contracted. Something seemed to torment her, something that would crush her spirit. She dragged me to the back of the house.

There was an open door with a steep staircase ending in darkness. The windows on that side of the house, too, were shut.

'They must have left,' I said softly and as consolingly as I could. 'Come on, let us go away.' But she wouldn't agree. Her face contorted with pleadings. She was almost hysterical. She wanted us to go up the steps. She wasn't afraid of the darkness or of the lizards that would be there. But I somehow managed to coax her away. Tears streaked down her face as we turned back.

Today the house is still there, but dilapidated and charred and roofless. Last year heavy rains swept the place and, it is said, lightning struck the building. But every time we pass by the house, Nargis looks at it searchingly. What is it she is thinking? Or recalling? I wonder.

40

Léopold Sédar Senghor

Négritude and Marxism

Léopold Sédar Senghor, poet-president of Senegal, has written much that deserves the attention of the student of African affairs. His main concern has been to throw *Négritude* – 'the collective Negro-African personality' – into relief by contrasting it with various non-African cultures and schools of philosophical and political thought: *Négritude* and ancient Greek culture, '*Latinité*', Arabism, Humanism, Socialism, Marxism. Senghor calls his synthesis of Arabism and *Négritude*, Africanism ('*Africanité*') and wants both Arabs and black Africans to share in a greater 'French Commonwealth'.

The encounter between *Négritude* and Marxism, passionate at the beginning, seems to have left no deep imprint on French-speaking Africa. Though Africa has its thoroughbred Marxists, the majority of leaders now in power have opted for a more flexible kind of 'African Socialism', supposedly in keeping with the continent's age-old communal structures.

At the rising movement of criticism which considers *Négritude* superannuated, Senghor flings his anathema: 'It is just as if Arabs said Arabism was out of date, the Americans that Free Enterprise was out of date, and the Soviets said the same about Communism. In my opinion, renouncing *Négritude* is a sort of inferiority complex.'

Négritude and Marxism

The various groups of the Negro-African élite, between the two world wars, were all formed in the mould of the same *French* mind, which was then oriented towards rationalism with a few musty whiffs of positivism. Whether collegians or students of the École Normale Supérieure, we were all given the same training. And we all obediently accepted the West's values: its discursive reason and its techniques. We thought that to emerge, or merely to survive as a race, we would have to steal the weapons of the conquerors, which, by the way, they were holding out to us, convinced that they would not be turned against them. It was our ambition to become negatives of the colonizers, 'Frenchmen with a black skin'. This went even further, since we would have blushed, had we been able to blush, at our black skin, our kinky hair, our flat noses, above all at the values of our traditional society, whose living and most vigorous expression was the Negro-African languages. I provoked a scandal in Dakar when in 1937 I advocated the 'return to the sources', the vernacular languages. Such was the abasement of the black man's soul in those days that we were resigned to being thought of as a *tabula rasa*, a race, almost a whole continent, which for 30,000 years had not thought anything, felt anything, written anything, painted or sculpted anything, sung or danced anything. A *nothing* at the bottom of the abyss which only knew how to implore and receive, a lump of soft wax in the hands of the white God with his rosy fingers and his sky-blue eyes.

Nonetheless, strongly though we renounced *being* – we could only *appear*, dressed as we were in gaudy alien rags – objectively speaking not all was lost yet. Our People had not renounced all. They continued to think, for example, that the *soul* of the black man was superior to the mind of the white. They continued to paint and sculpt, to sing and dance in their own style. What did they express? The communion of life forces, the beauty of black bodies:

> . . . the black man
> handsome with eyes closed, handsome on the sand.

The people ordered:

> With the silver metre
>   measure
> the indigo-coloured flank.

And the people secretly shamed us. The most lucid ones among us felt, even if they did not admit it, the *contradiction* in which they had secluded themselves. We were proud to be Frenchmen and despite everything, Negro-Africans. We would sometimes revolt at being considered mere *consumers of culture*. This caused me to be politely dismissed from my school, Libermann College.

Thus not everything was as yet lost. But it was Europe – such is the dialectic of life – it was France which was to make us discover the values of *Négritude* by activating in us along with the powers of the heart those of reflection, of co-reflection, to use a term of Teilhard de Chardin.

Whatever the friendship our fellow-students vowed us – and for the very reason that they felt obliged to do so – it did not take us long to feel different from them. We did not have the same reactions to facts and life in general. The way they were concerned about their future careers, their money-mindedness, and their enjoyment of good cheer were to me perpetual causes for amazement. At a deeper level, we did not react in the same way to the teaching of our professors nor to works of art. The lessons in order, clarity, and superior morality that the classical authors had to offer did not appeal to my sensibility with the same initial impact as their style and language and the sensual qualities of images and rhythms. We therefore felt different from our fellow students. This accounts for our habit of meeting on Sundays. Before long we were to form an 'Association of Students from Black Africa' and to stretch out our hands to those Caribbean and Malagasy students willing to join us. It was a scandalizing revelation – and we were actually proceeding from one discovery to another – when we detected Europe's inner contradictions: Here the idea was not linked to the act, nor the word to the gesture, nor morality to life, nor reason to the heart and, consequently, to art. We very nearly decried this as hypocrisy. At any rate, this was our disenchantment. What was to become of us? Never had our despair been so desperate.

But I have to stress over and over again that it was also Europe, that it was France which saved us by developing in us a faculty for reflection based on facts and on their comprehension, for critical self-appraisal, and especially by teaching us the values of Black Africa. It will be remembered that the First World War had, in the view of the most lucid minds in Europe, marked some degree of bankruptcy of civilization, i.e., their civilization, through its absurdity, as well as the spiritual and material ruins in its wake. How has this been possible, they asked themselves, when recovering their wits; is this our Reason, our Science, our Christian Morality? And then philosophers, writers, artists, and even scholars once more brought the old charges against them, those already listed at the end of the 'stupid nineteenth century'. But this time they went right down to the roots of things. Their criticism became radical and extolled the rehabilitation of intuitive reason and of the Collective Soul, of archetypal images rising from the abysmal depths of the heart, from the dark regions of the groin and the womb, in a word, the rehabilitation of primordial rhythms in accord with the very pulsations of the cosmos. The vocabulary of the ethnologists, who were just beginning to unveil Black Africa's secrets, was adopted; like them one spoke of life forces, whilst the scholars brought out the discontinuous and the indeterminate from the very heart of matter.

This was all the young Negro African élite was asking for. What the European élite praised was basically nothing but the values of *Négritude*. It is necessary here to define this word, as it lends itself to many contradictory interpretations, springing from polemics. *Négritude* is quite simply *the sum-total of the cultural values of the Negro world*. It is not racism but culture;

it is a situation understood and controlled so that it helps us to apprehend the cosmos by being in agreement with it. Because it is a symbiosis of definite determinants – ethnic as well as geographical – *Négritude* is rooted in them, taking on the colour of an original style, but historically it will soon go beyond them in the same way that life surpasses the matter from which it has arisen. However, this Teilhardian view of the concept was not the one we were to hold at the first onset, in the years between 1928 and 1935. *Négritude* as we had started to conceive of it, was a defensive and at the same time an offensive weapon, a weapon of hope rather than an instrument of construction. Among its values we only retained the ones that were opposed to those of Europe; to discursive, logical, instrumental, chrema-tistic reason. *Négritude* was intuitive Reason, reason-that-grasps and not reason-that-sees. To be precise, it was the *warmth of communion, the image-symbol and cosmic rhythm which instead of sterilizing by dividing, fertilized by uniting*.

This was going very far. We had regained our pride. Relying upon the works of the anthropologists, prehistorians and ethno-logists, who paradoxically were white, we proclaimed ourselves, in the phrase of the poet Aimé Césaire, the 'eldest sons of the earth'. Had we not dominated the world down to the Neolithic age, fecundated the civilizations of the Nile and Euphrates before they became the innocent victims of the nomadic white barbarians surging down from the Eurasian uplands? I have to admit that our pride was quickly transformed into racism. Even Nazism was acceptable to us as it bolstered our refusal to co-operate. Jean-Paul Sartre rightly defined *Négritude* as 'antiracist racism'. At that time we had the sincerity of youth and of passion. Everything that had anything to do with white Europe was insipid to us: her reason, her art, her women.

The triumph of Nazism and the Second World War were to bring us in turn to our senses. We finally understood that racism was hatred and violence and war, which took on universal and total proportions thanks to the new engines of destruction. Science was placed at the service of Death and not of Life. And then, we also had become conscious of the fact that racial purity was a myth. As early as the Neolithic, the hardly formed races had begun to mix. The first civilizations of the Nile, the Euphrates, the Indus were civilizations of mixed races, the joint work of black and white peoples, and this doubtless had made them a success.

How then could we thenceforth break the deadlock, things being what they were? Undoubtedly by letting Nature and History take their course. It was precisely History which since the Renaissance had brought us into contact with the European whites. But this contact had been one of conquest. It had not been free. It was not based on exchange but on domination, or at least on assimilation. Co-operation there was none but only conflict, the conflict between the earthenware pot and the iron one, about the outcome of which there could be no doubt. How can we get out of this new contradiction? we anxiously asked ourselves. The solution could only be found by a change of method. We had to give up our negative attitude, not let History take its course but in a positive way *make History ourselves by making it conform to Nature*. Marxism was to be our first instrument of liberation.

41

Ralph Opara

Lagos Interlude

Few African writers in English have broken so completely away from the traditional role of the artist as to expose their society to ridicule. The insider's-outsider's view implicit in Wole Soyinka's plays is only too rare. The reason may well be that the traditional role of the artist casts him as a spokesman for his society, and his modern counterpart has been forced to capitulate to the ignorance and prejudices of a foreign and sometimes even hostile audience. He has been so often the self-appointed apologist. Ralph Opara's cheerful piece about a Lagos that is now past is a satirical look at the élite.

Lagos Interlude

My cousin Nwankechukukere spent forty-eight hours in Paris. She is now an expert on the slim-look, the full-length look and all the possible combinations of 'looks' usually associated with Parisian *haute couture*. She also made an overnight stop in Rome and heard Maria Callas warbling her mellisonant way through Verdi's *Aïda* at La Scala. La Scala, unfortunately, happens to be in Milan, and Milan is quite some way from Rome. But then you never know the number of activities that could be fitted into an overnight stop. She is also an accomplished dancer, she probably tripped the light fantastic to the accompaniment of bedouin strings, in a tent somewhere north of Timbuctoo. But the Kano-bound plane makes no provision for refuelling in the middle of the Sahara.

Cousin Nwankechukukere came back with a wardrobe the size of the Eiffel Tower and such impressive ideas indicative of her profound study of de Gaulle, the Common Market and slimming. She had become a woman. She even changed her name. There was no fanfare about this. I had expected the usual insertion in the papers: 'I, formerly known, called, addressed as ... shall from today henceforward be known, called, addressed etc.' and the bit about 'former documents remaining valid'. But no. Cousin Nwankechukukere just changed her name to 'Nwa'. To me there was a delightful crunchiness in 'Nwan-ke-chu-ku-ke-re', a crunchiness redolent of fried corn and groundnuts eaten with coconut. It was a pity to lose all that. Furthermore Nwankechukukere as a name should give the bearer a superiority complex. It is a name which literally means 'She-who-is-made-by-God'.

Her new unpoetic and uncrunchy name she pronounced firmly with a French accent – which was rather like saying *s'il vous plait* with an Ibo accent. Indeed she taught me the gentle art of punctuating my sentences in English with *s'il vous plait*. This was a *sine qua non* in polite conversation. I have even heard her on occasions, at her abusive best, call an offending houseboy 'a pig-headed son-of-a-bitch, *s'il vous plait*'!

She did me the honour one day of asking me to take her in my car into the shopping centre on Lagos Island. My first reaction was naturally an appropriate one – surprise. It seemed to me most strange that after her pilgrimage to the Champs Élysées and the Arc de Triomphe (from where a Frenchman took off on an orbital flight), that she should ask for a form of transport much slower than a moon rocket. In fact I had misgivings over the ability of my decrepit four-cylinder wagon to live up to its reputation of good behaviour. It might develop stage fright or throw a tantrum. My reward for trouble-free motoring with my cousin as passenger to the Island and back to Lagos Mainland was a free lesson in the cha-cha-cha. They say that driving, like love, is a many splendoured thing. If a Dr Jekyll wanted a catalyst for his transformation into a Mr Hyde, he only needs to get behind a wheel and on to a road in Lagos. I have no reason to disbelieve this. I do know that driving in Lagos can be more than a many splendoured thing. It brings out the best in a man and the beast too – and the beast is the fellow in the driver's seat of the car behind. On this occasion, a veritable King Kong in the car behind, sat with all his King Kongly might on the horn of his car, playing, no doubt, a salutation to the African sun. My driving mirror told me that the fellow was not a taxi driver – only taxi drivers have the distinction of transforming car horns into battle sirens. My mirror also told me that the fellow was shaking his fist – the well-known gesture of impatient motorists. All this began when I drove into Herbert Macaulay Road on Lagos Mainland – and Cousin Nwa thought it was all *ça ne va pas*!

As we crawled to a busy road junction, a woman who had a basket on her head, a baby on her back and wings on her feet, decided to fly across the road. But with one hand clutching her basket and the other holding the baby, her feet seemed to lose all sense of direction. She zigzagged into head-on collision with a schoolboy in green uniform, turned right round, her arms flapping and ran for the kerb screaming, '*Olorun, Olorun-o*' (God, God).

I stepped sharply on my brakes. This sent Cousin Nwa flying into the windscreen and the driver behind into another fit of horn blowing. Now was my chance to do something about the nuisance behind me. I flung open my door, nearly knocking over a cyclist; he rode away invoking the goddess of Lagos waters to flood me out of my house. But I had no time for him. I strode purposefully towards the horntootler. I raised my right hand to point a big finger at him when – we recognized each other. 'Oh, hallo,' he said, 'I have been trying to attract your attention. I think the back tyre of your car is going flat.'

Now, that was hardly fair; I mean, the fellow might at least have let me unburden myself of some of the morning's accumulated irritations. I felt unjustly repressed, and apprehensive of the effect of this on my heart. I had read a few psychologists and their injunctions never to bottle up one's feelings. In the circumstances, all I could do was to say, 'Well, thank you very much, Olu.' I turned to do something about parking the car properly and getting out the spare wheel.

'Hey there.' This was from a policeman who suddenly appeared from nowhere. He was armed to the teeth with notebooks and ball pens. 'Park there,' he said, pointing at a section of the road. 'Yes, certainly – of course – em, if you say so.' I smiled. 'I say so!' He barked. I stopped smiling. He carefully selected a pen to match the notebook in his hand. 'Obstruction; that's what it is. Obstruction. Do you know you are causing obstruction – in traffic – eh?' 'Wait a minute constable – eh, officer, I merely stopped to – em – park to change a flat tyre.' 'Obstruction – causing obstruction – don't you know traffic must go on?' At this he flicked open a blank page of his notebook, and turned the bonnet of my car into a writing desk. 'Give me your *particular*.' He fixed a gaze at Cousin Nwa. 'I beg your pardon,' I said. I think Cousin Nwa almost giggled but thought better of it.

'You don't hear me? Give your particular,' repeated the policeman and he flicked open another page of his notebook and changed his blue pen for a red one. Cousin Nwa now switched on what she thought was a most disarming smile, turned to our man and said:

'Please officer, my cousin is driving me into Lagos Island to shop, *s'il vous plaît*.' He fixed her with a look which implied: 'Young lady, you better look out,' but he said, 'That question is not relevant to this matter, sir – madam.' And Cousin Nwa did a most surprising thing. She shut up – and sought refuge in the centre pages of a daily paper. 'Well, well, well, where is your particular?' He flicked open a third page but did not change pens. 'Give me your licence, driving licence, motor licence, insurance licence – everything.'

At this point a police van in which our policeman had driven up and which was parked not very far from the scene, passed by. The man at the wheel smiled and nodded to our man. The smile meant everything in the sentence, 'Carry on, old chap, you have landed your fish.'

'You see, officer,' I began – 'You are wasting time. Give me the particular. Your name? Age, address?' He paused as he wrote these down. The next thing naturally would be to inquire into my marital status, financial status, age next birthday, father's tribe, mother's tribe, religious denomination ... but he did not seem to want these. 'O.K.' he said, 'where the licence?' I reached for my brief case on the back seat of the car, but the licence was not in it. That confirmed his suspicion; I did not possess any. 'I'm sorry officer, but the licence is on my writing desk at home. It should have been in my brief case.' 'Ho,' he cried, 'you think you fool me.' A third notebook appeared; the red pen disappeared. 'Well, your licence is not here. Therefore you are a learner. Therefore you are driving without a licence,' he paused, 'then you are a learner!'

A few passers-by were taking some interest in all this. A man in a yellow shirt got off his bicycle, rolled up to Cousin Nwa's side and took a solid front-line position. It was not clear whether he wanted to hear every word that passed between the officer and myself. Detectives have been known to wear yellow shirts. The next cyclist who had obviously seen this sort of motorist-policeman situation on several occasions, did not try to stop, he merely shouted 'I go drive myself' which was his way of telling everybody within ear-shot that I could not afford a driver. This was the truth of course. But his tone of voice suggested that this was an unpardonable sin. Perhaps he was a dedicated Trade Unionist who had made a pilgrimage to a certain place behind the Iron Curtain and now spoke out loud and clear on behalf of down-trodden commercial drivers, deprived of jobs by the likes of me. Anyway the policeman's voice was louder and clearer as he declared: 'Yes, that is how you people drive in Lagos. No licence! You are a learner. Yes, I think so.' He looked at Cousin Nwa to confirm this, but she instead opened her handbag, took out a dainty little handkerchief and dabbed at a small bead of perspiration on her forehead. Mr Yellow-shirt thought this was most elegant and said in admiration, 'Ah, sissy!' The word 'Sissy', a corrupt form of sister, was a general term for 'young lady'. But Cousin Nwa did not take kindly to this form of address and did the most inelegant thing that day. She told Yellow-shirt, 'Go home and mind your own business.' Whether she expected Yellow-shirt to execute a D'Artagnan bow, I don't know. But what Yellow-shirt did do was not to be found in any Encyclopaedia of Good Manners. He made a rude sign at Cousin Nwa and made her taste a few choice expressions from his larder of Yoruba invectives. He rounded the whole business off with; 'Get away, you think I no know you. I see you before at Yaba roundabout,' which was his way of saying that Cousin Nwa walked the streets at night, *s'il vous plait*!

The audience cheered – especially a hawker with an assortment of articles ranging from clothes pegs to leather watch-straps. Now he did not exactly show the kind of tact expected of an experienced salesman. He sidled up to Cousin Nwa, thrust a pair of sunglasses in her hand and said: 'Madam will buy? Four shillings and sixpence only.' My cousin, who had passed through a thousand and one emotional stages in the few seconds following Yellow-shirt's insult, did what came naturally. She threw the sunglasses out of the car, and covered her face with her hands. The hawker did a marvellous dive, a smart wicket-keeper he was, and caught the sunglasses. But then he dropped quite a few of the clothes pegs, woollen socks, watch straps and other sunglasses. Yellow-shirt quickly picked these up for him and with a grin the hawker promptly asked Madam to buy a lady's watch since she did not like sunglasses.

Cousin Nwa was a thoroughly confused woman, not knowing what to do about Yellow-shirt or the hawker. But swiftly and surely, inspiration came and with a voice which would have done credit to any drill-major, she shouted: 'Officer, arrest this man.'

This request did not exactly specify whether she meant Yellow-shirt or the hawker. The hawker looked at Yellow-shirt; Yellow-shirt looked at the hawker. And I thought they were going to toss a coin to determine to whom the honour was due. Now the policeman, still standing on my side of the car, was just then assuring me for the fourth time that he was convinced I was a learner-driver. He was in fact prepared to have a bet on it. This was a financial proposition that interested me very much. But Cousin Nwa cut into this frank and fair discussion with: 'Officer, arrest this man.'

Yellow-shirt and the hawker did not like this insistent appeal to the policeman. Apparently they were, in their private lives, God-fearing, water-drinking, law-abiding, tax-paying citizens. And nothing must tarnish their record. Perhaps this accounted for the strange turn of events. The hawker appealed to everyone around to bear witness that he meant no offence and that if a man asked a young lady to purchase a pair of sunglasses to protect her eyes from the wicked sun, did the man do wrong? Yellow-shirt thought the hawker was trying to pass the buck. 'Me and you,' he declared, holding the front of the hawker's singlet, 'me and you, na who make the sissy vex. Eh?'

The audience refused to take sides. Said the hawker, 'Leave me.' Replied Yellow-shirt, 'Leave me.' And they left each other; this they did either to emphasize the peace-loving aspects of their characters or because the policeman had brought out another notebook and a blue pen. The audience was naturally disappointed – and one or two muttered under their breath '*ojo, ojo*' – the Yoruba for 'coward'.

Cousin Nwa could not quite see why the Black Maria had not rolled up to whisk away the miscreants. So she urged, for the umpteenth time, 'Officer, arrest this man.'

The policeman opened the fifth page of his notebook, wrote something and said to me; 'Bring your licence and show me at the station by 5 p.m. today.' At that he shut his notebook, returned the pen to his pocket and marched away to deal with more obstructions farther up the road.

And that you may say was the end of my privilege of taking Cousin Nwa shopping, *s'il vous plait*.

42

Wole Soyinka

Salutations to the Gut

Wole Soyinka is the most versatile of African writers in French or English; he has not only written poems, short stories and plays, but is the single major example amongst the English writers capable of standing outside his culture with the serious capacity for laughter. When he has advocated a cause it has always been in the separate guise of citizen.

The piece that follows is more like some of his early poetry. There is the play of wit and the deep underlying respect for Yoruba culture; in the early poetry this becomes the black man's dignity. The humour is never at the expense of the culture, and if at times the sound of laughter appears to be European, this is perhaps his dramatist's ear for levels of sound.

Salutations to the Gut

Sheer poetic luxuriance of a hundred '*oriki*' redeems us. Fantasies of hawking-cries that startle a hungry afternoon, spun casually by the most indifferent looking nubile that ever sold bean pottage transform us. Currants of euphonious names in a world that moves ever nearer an inhuman vitamin pill age – *sokoyokoto* (lubricate-the-husband), *koniilo* (he-shall-not-budge), *moyinmoyin elemi meje* (moyinmoyin of the seven souls) – these elevate the Yoruba above the common herd of gluttons, prepare us for the adventure of direct experience with the leading race of lyrical gastronomes. It is sad that daily the business of the world becomes more hurried, and the few who still possess leisure lack true poetry of food; they roll off the table in the instant slumber of gorged swine oblivious of past content, for all food is the same to them. Not so the Yoruba, for he is the true hedonist who has felt in every morsel the soul of the open kitchen. Inspired he rhapsodizes, conceding immortality to fruit and flesh even as his teeth curtail their sacrificial existence. For the Yoruba is aware that nature is a vulgarian, his task as the artist is to tune its rawness to the fine receptivity of man.

Realist or dreamer, man must accept a Beginning. Without craving, supply would be an indulgence, reprehensible and superfluous. Hunger is the cry of a god, and two gods do the humans worship – the Head and the Stomach. The Head may be ignored, for this cult is the mere corruption of a degenerate civilization. Let the so-called progressive world continue to equate the human head with termites and cockroaches, fed on a dry diet of books; the Head is still subservient to the Stomach. We know the body will survive without Head sustenance, but the Stomach, the god that rumbles and thunders when sacrifice is late, this god cannot be slighted. Epicureanism therefore embraces more than a philosophy or a science; it is a religion. And the Yorubas, a realistic race of hedonists, approach the Deity of Hunger with the same mixture of gravity and humour as is dictated by their ready acceptance of life values:

> *Ebi npa mi, olose nkiri*
> *Bi ngo we'nu ngo le we 'de*

Hungry I am, and the soap-hawker keeps calling / if my inside is dirty I will not wash my skin.

Revelation of this universal wisdom has not, in this instance, by-passed the European. Dr Johnson, the great man of discourse, once declared: 'A man is in general better pleased when he has a good dinner upon his table, than when his wife talks Greek.' Dr Johnson's choice of words was divinely guided. Classical Greek is indeed the language of Stomach in spiritual possession.

But let us continue our adventure with the Yoruba in search of the attributes of this divinity. Another epigram will take us further, it is a gem of Yoruba wit and mischief even in deeply religious matters:

> *Ebi o pa 'male, o ni oun o j'aya:*
> *Ebi pa Sule o j'obo.*

Full-bellied, the Moslem swears he will break no taboo / when Hunger seized Sule he wolfed a monkey.

And if infidels there are who still doubt the power of the divinity to turn a fanatic into an apostate, they have only to consider the history of the European soldier or explorer who, emaciated in desert wastes, in Arctic colds or the unresponsive seas, resorted to cannibalism as the ultimate appeasement of the god. Few deities ever demand this extreme sacrifice. Historians claim that what Napoleon hid in the pocket of his waist-coat was nothing other than a piece of human flesh which he secretly nibbled on the harrowing retreat from Moscow. This has never been convincingly proved, and Napoleon's memoirs do not even hint at the subject. We are thrown back, in fact, on that great explorer Jonathan Swift, for a scientific appraisal of the palate values of human flesh. Coyly, and in the modern manner of the British, he passes the credit to the Americans, but since Swift travelled extensively under the name of Gulliver, we are left in no doubt at all that he has given the world the benefit of his own experience. For there was no voyager of those uncertain days who did not, at least once in his existence, perform the Ultimate Oblation to the Immovable One.

I have been assured by a very knowing American of my acquaintance in London, that a young healthy child well nursed is at a year old a most delicious, nourishing and wholesome food, whether stewed, roasted, baked or boiled; and I make no doubt that it will equally serve in a fricassee or a ragout.

He is, beyond doubt, the Divine Discoverer of new dietetics, Destroyer and Conquerer of old-fashioned abominations.

On the testimony of creative humans through the ages, Hunger is Divine Inspiration, Begetter of Masterpiece. Poets court him, and the monuments of art are inscribed to him.

Ebi Opapala: It is time we corrected the heinous metaphysical fallacy. Hunger, not Sex, is the First Principle. The presiding Principle of the first fertility dance was not *Obatala*, but *Opapala* (an easy confusion in written, much more in oral records). The dance of the bush-rat fascinated and drawn remorselessly to the waiting cobra is a more pristine, more elemental dance than the exhibitionist struttings of the peacock. Sex fantasies merely intrude in dreams; real dominance is attested by the nightmares of the over-laden belly and the mad, visionary apotheosis of the vegetarian hermit. Collective evidence of these is found in the *oriki* of the Yoruba:

> *O g' aja f' owo m' eke*
> *Ebi Opapala*
> *O sun sile ro dun-dun*
> *O sun sile ka gi aja*
> *Ebi o pa mole o ni oun o je aya*
> *Ebi pa Sule o j' obo*
> *Iwo ko jeun sun*
> *O ji, o ni o la alakala*
> *Ki o to sun ki o ti ri irikuri*
> *Ebi lo pa orisa oko*
> *To fi ti ina bo ogba isu kan*
> *Ebi npa mi ko se fi ife wi.*

Bends you double belly clutching/Hunger the All-powerful/Try to sleep the big drum rumbles/Try to sleep your eyes rove round rafters/Full-bellied the Moslem swears he will break no taboo/ When Hunger seized Sule he wolfed a monkey/Supperless to bed, you woke/Complained of horrors and night fantasies/Did not your tribulations dear friend/Begin right from your waking hours/It was Hunger that maddened the Farm Deity/Goaded him to set fire to the yam plot/'I am famished' is said with a bellow/Not piped with a thin whistle.

And now that to *Opapala* has been rendered His due, let us now, still of course in the same spirit of worship, examine some of the votive offerings.

Emele, Afonj'okun! It could only refer to one food. Experience has simplified the often impossible task of translation; only one food is retentive of heat – *Emele*, that leaps to scald the stomach! The first incautious morsel of this steaming yam flour preparation is not forgotten in a hurry, and yet no true disciple does not again and again sear his gut linings, such being the compulsive nature of its 'subtle goodness'. It is the masocho-hedonistic cycle of the true followers of the First Cause – pain becomes pleasure which is in turn stimulated by pain. The Yorubas understand this well, but to the uninitiated European, the liberality of hot peppers in Yoruba cooking must always remain a cross of uncompensated torture. Sweet aftermath is only a blind, a deceptive consolation, pleasure is actually conjunct with the experience of sweat and rheum through pepper, and fractional oesophageal paralysis from the retentive heat of *Oka, Amala, Emele Afonj'okun.*

> *Emele,* that leaps to scald the stomach
> Whose subtle goodness rolls round
> Each finger of the Right
> Mellows to the turning of the hand
> For you cannot sink it merely
> Like *gari* which soon turns to *eba*
> It shares its secret only with the hand
> That sets the pot on fire.

However, even above *oka* no discriminating palate on the coast of West Africa will hesitate to place the pounded Dome without a blemish! And here we have another cause of the long confusion that has surrounded the First Origin, for *iyan* is also the favourite food of *Obatala*, but *Obatala's* preference in this case has no root in epicureanism, the reason is one of simple colour discrimination.

Kokoro funfun ona ofun! Once again, the precision of this image leaves no room at all for alternatives; it can refer only to the pounded yam. I cannot ever exaggerate the triumph and ecstasy of this poem; without a doubt, it is the most euphoric of Yoruba paeans to food. I cannot think, to return to our first example, of a single line in any poem whose image leaps with equal clarity and abandon to the appreciative centre of the Adam's apple. It causes a distinct gulp, creates an instant vacuum for every future poetic preception. *Kokoro funfun ona ofun!* The simple alliterative image means 'Plump white slug in the throat's passage'.

> *Iyan O ! Iyan !*
> *Iyan O ! Iyan !*
> *Alelerekange*
> *Kokoro funfun ona ofun*
> *Iyan funfun lele . . .*
> *Osupa abe iti*
> *Aran ma de' le ole . . .*
> *Iyan ti dundun ki ki ki, ti ko le ki tan*
> *Ti gudu-gudu fi nse orin ko . . .*
> *Osupa abe iti*
> *Aran ma de' le ole.*

Iyan O!/Slithers down to cool the chest/child of the mortar, master of the pestle/Plump white slug in the passage of the throat/White as the egret – *iyan*!/Dressed in *isapa* – *iyan*!/Trousered in melon – *iyan*!/*Iyan* – Ah, *iyan*!/Praise him – the sick man calls him with a nasal mumble/Can't you hear me – it is *iyan*. I shall eat today!/Moon of the undergrowth/Whose radiance touches not the idler's home/The male drum sang his praises but found no end/And the treble drum turned him into an eternal ballad/Still cry I – white as the egret – *iyan*! Rotund morsel in the hollow of the right hand/A moment to the crook of the nose and it vanishes with a sleight of hand/There is nothing on earth like *iyan* eaten on the farm/There is no one to invite/There is no one to decline/There is no power of mischief that upsets its soup.

Let the relations of *Opapala* on the Greek side, the much vaunted disciples of Dionysus, match that for rapture, for sheer epicurean abandon!

But I find the modern inheritors of Greek gastronomic ecstasy, the European torch-bearers of epicureanism, to be prone to exaggeration, to be lacking in a fundamental sensitivity to food. Poetry of the gut must sustain a profound snobbishness, an awareness of universal food values and a refusal to compromise for the sake of petty national prestige. Insularity however has played sad havoc with British epicurean values. What other than a deadness of taste buds, a corruption of the tonsils could prompt these profane lines to an old bottle of dry sherry?

> Hail, thou whose inner self so far
> Exceeds thine outward show.
> Hail! wakener of appetites,
> Diffuser of a glow.

Indeed, should the object of adoration here be less than a flagon of rare sherry? But no, that verse is none other than Stephen Gwynn's hymn to S A U S A G E S ! This surely is enthusiasm gone mad, a lack of gastronomic dignity the like of which a son of *Opapala* would never exhibit. And I had always believed that apple dumplings were a mere parental device to persuade the doctor's apple-a-day on children. But no again! Coleridge, on the testimony of John Gay maintained that, 'a man cannot have a pure mind who refuses apple dumpling'; fortunately, spiritual judgements from the authority of any Englishman passed a long time ago. Elysium might then be discovered, guarded by St Coleridge with a bowl of apple dumpling and a spoon, barring admittance to every throat of rejection.

Tantalized then by Stephen Gwynn, let us turn again to the Yoruba for a cup of solace – *Alimotu* ... *Lanihun* ... The Yorubas say that 'the pot that will eat of good things, its bottom first must feel the heat'. The pursuit of the milk of the straight rib has been spattered with blood and bones, for *Opapala* is a demanding god. The palm tree tapper plies a most dangerous trade, and his perch often proves treacherous. But *Alimotu* is the inspiration of Amos Tutuola whose book *The Palm Wine*

Drinkard is the eternal Odyssey of man in pursuit of the ultimate thirst quencher. It is a Quest indeed, a Spiritual Quest, but let us be certain of our spirits. The spirituality is of *Opapala*, and the 'mysticism' a regressed primordial consciousness, collective, of the earliest unicellular drinking men. Tutuola's myth is ancient as the innermost ring of the deepest sunk palm rib in historical peat, his vision of the spirit world is realistic, his agency intuitive, a divine intimation from the First Cause and Final Presider of the spirit world, *Opapala*.

> *Alimotu akengbe*
> *Lanihun inu aha*

So begins the *oriki* to the flow of the one true distilling plant, a cup of whose sacrament raises man froth-like on to the mystic layers of consciousness, opens his spiritual eye to behold the misted Form of the First Cause, the Primal Muse Divine – *Ebi Opapala!*

> *Alimotu* of the gourd
> *Lanihun* in the fibrous clump
> Dawn it is that heralds your approach
> When evening comes, the drum crook taps
> Taps, taps in gladness
> Mistress of tuppence only, yet
> Chased the millionaire into the forest.
> You are that which the horse drank
> Drank, drank, and forgot his horns
> You are that which the cock drank
> Drank, drank, and forgot to urinate
> You are that which the guinea-fowl drank
> Drank, till a cry pierced his throat
> And he took to the wilds.

43

Bakare Gbadamosi

A Wise Man Solves His Own Problems

This was translated from Yoruba and has a Tutuolan ring about it: in the use it makes of Yoruba allusions; in the mode of direct address to the reader; and in the moral nature of the whole piece. But here the resemblance ends, for Bakare Gbadamosi is more secure in the world of Yoruba folk-belief where men, gods and animals intermingle. Tutuola strings together his material, shaping it into the novel-form; Gbadamosi invents completely new material. He is therefore like and yet unlike the oral artist, for the substance he allows himself never belonged to the oral spokesman, whereas the raw bones of this material did.

A Wise Man Solves His Own Problems

The foolish man holds a fish by its tail – the wise one holds it by the head. Some problems seem beyond solution by either the wise or the foolish man. That is the time, when the wise man must stop asking for advice and must settle down to solve his own problem.

In the olden days there lived a man called Alatishe – that is to say: 'the wise one who solves his own problems'. Alatishe had huge money and many wives. The senior wife had borne him three children – the rest were yet childless. Everybody thought Alatishe was a very happy man. But as life is filled with sweetness – so it is filled with difficulties. As the world is filled with valleys so it is filled with hills. The world can change overnight. One day Alatishe's eyes began to pain him, and he began to spend money to cure his eyes. For the eyes are the father of the body. But all was in vain and he became blind.

My friend, we experience many tribulations in this world. We only pray that we will not meet more tribulations than we can cope with. But it happened that a new misfortune befell Alatishe. He lost the privilege of sleeping with his wives. This second misfortune brought even greater sadness to Alatishe. He ran from one herbalist to another. But all their efforts came to nothing. The only result of all his efforts was, that people began to notice him everywhere and they were talking about him wherever he went. The herbalists continued to tell their lies and they robbed him of his money. But Alatishe thought: the man who refuses to buy lies will never buy a truth.

But let me not prolong the breath of the story – all his money came to an end. Only his land and some houses were left. His senior wife stood by him during his troubles, so did the junior one. But all the others deserted him for many women are like 'the tree breaks and birds fly'. When the senior wife observed that her husband could not go into his wives any more she became happy. And she thought within her stomach: my children will remain the only ones to divide Alatishe's property after his death. But the junior wife was not happy: for the only way to reach the top of a palm tree is to climb it. And she loved Alatishe well and did not desire any other man. Often she wept with Alatishe saying: our own part in this world has come to an end. But man knows today, while God knows tomorrow. Moreover, endurance is the sacrifice that God is likely to accept.

One day Alatishe was sitting in front of his house thinking about his life, when suddenly a wood pigeon appeared. It looked worried and it was panting like a hunter's dog. The pigeon said to Alatishe: My blind father. Do not suffer me to die a hot death. I was sitting quietly by myself, not committing any offence, when a large black hawk appeared, wanting to kill me. It is running after me now. If you can help me – so I don't end up in its belly – I will also help you so that your eyes will open. When Alatishe heard this, he took the dove and put it under his gown.

Soon the hawk arrived. He moved his head up and down like a palm wine tapper, and he began to pray for Alatishe: May the owner of today and tomorrow never allow you to feel hunger. For this hunger is killing me today. Wherever you may be hiding the dove – please let me eat it! If you can do that for me, I will also help you. And you will be able to sleep with your wives again as before, and you will have as many children as you like.

Alatishe was confused: was it good to have many children and never be able to see them? Or was it better to be able to look at his beautiful young wife every day and not be able to sleep with her?

Then he called his senior wife and asked her to help him to decide. The senior wife said: If you do not know what has brought darkness to a certain place, you will not be able to know how to walk safely in that darkness. Then Alatishe repeated the whole story of the pigeon and the hawk to her. Then she said to him: You must never allow the pigeon to buy a hot death, so that you may be able to see again. It is not good for you to be in darkness. And if it is God's wish that you may have more children – then surely your own children will bear new children for you. Even if your power comes back to you – you would soon lose it again, because you are getting old. But if you regain your eyesight, it will stay with you for the rest of your life. You must never allow the hawk to kill the pigeon. After all – it is just ordinary hunger the hawk is feeling, but the dove does not want to taste the bitterness of death. So let the hawk find his own food.

This reply did not satisfy Alatishe, and so he sent for his junior wife. Her own advice was quite different to that of the senior wife. She said: I beg you my husband, I beg you with my head, the head on which you paid a dowry, please let the hawk kill the pigeon, so that you may regain the power to sleep with women. For I too want to have children for you – even if it is only one. After all: since you have become blind, there is no difference to you between the Sun, the moon and the stars. What do you want to do with eyes? It is better for you to have more children and God to help me not to die a barren woman.

When he had heard the different advice given by his two wives, Alatishe hung his head like a banana leaf, thinking seriously. Whether he would follow the senior wife's advice or the junior one's – he could never be fully satisfied. And as he was thinking which way to turn the hawk was shouting over his head and the dove was trembling under his garment. Then he said to himself: it is I, Alatishe, who must solve my own problem. Then wisdom entered his head. He sent his young wife to buy another pigeon and hid it under his cloak, then he said to the hawk: If I satisfy your hunger – will you fulfill your promise? The hawk said: Yes, but when hunger has entered the belly, there is no room for other matters. So Alatishe gently put his hand under his gown and he dropped the dove. The hawk pounced on it so quickly that he did not realize that it was another pigeon. The hawk was so grateful that he fulfilled his promise. And Alatishe to his delight felt that the blunt knife had been sharpened. When the hawk had left, the dove too showed her gratitude and Alatishe regained his sight.

Now a big change came into Alatishe's life. As soon as the wives heard that he had regained his strength they returned to him and bore him many more children. And money once more found his house a comfortable place to dwell in.

Thus the man who succeeds in the end is always the wise one who does not listen to much advice but who knows how to solve his own problem. For no other person ever has your own interest fully at heart. Even your own wife may not care, whether you go blind or even impotent.

44

Cheikh Hamidou Kane

The City of the Future

Samba Diallo, a young Diallobe from Northern Senegal, comes to Paris to study philosophy and to learn the secret of the West: 'to win without being right'. He gets caught between the rationalist and materialist creed of the West and the spiritual message he has been carrying from Black Africa. Though adhering to his beliefs under the impact of the Western way of life and thought, Samba Diallo finally realizes, 'I have become the two'. His God – who never was the Merciful one of whom the Koran says, 'We are closer to Him than His jugular vein', but rather the Inscrutable One whom Samba's father qualifies as 'no relative of ours' – this God eludes him. And in the urban stone-desert of Europe, the Islamic-African mystic's 'closeness to death' and his intimate communion with nature are engulfed by an inner void, by what Samba Diallo calls '*une grande absence*'. So, when he returns to Africa, a hybrid and traitor to the old order, the 'Madman', a figure symbolic of the violent backlash of religious fanaticism, stabs him to death.

Despite its cerebral design as a dramatized *theological tract*, *L'Aventure ambiguë* has a strangely haunting poetic quality only to be found rarely in the best of Mongo Beti and Sembène Ousmane. It is the heart-rending attempt by the young author, then an economist in the making, to cling to his spiritual roots. *L'Aventure ambiguë* was published in 1961, but had been written by 1952.

The City of the Future

The earth seemed to end in an abyss at the horizon. Above this horizon the sun was dangerously suspended. The liquid silver of its heat had been resorbed, though the light had lost none of its splendour. The air had only taken on a red hue, and in this lighting the small town seemed suddenly to belong to a strange planet.

Paul Lacroix, standing behind the closed window, was waiting. What was he waiting for? The entire small town was waiting too, in the same dismayed expectation. The man's look strayed over the sky where long bars of red rays joined the dying sun to a zenith already invaded by an insidious shadow. 'They are right,' he thought, 'I can quite believe that this is the moment. The world is coming to an end. The moment is fragile. It may break; then time will be obstructed. No – ' Paul Lacroix had almost pronounced this 'no'. With an abrupt gesture he brought down over the scarlet window-pane the green curtain which hung above it. The office was turned into a glaucous aquarium. Paul Lacroix went slowly back to his chair.

Behind the table, Samba Diallo's father had remained motionless as if indifferent to the cosmic drama which was being enacted outside. His white boubou had turned violet. The way it fell down in frozen folds around him made him look like a stone statue. 'Jean is right,' Lacroix thought, 'he does look like a knight of the Middle Ages.'

He spoke to the man. 'Does this twilight not perturb you? Me, I find it upsetting. Right now it seems to me to be nearer to the end of the world than to the night.'

The knight smiled. 'Don't be afraid. I predict you a peaceful night.'

'So you don't believe in the end of the world?'

'On the contrary, I even confidently expect it.'

'That's what I thought. Here all believe in the end of the world, from the untutored peasant to the most cultured people. Why is this so? I have been wondering, and only today, while looking at the twilight, have I begun to understand.'

The knight looked at Paul. 'Now it's my turn to ask you. Do you really not believe in the end of the world?'

'Of course not. The world will have no end. At least, not the kind of end your people here are expecting. I am not saying that a catastrophe may not destroy our planet ...'

'Our untutored peasant does not believe in this episodic and accidental end. His universe does not allow of any accident. It is more reassuring than yours, despite all appearances.'

'That may well be so. Unfortunately for us, my universe is the true one. The earth is not flat; it does not have any declivities sloping down into the abyss. The sun is not a candelabrum fixed on a canopy of blue china. The universe which science has revealed to the West may be less palpably human, but you have to admit that it is more solid ...'

'Your science has revealed to you a round and perfect world in infinite motion. It has recovered this world from chaos. But I think that in this way it has laid you open to despair.'

'By no means. It has freed us from ... childish and absurd fears.'

'Absurd? Absurd – that's what the world without end is. When would one know truth, the whole truth? As far as we are concerned, we still believe in the coming of truth. We are hoping.'

'So that's it,' Lacroix thought. 'The truth which they don't have now, which they are incapable of wresting from nature, will, they hope, be revealed to them by the end. The same with justice. All that they want and don't have they expect from the end instead of trying to conquer it now.' But he did not express his thought. He simply said, 'As far as we are concerned, we conquer a little more truth each day through science. We don't wait ...'

'I was sure that he wouldn't understand,' the knight mused. 'They are so fascinated by the yield of the tool that they have lost sight of the infinite immensity of the whole work in hand. They do not see that the truth which they discover each day is each day becoming more stinted. A little truth each day ... of course, it's necessary. But Truth itself? To have the one, is it necessary to renounce the other?'

'I think you understand very well what I want to say. I am not disputing the quality of the truth revealed by science. But it is a partial truth, and as long as there is a future, all truth will be partial. Truth has its place at the end of history. But I see that we are taking the deceptive path of metaphysics.'

'Why do you say "deceptive"?'

' "To each word can be opposed another one." Did not one of your Ancients say this? Tell me frankly whether this is not your belief even today.'

'No. And please don't refrain from going into metaphysics. I should like to know your world.'

'You know it already. Our world is the one that believes in the end of the world, which hopes for it while fearing it at the same time. That's why just a little while ago I felt a great joy when it seemed to me that you were in anguish, standing at my window. Look, I said to myself, he has a presentiment of the end ...'

'No, to tell the truth, it was not anguish. It didn't go quite as far ...'

'Then I wish you from the bottom of my heart that you may regain this sense of anguish at the sight of the dying sun. I ardently wish it for the West. When the sun dies, no scientific certainty should keep us from weeping over it, no rational evidence from wondering whether it will be born again. You are slowly dying under the weight of evidence. I wish you that anguish like a resurrection.'

'What would we be born to?'

'To a deeper truth. Evidence is a surface quality. Your science is the triumph of evidence, a proliferation of the surface. It makes you the masters of the external world but at the same time it exiles you there more and more.'

There was a moment of silence. Outside, the evening drama had come to an end. The sun had fallen. Behind it an imposing mass of scarlet clouds had almost disintegrated in its wake like a monstrous trail of curdled blood. The red splendour of the air had gradually grown softer – an effect of the shadow that slowly invaded space.

'It's a strange thing,' Lacroix was thinking, 'this fascination nothingness holds for those who have nothing. They call their nothingness the Absolute. They keep their backs turned to the light while looking fixedly at the shadows. Has this man no awareness of his poverty?'

At this moment the knight's voice arose. It was deep and meditative as if he were speaking to himself, 'I wanted to tell you all the same . . .' He hesitated.

'What did you want to tell me, Sir?'

'I wanted to tell you that in the end it was I who put my son in your [European] school.'

'It's a pleasure to hear it from you.'

'I have put my son in your school and I have prayed to God to save us all, you and ourselves.'

'He will save us, if He exists.'

'I have sent my son to your school because the external world which you have held at bay was invading us slowly and destroying us. Teach him to stem the external world.'

'We have stemmed it.'

'The external world is always on the offensive. If man does not conquer it, it destroys him and makes him a tragic victim. A wound one neglects does not heal, but festers till it becomes gangrenous. A child that is not educated regresses. A society that is not governed is destroyed. The West builds up science against the invading chaos as one puts up a barricade.'

At that moment, Lacroix had to fight the compulsive temptation to operate the electric switch which was within the reach of his hand. He would have liked to scrutinize the shadowy face of the man sitting motionless in front of him. In his voice he detected a quality which intrigued him and which he would have liked to connect with the expression on his face. 'But if I switch on,' he thought, 'it may well happen that the man falls silent. It's not to me that he is talking, it's to himself . . .' He listened.

'Each passing hour adds a little more fuel to the crucible in which life is amalgamating. We have not had the same past, you and me, but we shall definitely share the same future. The era of solitary destinies is over. If you look at it in this way, the end of the world has certainly come for every one of us, for nobody can live out of the sheer perseverance of the self anymore. But from our long manifold ripening processes a son will be born to the world, the first son of the earth, and also the only begotten one.'

Lacroix felt him turning slightly towards him in the shadow. 'Mr Lacroix, I accept this future. My son is the proof of this. He will contribute to building it. I want him to contribute to it, no longer as a stranger coming from afar but as an artisan responsible for the destiny of the city.'

'He will teach us the secrets of the shadow. He will lay bare to us the sources from which your youth quenches its thirst.'

'Don't exaggerate, Mr Lacroix! I know that you don't believe in this shadow, nor in the end. What you do not see does not exist. The instant carries you like a raft on the luminous surface of its round disk, and you deny the whole abyss that surrounds you. The city of the future will, thanks to my son, open its windows on to the abyss, from which great gusts of shadow will come over our dried-out bodies and our thirsty foreheads. I wish this opening with all my soul. Such must be our work in this city about to be born, and we all must contribute: Indians, Chinese, South Americans, Negroes, and Arabs, all of us, gawky and pitiable, we the underdeveloped who feel out of place in a world of perfect mechanical adjustment.'

It was now completely dark. Lacroix, motionless, heard this strange prayer in the shadow, 'God in whom I believe, if we do not succeed, let the Apocalypse come! Then deprive us of this freedom we have not known how to use. May Thy hand then fall heavily on the great obliviousness. May the sovereignty of Thy will throw the stable course of our laws into disorder . . .'

Biographical Notes

AKIGA was born in Nigeria about 1898, the son of a black-smith. He began living with a missionary when young and became converted. During his later journeys among the Tivs he had the idea of writing a book, with his father and other village elders as his chief informants.

MILLER O. ALBERT is the pen-name of one of the Onitsha writers. He describes himself as an 'author and journalist' and has published *Rosemary and the Taxi-driver* and *Saturday Night Disappointment* in the Onitsha series. Both books caution the reader that the characters are fictitious and 'whoever hits his head at the ceiling does it at his own personal fatal risk'.

DAVID ANANOU was born in Togoland and has published one novel in French. His book *Le fils du fétiche* shows him as being very pro-Western. The Epilogue of the book is the author's viewpoint; he says, 'What kind of progress will be effectively realized in a country which is still in the chain of a thousand superstitions?'

MONGO BETI was born in 1932 in Mbalmayo, Cameroon. He attended school in Yaoundé and took his *baccalauréat* at the *lycée* in 1951. In France he studied literature at the Sorbonne and is now a university lecturer. He has published four novels.

NAZI BONI was born in 1912 at Bouan, Upper Volta. He was once a deputy in the French National Assembly. He now lives in Dakar and has published one novel. Very much a traditional-ist, his novel shows his interest in legends.

ADELAIDE CASELY-HAYFORD was born in Sierra Leone in 1868 and educated in Britain and Germany. In 1903 she married the Ghanaian lawyer and writer E. Casely-Hayford and in 1944 went to Freetown with her daughter. She died at the age of 91.

Biographical Notes

E. CASELY-HAYFORD was born in 1866 and died in 1930. He went to Cambridge and studied to be a lawyer. He edited *The Gold Coast Leader* and served on the Gold Coast Legislative Council from 1916 until his death.

R. R. R. DHLOMO was born in South Africa and became a trained teacher. He was a regular contributor to, then editor of, a popular Zulu weekly. He wrote in Zulu and English and is best known for *An African Tragedy* (1928).

SPEEDY ERIC is one of the pen-names of an Onitsha writer. In a magazine that these authors launched in May 1962 they spoke of how 'Author is a prouder title than king' and emphasized the didactic nature of their work, but Speedy Eric's novelette is semi-pornographic.

BAKARE GBADAMOSI was born and educated in Nigeria and has collaborated with Ulli Beier on a number of translations of oral Yoruba poetry. More recently he has turned his attention to writing short stories in Yoruba which show his interest in and knowledge of the Yoruba way of life.

ALEX LA GUMA was born in 1925 in Cape Town, South Africa. He was among the accused in the South African 'treason' trials. He was at one time a columnist for a weekly Cape Town paper. He now lives in Britain.

PAUL HAZOUMÉ was born in 1890 in Dahomey. He is a French-trained ethnologist. He is retired and apart from *Doguicimi* (1938) he has written papers of sociological interest.

LUIS BERNARDO HONWANA was born in 1942 in Lourenço Marques, Mozambique, and attended secondary school there. He worked as a journalist in Beira, after financial circumstances forced him to discontinue his secondary education.

EDWARD BABATUNDE HORATIO-JONES was born in 1930 in Lagos and educated in Sierra Leone and London. He has lived in Paris and Germany (where he studied theatre in Berlin), worked as a film reporter at the Nigerian war-front, and is now with Carlo Ponti in Italy. A man of varied tastes, he has completed several novels still waiting publication.

CHEIKH HAMIDOU KANE was born in 1928 in Matam, Senegal. He studied philosophy and law in Paris and in 1960 became governor of Thiès Province. He has worked in Lagos with

UNICEF. His single novel, from which an extract is reprinted here, demonstrates some of the conflicts in his own upbringing.

JONATHAN KARIARA was born in the Nyeri District of Kenya in 1935. He studied English at Makerere University College, Kampala, Uganda, from 1955 to 1960 and is now with the East African Literature Bureau. He has published short stories and has travelled widely in West Africa and Europe.

SADRU KASSAM was born in 1941 in Mombasa, Kenya, and after local school went to Makerere in 1963 where he read English. He is now a teacher and writes short stories. He hopes to publish a novel shortly.

AKÉ LOBA was born in 1927 in Ababo Baoulé, Ivory Coast. He worked on his father's farm, and then went to France, where he worked as a labourer and in factories, before studying agriculture. He is now his country's ambassador to the Federal Republic of Germany.

D. N. MALINWA was born and educated in Tanzania. He has written poems and short stories but his poetry lacks the language appeal of his prose. He lives and works in Dar-es-Salaam.

JEAN MALONGA was born in 1907 in Congo (Brazzaville). After attending local schools he went to France in 1946 as a member of the French National Assembly.

CASEY MOTSISI is a Johannesburg journalist. He was once a frequent contributor to *Drum*. He lives in South Africa and writes occasional short stories.

EZEKIEL MPHAHLELE was born in 1919 in Pretoria. He started training as a teacher but, forced to give this up, he worked for *Drum* and took external degrees. In 1957 he left for Nigeria, where he was an extra-mural tutor with the University of Ibadan. Later he lived and worked in Paris, Nairobi and Denver, Colorado. At present he is a professor of English in Zambia.

JAMES NGUGI was born at Limaru, Kenya, in 1938 and educated in Kenya and at Makerere, where he read English. He did post-graduate work at Leeds University and has now returned to teaching in East Africa.

S. Y. NTARA was born in Malawi and wrote the biography of a chief in Cewa which was translated into English in 1949. His

Biographical Notes

work shows his interests – the intrusion of a new way of life on the traditional patterns.

E. E. OBENG was born in Ghana and wrote the first truly West African novel, in 1943. Obeng saw the function of the African artist as one which could not afford to be aesthetic alone. For him his novel had to teach the literate about the meaning of their emancipation.

OKENWA OLISA is an Onitsha pamphleteer from Nigeria. He writes under various pen-names including 'Master of Life' and 'Strong Man of the Pen' and has written novelettes, plays and factual accounts. He was the manager of the Okenwa Correspondence College in Onitsha.

RALPH OPARA was born in 1933 in Nigeria and educated at Government College, Umuahia, and the University of Ibadan, where he read English. He was formerly Head of Talks for the Nigeria Broadcasting Corporation.

SEMBÈNE OUSMANE was born in 1923 in Ziguinchor-Casamance, Senegal, and educated there. He was in turn mason, mechanic, soldier and dock-worker. When he turned to writing novels he was able to bring to his work the vitality of a varied experience.

FERDINAND OYONO was born in 1929 in Ngulemakong, Ebolowa, Cameroon. He went to secondary school in France in 1950 and studied for his doctorate of law in Paris. He is now a diplomat in Monrovia.

SOL T. PLAATJE was born in South Africa. Though educated only up to primary school level, he supplemented this by private reading. He was employed as a court-interpreter and spoke Dutch, English, German, Afrikaans and four Bantu languages. His publications include a novel, *Mhudi* (1930), as well as a political book and Shakespeare translations.

ABDOULAYE SADJI was born in Rufisque, Senegal, in 1910 and died in 1961. He attended in turn the Koranic school, the French elementary school and a training college, obtaining his diploma in 1929. In 1932 he obtained his *baccalauréat* and became an inspector of elementary schools in Senegal.

SALIM BIN ABAKARI wrote in 1896 (in Swahili) an account of his journeys to Russia and Siberia with his German employers.

His account is important, for it shows him as a man who was a keen observer and a sympathetic recorder of alien customs.

JOHN MENSAH SARBAH was born in 1864 and died in 1910. He was educated in England and was the first Gold Coaster to be called to the bar. In 1901 he became a member of the Legislative Council and was awarded the C.M.G. in 1910.

SEGILOLA was probably the pseudonym of Isaac B. Thomas, the editor of a Lagos newspaper. 'Segilola' published her life-story in 1929. The serialized story was intended for a didactic purpose. Thomas died in 1930.

LÉOPOLD SÉDAR SENGHOR was born in 1906 in Joal, Senegal, and went to the local *lycée*, then the Sorbonne. He taught for some years and fought during the war. Later he entered politics and became first Deputy, then a Minister, and in 1960 finally President of independent Senegal.

A. B. C. SIBTHORPE arrived in Freetown as a child and a freed slave. He lived in Gloucester, near Freetown, and attended the C.M.S. Grammar School in 1852, but left two years later to train as a teacher. Besides writing a history and geography of Sierra Leone, he was also a painter.

OUSMANE SOCÉ was born in 1911 in Rufisque, Senegal. After local schooling, he studied to become a veterinary surgeon. He is at the moment Senegal's ambassador to the United States and the United Nations. He is the former editor of the monthly *Bingo* in Dakar.

CASTRO SOROMENHO was born in 1910 in Chinde, Mozambique. He is white and has been a journalist and a newspaper editor. He writes in Portuguese. He lived for some time in Angola but has returned to Mozambique.

WOLE SOYINKA was born in 1935 in Abeokuta, Nigeria. He studied at the Universities of Ibadan and Leeds, reading English at Leeds. He has taught at two universities in Nigeria, and has had his plays performed throughout the world. Recently he has been imprisoned without being charged by the Federal Nigerian Government.

ISAAC B. THOMAS (*see* Segilola)

SÉKOU TOURÉ is President of the Republic of Guinea. Born in 1922 at Farannah, he went to Koranic then primary school and later on to the French technical school at Conakry. After a number of jobs, he became committed to the labour movement and in 1958 led his country to independence.

K. TSARO-WIWA was born in Nigeria and read English at the University of Ibadan, graduating in 1966. He was a post-graduate student in drama, a university lecturer and is now a Civil Commissioner in the Rivers State Government.

AMOS TUTUOLA was born in 1920 in Abeokuta, Nigeria, and only educated up to primary school. He was in turn farmer, blacksmith, coppersmith with the R.A.F. and, after the war, messenger in Lagos. He is now a storekeeper with the Nigerian Broadcasting Corporation, Ibadan.

TIMOTHY WANGUSA was born in 1942 in Bugisu District, Uganda. He read English at Makerere University College before proceeding to Leeds in 1967 for a Master's degree. A writer of both prose and poetry, some of his poetry has appeared in *The East African Journal* and recently in a Commonwealth anthology.